VIRGINIA WOOLF AND THE
MIGRATIONS OF LANGUAGE

Virginia Woolf's rich and imaginative use of language was partly a result of her keen interest in foreign literatures and languages – mainly Greek and French, but also Russian, German, and Italian. As a translator she naturally addressed herself to contemporary standards of translation within the university, but also to readers like herself. In *Three Guineas* she ranged herself among German scholars who used *Antigone* to critique European politics of the 1930s. *Orlando* outwits the censors with a strategy that focuses on Proust's untranslatable word. *The Waves* and *The Years* show her looking ahead to the problems of postcolonial society, where translation crosses borders. In this first in-depth study of Woolf and European languages and literatures, Emily Dalgarno opens up a rewarding new way of reading her prose.

EMILY DALGARNO is Professor Emerita at the Department of English at Boston University.

VIRGINIA WOOLF AND THE MIGRATIONS OF LANGUAGE

EMILY DALGARNO

CAMBRIDGE
UNIVERSITY PRESS

709890459

CAMBRIDGE UNIVERSITY PRESS
Cambridge, New York, Melbourne, Madrid, Cape Town,
Singapore, São Paulo, Delhi, Tokyo, Mexico City

Cambridge University Press
The Edinburgh Building, Cambridge CB2 8RU, UK

Published in the United States of America by Cambridge University Press, New York

www.cambridge.org
Information on this title: www.cambridge.org/9781107010185

First published 2012

Printed in the United Kingdom at the University Press, Cambridge

A catalogue record for this publication is available from the British Library

Library of Congress Cataloguing in Publication data
Dalgarno, Emily.
Virginia Woolf and the migrations of language / Emily Dalgarno.
p.   cm.
Includes bibliographical references and index.
ISBN 978-1-107-01018-5 (hardback)
1. Woolf, Virginia, 1882–1941 – Knowledge – Language and languages.   2. Woolf, Virginia,
1882–1941 – Knowledge – Literature.   3. Woolf, Virginia, 1882–1941 – Knowledge – Translating and
interpreting.   4. Woolf, Virginia, 1882–1941 – Language.   5. Translating and interpreting –
Philosophy.   I. Title.
PR6045.072Z58145   2012
823'.912–dc22
2011011415

ISBN 978-1-107-01018-5 hardback

In memory of
Imre Gyula Izsák
Astronomer
(1929–65)

Contents

Preface   *page* viii
List of abbreviations   x

   The migrations of language: introduction   1

1 Translation and ethnography in "On Not Knowing Greek"   18

2 *Antigone* and the public language   38

3 Tolstoy, Dostoyevsky, and the Russian soul   69

4 Proust and the fictions of the unconscious   97

5 Translation and iterability   133

6 Assia Djebar and the poetics of lamentation   156

   Conclusion   189

Bibliography of works cited   196
Index   212

Preface

Throughout this work I have continued to ask how the richness and historical depth of Woolf's language become apparent in the context of translation. Woolf's expressed desire to transform the English language always seemed to me a measure of her ambition and stature as a writer, and a goal scarcely to be imagined. A study of her vocabulary shows that she gave us relatively few new words.[1] How then did transformation come about? After "On Not Knowing Greek" her thoughts on translation are scattered throughout her fiction, essays, and diaries. Although her response to works of Russian fiction and to Proust shaped her writing practice significantly, there is no further essay on translation, perhaps because the language of the Victorian translator of Greek was no longer suitable, and others were not yet in circulation. Like the German Hellenists of her generation she learned that the translation of classical texts can be used to mount challenges to the ideology of national governments. Reading Proust with Vita Sackville-West suggested to Woolf that the language of gender comes into existence on the borders of consciousness, at the moment of awakening. Such a study enhances our sense of her language as responding to its history, and hospitable to the rhetorical strategies of other western languages.

The experience of a semester at the Camargo Foundation in Cassis greatly enhanced my understanding of translation and the social and political relationships among languages. My thanks to the Director, Michael J. Pretina, who arranged seminars with other fellows, and glimpses of the culture of Marseilles that widened the scope of my study, to include not only my chapter on Proust, but also work on Assia Djebar.

I particularly wish to thank the Society of Authors as the Literary Representative of the Estate of Virginia Woolf, for permission both to cite short extracts from her work and to quote from holograph material in several

[1] Rowena Fowler, "Virginia Woolf: Lexicographer," *English Language Notes* 39 (2002), 54–70.

collections. For permission to read Woolf's notes on Tolstoy, I thank the Mortimer Rare Book Room, Smith College, Northampton, Massachusetts. The curator of the Smith College Museum of Art has graciously given permission to print the image of Woolf that appears on the jacket. My thanks to the Henry W. and Albert A. Berg Collection, the New York Public Library, for permission to cite Woolf's reading notes, and to the British Library for permission to cite a passage from "The Hours" holograph. My thanks to Albin Michel of Paris for permission to cite several of the works of Assia Djebar.

My thanks to the editors of *Modern Fiction Studies* for permission to reprint an earlier version of chapter three; and to the editors of *YES* (2006) for permission to reprint an earlier version of chapter five.

I acknowledge with deep gratitude the criticism and encouragement of colleagues and friends who were resident at the Camargo Foundation in 2004, especially Robert Aldrich. Among my colleagues in the US who read individual chapters special thanks to: Irline Francois, Laura Korobkin, Jeffrey Mehlman, Robin Feuer Miller, Stephen Scully, and especially Mark Hussey and David Wagenkecht. Thanks also to many supportive friends: Julia Bader, Gillian Cooper-Driver, Anne Gaposchkin, Arthur Kaledin, Louis Kampf, Jane Lilienfeld, Alan Spitzer, Holly Zaitchik, my cousin the late Jean Vetter, Andrew Izsák, and Kim Wright.

I thank Ray Ryan, Senior Commissioning Editor, English and American Literature, Cambridge University Press, for his patience and encouragement. I should like also to thank Maartje Scheltens, Editor, for guiding me through the production process. My thanks as well to Caroline Howlett for her care in editing the text. Thanks also to the anonymous referees whose suggestions made this a better book.

Abbreviations

Works by Virginia Woolf: I have used the Hogarth Press "Definitive Collected Edition" of Woolf's fiction except when otherwise noted.

APA	*A Passionate Apprentice: The Early Journals 1897–1909*, ed. Mitchell A. Leaska (New York: Harcourt Brace Jovanovich, 1990)
BA	*Between the Acts*
CDB	*The Captain's Death Bed*, ed. Leonard Woolf (1950)
CSF	*The Complete Shorter Fiction*, ed. Susan Dick (New York: Harcourt Brace Jovanovich, 1985)
D	*The Diary of Virginia Woolf*, vols. I–V, ed. Anne Olivier Bell (New York: Harcourt Brace Jovanovich, 1977–84)
DM	*The Death of the Moth* (1947)
E	*The Essays of Virginia Woolf*, vols. I–IV, ed. Andrew McNeillie (New York: Harcourt Brace Jovanovich, 1986–94); vol. V, ed. Stuart N. Clarke (2009)
Hol W	*The Waves: The Two Holograph Drafts*, ed. J. W. Graham (1976)
JR	*Jacob's Room*
L	*The Letters of Virginia Woolf*, vols. I–VI, ed. Nigel Nicholson and Joanne Trautmann (New York: Harcourt Brace Jovanovich, 1975–80)
M	*The Moment and Other Essays*, ed. Leonard Woolf (New York: Harcourt Brace Jovanovich, 1947)
MB	*Moments of Being: Unpublished Autobiographical Writings*, ed. Jeanne Schulkind (New York: Harcourt Brace Jovanovich [1976], 1985)
MD	*Mrs. Dalloway*
ND	*Night and Day*
O	*Orlando*
RO	*A Room of One's Own / Three Guineas*, ed. Michèle Barrett (London: Penguin, 1993)

TG	*Three Guineas*
TL	*To the Lighthouse*
TP	*The Pargiters*, ed. Mitchell A. Leaska (New York: Harcourt Brace Jovanovich, 1977)
VO	*The Voyage Out*
W	*The Waves*
Y	*The Years*

Woolf's holograph notes in the Henry W. and Albert A. Berg Collection of English and American Literature are referenced by reel numbers.

The migrations of language: introduction

The need to change the structure of the English sentence in order better to meet the requirements of women writers is a constant theme in the work of Virginia Woolf.[1] She wrote during a period when the goals of translation were undergoing fundamental changes that enlarged and facilitated that project. The British translator who was compelled to observe the ethnocentric standards of Greek translation in the university evolved within a few decades into a figure whose aim, in response to the demands of colonial readers, was to mediate between cultures. It is the argument of this book that although Woolf read translations to acquaint herself with the diverse cultures of the world, as a writer she quickly learned to use translation as a means to resist the tendency of the dominant language to control meaning, the first step to remodeling semantics and syntax. My work is oriented towards the classic essays on translation by Roman Jakobson and Walter Benjamin, and several works by Jacques Derrida that link translation to larger questions of nationality and otherness. When read together with Woolf's essays and the scenes of translation in her novels they reveal the scope of her attempts to redesign the sentence and to recreate the dominant language.

Throughout her career Woolf moved with ease among her roles as writer and as reader, translator, and publisher of foreign texts. Over the twenty or so years that she studied Greek she translated a number of texts, notably *Agamemnon*, undertaken while she was drafting *Mrs. Dalloway*. Like others of her class she read French, although unlike Lytton Strachey and Vita Sackville-West she was not bilingual. She and Leonard studied Russian briefly, and her numerous essays on Dostoyevsky, Turgenev, and Tolstoy, together with the work of the Hogarth Press, helped to develop a British readership for Russian fiction. Two notebooks are filled with her exercises as

---

[1] In "Life Sentences" Molly McQuade surveys passages from *A Room of One's Own*, Woolf's short stories, and the essay "Craftsmanship" which detail her vision of a new sentence. *Woolf Studies Annual* 14 (2008), 53–67.

she studied Italian. She evolved a position in which she might use a translation to read an entire work quickly and grasp it as a whole, while retaining her student's understanding of the structure and limits of the original language. Although she both deplored and supported the need for translation, she was clearly someone for whom foreign languages redrew the map of the world.

Woolf began her study of foreign languages in a university program. She was enrolled in the University of London King's College Ladies' Department from 1897 to 1901. There from the ages of fifteen to nineteen, she "reached degree-level standard in some of her studies" of history, Greek, Latin, and German.[2] From 1897 to 1900 she studied Greek with Professor George Warr, Professor of Classical Literature at King's.[3] But her grasp of Greek grammar was slim, if we are to believe the account, written in 1903, of her subsequent lessons with Janet Case: "Then there was our grammar. Many teachers have tried to break me in to that – but with only a passing success. Miss Case went to the root of the evil; she saw that my foundations were rotten – procured a Grammar, & bade me start with the very first exercise – upon the proper use of the article – which I had hitherto used with the greatest impropriety" (*APA*: 183). Whereas Woolf responded "with literary delight" to a line, Miss Case kept the emphasis on grammar and the teaching of morality. Perhaps in this early exchange with the instructor she came to love we can see Woolf composing an image of herself studying Greek at home as an outsider and a critic of institutionalized learning that was somewhat at odds with her actual experience. In other words, the image of Woolf as self-taught that appears in many biographies accepts at face value the picture of herself that she carefully cultivated, for instance in this letter of 1932 to a would-be biographer. Warning him not to confuse her life with the positions she took as a novelist and in *A Room of One's Own*, she offered this disavowal: "Partly for reasons of health I was never at any school or college" (*L5*: 91). Hermione Lee has explored the various functions of the letters and the diary, and concluded that both are "full of exaggeration and invention."[4] For my purposes the King's College records and the early diary ground the theory of the subject in an image of her education that Woolf was at pains to construct for her readers.

[2] Christine Kenyon Jones and Anna Snaith, "'Tilting at Universities': Woolf at King's College London," *Woolf Studies Annual* 16 (2010), 4. The article reproduces the College records of registrations, syllabi, and class lists.

[3] *Ibid.*, p. 15.

[4] Hermione Lee, *Virginia Woolf* (London: Chatto & Windus, 1996), chapter one, "Biography," pp. 3–20.

Woolf's early tuition insured that somewhat later, when she read Sophocles and Aeschylus in translation, she responded to language as a student trained in a particular pedagogical theory. Reading *Agamemnon*, she commented on "the immeasurable difference between the text & the translation" (*D1*: 184). Her own translation of *Agamemnon*, based largely on the bilingual text of A. W. Verrall (1904), shows her attention to individual words that she retranslated in the margins of the Greek text. It is an approach that reveals her dependence on a now outdated model that envisions the adequate substitution of one word for another, and a translator whose task is to follow certain abstract rules. At the same time her interest in the semiotics of prophecy, the sense that language speaks Cassandra, demonstrates an emphasis on the signifying powers of language, as in her translation of this line from the chorus: "To this sign thou art prayed to let the event accord."[5] In my view there she might have remained, invisible in the margins of someone else's translation, were it not for a redefinition of translation as cultural process as well as product, an approach that makes it possible now to study its effect on her writing practice.

Translation cannot be confined to the substitution of one word or one text for another. Woolf's work as a translator of Greek is clearly the second of Roman Jakobson's three kinds of translation, which he labeled "1) Intralingual translation or *rewording* is an interpretation of verbal signs by means of other signs of the same language. 2) Interlingual translation or *translation proper* is an interpretation of verbal signs by means of some other language. 3) Intersemiotic translation or *transmutation* is an interpretation of verbal signs by means of signs of nonverbal sign systems."[6] Although intralingual translation often involves circumlocution, the unit of translation from one language to another is larger, so that "messages in one language" are substituted for messages in another. Since the overall problem concerns "equivalence in difference," the translator is forced to become an interpreter of that difference, and the subject of translation cannot be confined for long within formal criteria.[7] In Woolf's work inter- and intralingual questions of translation often intersect in the same passage, at the point where the ambiguity and contradictions of history have made the sign untranslatable, as for instance in *Orlando*, where the gypsies cannot translate the word *beauty*, because in their culture the concept does not exist.

[5] I discuss the matter more fully in *Virginia Woolf and the Visible World* (Cambridge: Cambridge University Press, 2001), p. 70.
[6] Roman Jakobson, "On Linguistic Aspects of Translation," *On Translation*, ed. Reuben Brower (Cambridge, Mass.: Harvard University Press, 1959), 233.
[7] *Ibid.*

Translation, argues André Lefevere, is the sign of openness both to another literature and to transformation, "depending on where the guardians of the dominant poetics, the dominant ideology stand. No wonder, therefore, that there have been attempts to regulate translation, to make sure it does not exert any subversive influence on the native system, to use it to integrate what is foreign by naturalizing it first."[8] Woolf's major essay on translation, "On Not Knowing Greek," refers to the decades-long controversy about the teaching of Greek in British schools and universities. Although she avoids taking sides, the title itself is drawn from Arnold's play on "knowing" in "Literature and Science" (1885). Her essay engages Arnold's criticism in "On Translating Homer" (1861) of a translation of the *Iliad* by another classical scholar, Francis Newman, whose career was oriented towards the needs of students and common readers. Although Arnold criticized the archaic diction of Newman's *Iliad*, his larger aim was to defend an academic elite that could impose its standards on readers outside the university. In her essay Woolf silently inhabited Arnold's position while aligning her values with Newman's.

In fact what is missing from such debates are the political and economic conditions in which translations are produced and consumed. Perhaps owing to her position outside the university Woolf was able to shift the debate from Arnold's assertions about the proper language of translation to ask, by whom are translations produced and used? That is, she broadened Arnold's emphasis on the interlingual aspects of translation by introducing into the discussion her experience of the history of struggle and contradiction in British education. Since the 1980s the study of translation practices has focused on questions about translation as a cultural process, and its connections with literary criticism, philosophy, and other disciplines. Woolf's emphasis in "On Not Knowing Greek" on Greek climate and social customs suggests that by 1925 she had begun to entertain some of these larger questions, as she came to recognize the ethnocentric limits of purely linguistic criteria.

Nor did Woolf's challenge to the "guardians of the dominant poetics" stop with her mimicry of Matthew Arnold. She used the role of translator to position herself in national controversies. When she cited a line about love from Shelley's translation of the *Symposium*, so controversial that it remained unpublished during his lifetime, she freed herself to refer to a

---

[8] André Lefevere, "Why Waste our Time on Rewrites?: The Trouble with Interpretation and the Role of Rewriting in an Alternative Paradigm," *The Manipulation of Literature: Studies in Literary Translation*, ed. Theo Hermans (London and Sydney: Croom Helm, 1985), 237.

division within the national language about discussion of homosexuality, as if translation were about crossing social borders as well. Derrida argues that translation often has such an effect on the native language: "Babelization does not wait for the multiplicity of languages. The identity of a language can only affirm itself as identity to itself by opening itself to the hospitality of a difference from itself or of a difference with itself."[9] In *Aporias* Derrida redefines this philosophical term as crossing a border into what is not permitted or not possible. It lies at the heart of translation, since one type of aporia separates nations, languages, and cultures; another "domains of discourse," to which he added a third, the separation between concepts or terms.[10] As soon as a line is drawn, whether a threshold, an edge, "or the approach of the other," aporia manifests itself as a division of the self. In Woolf's essay Shelley's translation of the *Symposium* marks a well-defended border within the domain of the English language. In this essay and in *Orlando* Woolf treated the public silence about same-sex love (outside the courts that is) as a problem of untranslatability, that is as a struggle too recent and intense yet to be named in the dominant language. Whereas Jakobson's linguistic definition of the intralingual may be a neutral circumlocution, in Woolf's essay intralingual translation becomes an occasion to demonstrate a position of openness in a national controversy.

Woolf's figure of Antigone, when read in the context of the European redesign of classical studies, poses a challenge to Fascism precisely at the intersection of intra- and interlingual translation. Following the excavations of Greek sites in the early twentieth century German scholars broadened the field of classics to include archeology. *Altertumswissenschaft*, as it was called when imported into British universities, made possible the professional study of the classics by women. In writing *Three Guineas* Woolf rejected the temptation to turn *Antigone* into propaganda, choosing instead to structure her essay along the lines of the scene in which Antigone confronts Creon, as an occasion to resist the public language by challenging old vocabularies. In so doing the female subject, while forced to speak a dominant language not of its making, seeks to avoid ventriloquism. The image of the brother's grave as the site of a mourning cry that combines grief for the dead with resentment of his social privileges illustrates the social contradictions of Antigone's position. In *Three Guineas* translation marks the place where the socially disempowered subject encounters a history that

---

[9] Jacques Derrida, *Aporias*, trans. Thomas Dutoit (Stanford: Stanford University Press, 1993), p. 10.
[10] *Ibid.*, p. 23.

she cannot read. The radio brings together the "ancient cry" that is heard in *Antigone* and *Three Guineas* with the problems of representation and translation that are associated with female mourning. Just as German scholars used classical texts to interrogate Fascist ideology, interlingual translation is the starting point for Woolf's intralingual challenge.

Whereas Woolf was the ideal reader of Greek poetry published in a bilingual tradition, the reader of fiction in a language not well known in England was in a different position. As a publisher, a reviewer, and a would-be translator of Russian she came to understand what it takes to market a translation. When British readers began to read Russian fiction Virginia and Leonard seized the opportunity to publish a number of translations that significantly changed the position of the Hogarth Press. Whereas it had been a small press that published the works of friends, publication of Russian fiction gave it a stake in international modernism. Both made an attempt to learn Russian, and Virginia collaborated with S. S. Koteliansky in the translation of "Stavrogin's Confession," a suppressed chapter of Dostoyevsky's *The Possessed*. Her reviews of several translations from Russian, 1917–25, helped to create the British market for work by Dostoyevsky and Tolstoy. Yet as a critic she saw translation of the Russians as a "mutilation": "When you have changed every word in a sentence from Russian to English, have thereby altered the sense a little, the sound, weight, and accent of the words in relation to each other completely, nothing remains except a crude and coarsened version of the sense. Thus treated, the great Russian writers are like men deprived by an earthquake or a railway accident not only of all their clothes, but also of something subtler and more important – their manners, the idiosyncrasies of their characters" (*E4*: 174). Although translation had been useful to her as a student of Greek, reading Russian, a language she did not command, put her in the company of those "who have had to depend, blindly and implicitly, upon the work of translators" (*E4*: 174).

Although Woolf's interest in Russian fiction eventually waned, her interest in Tolstoy was most in evidence at the end of her career. She wrote of Tolstoy as bringing the universe into view: "even in a translation we feel that we have been set on a mountain-top and had a telescope put into our hands." Although in her notes she praised him for his ability to engage the readers' emotion and feeling, while drafting *The Years* she turned to *War and Peace*, with its digressions on history, as a model of the essay-novel that aligns family history with that of the nation. As her diary shows, she was especially drawn to the second Epilogue, where Tolstoy engages the problems of patriotism and the nation, although much of this emphasis was lost when *The Years* was cut and revised for publication. When Eleanor Pargiter completes the sentence begun by the foreigner Nicholas, Woolf suggests that translation is a sentence completed by another, and that such translation is the condition of historicity. Yet her readers, like Tolstoy's, reacted with incomprehension if not hostility to the mix of fiction with history.

Not only did Woolf not cite lines in Russian, as she had lines in Greek, but her constant comparison of Russian to English texts, although in one sense it domesticates the foreign, in another constantly emphasizes their foreignness. Reading Chekhov she was reminded that whereas in Victorian fiction there is closure – lovers are united – in his stories "the soul is ill; the soul is cured; the soul is not cured. Those are the emphatic points in his stories" (*E4*: 185). The novels of Dostoyevsky "are composed purely and wholly of the stuff of the soul" (*E4*: 186). The quality of meaning "on the far side of language" (*E4*: 45) that drew her to the Greeks was replaced by a spiritual hunger expressed in the language of feeling and soul. The change involves more than vocabulary, for whereas "the far side" refers to the suggestive capacity of the Greek language, the language of the soul reflects more directly on the reader's spiritual hunger. In some sense the Russians led Woolf gradually to see in Proust a writer whose sense of the soul was more available to her, in a language that she could read.[11]

Since languages do not share the borders of political units, the sense of language as an intellectual domain challenges the linguistic tradition that coincides with the idea of the nation. Woolf's diary records an evening in 1927 spent at Long Barn, when Harold Nicolson maintained that the fact of the British Empire made Australia more important than France. Woolf intervened on the side of growth and change: "Also, I said, recalling the aeroplanes that had flown over us, while the portable wireless played dance music on the terrace, 'can't you see that nationality is over?'" (*D3*: 145). In 1940, in "The Leaning Tower," she protested on behalf of the common reader: "literature is common ground. It is not cut up into nations; there are no wars there" (*M*: 154). Whereas in Nicolson's idealized monolingual culture, imperial geography subordinated linguistic diversity to national identity, literature as "common ground" opens the way to a world in which

---

[11] Pierre-Eric Villeneuve writes of "Woolf's and Proust's common admiration of the Greeks and their exploration of the character's soul in fiction," "Communities of Desire: Woolf, Proust, and the Reading Process," *Virginia Woolf and Communities: Selected Papers from the Eighth Annual Conference on Virginia Woolf*, ed. Jeanette McVicker and Laura Davis (New York: Pace University Press, 1999), 23.

technological developments have diminished the significance of national boundaries.[12]

A central paradigm of translation, the story of the Tower of Babel in Genesis, arises in the context of a struggle among nations. The story is introduced by the genealogies of "the sons of Shem, by their families, their languages, their lands, and their nations" (Gen. 10:31). At a time when all men spoke one language that had few words, men proposed that we "build ourselves a city, and a tower with its top in the heavens, and let us make a name for ourselves, lest we be scattered abroad upon the face of the whole earth." The Lord, seeing that "nothing that they propose to do will now be impossible for them," confused their language and "scattered them abroad from there over the face of all the earth, and they left off building the city" (Gen. 11:6–8). The building of the Tower is represented as an interval in a narrative about the sons of Shem, who colonized the world after the Flood. Translation is an attempt to recapture an earlier ideal society where men could communicate, and history since Babel rests on linguistic confusion: "Therefore its name was called Babel, because there the Lord confused the language of all the earth" (Gen. 11:9).

The Biblical narrative is implicit in Benjamin's "The Task of the Translator" (1921), for instance in his emphasis on kinship and on an "original": "If the kinship of languages is to be demonstrated by translations, how else can this be done but by conveying the form and meaning of the original as accurately as possible?"[13] The significance of kinship is that "In the individual, unsupplemented languages, what is meant is never found in relative independence, as in individual words or sentences; rather, it is in a constant state of flux – until it is able to emerge as the pure language from the harmony of all the various ways of meaning."[14] Since all languages are relatively distant from revelation, translation "envelops its content like a royal robe with ample folds. For it signifies a more exalted language than its own and thus remains unsuited to its content, overpowering and alien."[15] So that language may be seen as "fragments of a greater language, just as fragments are part of a vessel, . . . it must in large measure refrain from

[12] "Over the last decade, studies within a variety of disciplines have unmasked the idea of homogenous (national) languages and cultures as a central mechanism mobilized by Western nation-states to inculcate a common identity upon their citizens." Reine Meylaerts, "Heterolingualism in/and Translation: How Legitimate Are the Other and his/her Language? An Introduction," *Target* 18 (2006), 1.

[13] Walter Benjamin, "The Task of the Translator," *Selected Writings*, vol. 1: *1913–1926*, ed. Marcus Bullock and Michael W. Jennings (Cambridge, Mass.: Belknap Press of Harvard University Press, 1996), p. 255.

[14] *Ibid.*, p. 257.   [15] *Ibid.*, p. 258.

wanting to communicate something."[16] Benjamin thrusts aside the notion of the fidelity or license of a translation, to make a point not about the text but about the relationship of languages to each other. "It is the task of the translator to release in his own language that pure language which is exiled among alien tongues, to liberate the language imprisoned in a work in his re-creation of that work."[17]

"The Task of the Translator" remains at the heart of contemporary theories of literary translation. Antoine Berman, who considers it the central text of the twentieth century on translation, notes that in a philosophical or religious tradition commentary and translation are inter-dependent. In fact commentary on the original inevitably leads to retranslation. He cites the correspondence in which Benjamin revealed his reluctance to translate Baudelaire's *Fleurs du mal*, to which the essay was to serve as a prologue. Although Benjamin translated *Sodome et Gomorrhe* (the manuscript of which is lost), and another volume of *La recherche* with Franz Hessel, Berman suggests that Benjamin's theory of translation points to a continuing tension between the experience and the theory of translation.[18] By titling his text "The Task of the Translator" rather than "The Task of Translation" Benjamin kept the emphasis on the subjectivity of the translator, where the tension between experience and theory plays out.

As a contemporary of Benjamin in postwar Europe, Woolf had had similar experiences: she too was an avid reader of translations and on a smaller scale had some experience of translation. She shared some of his goals: her criticism of language that is devoted to communication, and of the narrow view of translation as fidelity to an original. Independently of Benjamin she assumed the translator's task of recreating one's native tongue. But her particular spirituality and distrust of the Bible would not have been at home with Benjamin's religious messianism, or his conception of "pure" language.[19] Her understanding of translation was more in line with the questions that Paul de Man put to Benjamin's essay, stemming from the sense that a translation disrupts our presumptive ease within our native language, and works to alienate the reader. When de Man asks why the translator is at the center of Benjamin's essay: "The text is a poetics, a

---

[16] *Ibid.*, p. 260.   [17] *Ibid.*, p. 261.
[18] Antoine Berman, *L'âge de la traduction: "La tâche du traducteur" de Walter Benjamin, un commentaire* (Paris: Presses Universitaires de Vincennes, 2008), p. 36.
[19] Hilary Thompson reads the character of Septimus Smith as "a harbinger of arrested messianism" in terms of Benjamin's concept of "the exception," in "Time and its Countermeasures: Modern Messianisms in Woolf, Benjamin, and Agamben," *Modernism and Theory: A Critical Debate*, ed. Stephen Ross (London and New York: Routledge, 2009), 86–98.

theory of poetic language, so why does Benjamin not go to the poets? Or to
the reader, possibly; or the pair poet-reader . . . ?" the question leads directly
to Woolf's focus on translation that meets the needs of an expanding group
of readers outside the university.[20]

We might say that Woolf staked her position on a sense of the linguistic
confusion of Babel, which in the context of *Antigone* enabled her to ask: by
whom are languages constructed, and to what ends? To those who experience diaspora, the story of Babel poses an immediate ontological problem.
Derrida, an Algerian Jew, positioned among Hebrew, Arabic, and French,
deconstructs the metaphysical tradition and the possibility of a transcendental signified as independent of language. He turns to Saussure's qualified
endorsement of the sign. Translation upholds the difference of signifier/
signified: "In effect, the theme of a transcendental signified took shape
within the horizon of an absolutely pure, transparent, and unequivocal
translatability. In the limits to which it is possible, or at least *appears*
possible, translation practices the difference between signified and signifier.
But if this difference is never pure, no more so is translation, and for the
notion of translation we would have to substitute a notion of *transformation*:
a regulated transformation of one language by another, of one text by
another."[21] Woolf's language constantly remarks the historical contingency
of the sign, especially in *Three Guineas*, where although "we have no time to
coin new words," much of the discussion challenges the vocabulary of
patriarchy (*TG*: 131). Implicit in her project for "a female sentence" is the
need for *social* transformation. In my view her sense that social transformation begins with language makes her work compelling to writers who are
struggling against their colonization.

Whereas many studies of translation in the twentieth century have been
oriented towards Spanish and the culture of the New World, Woolf's knowledge of French invites instead a focus on a postcolonial reading of the myth
of Babel in the context of the Francophone diaspora.[22] I want to turn to
Philip Lewis' "The Measure of Translation Effects" (1985), an essay that is
central to my argument. It in turn responds to Derrida's essay on the
apocalyptic tone of contemporary philosophy, "D'un ton apocalyptique

[20] Paul de Man, "Conclusions: Walter Benjamin's 'The Task of the Translator,'" *The Resistance to Theory* (Minneapolis: University of Minnesota Press, 1986), p. 80.
[21] Jacques Derrida, *Positions*, trans. Alan Bass (Chicago: University of Chicago Press, 1981), pp. 19–20.
[22] For instance the argument of Eric Cheyfitz's *The Poetics of Imperialism: Translation and Colonization from "The Tempest" to "Tarzan,"* is "that translation was, and still is, the central act of European colonization and imperialism in the Americas" (New York and Oxford: Oxford University Press, 1991), p. 104.

adopté naguère en philosophie" (1981). In it Derrida builds on a work by a scholar who was also an Algerian Jew, André Chouraqui's *Liminaire pour l'Apocalypse*. Derrida seeks the origin of the apocalyptic tone in Revelation, in which John of Patmos reports what he heard and saw (Revelation 22:8). He transmits the message that the angel transmits from god, which Derrida suggests is a transcendental condition of all discourse ("l'apocalyptique ne serait-il pas une condition transcendantale de tout discourse").[23] What makes the essay difficult is Derrida's multilingual discussion of individual words that confronts the limits of the reader's knowledge of languages, since he cites ancient Greek, Hebrew, French, and German. Chouraqui's project, as Derrida represents it, was to recover from lost Aramaean and Hebrew texts whose traces have disappeared an original Hebrew under the extant Greek text, as though he were translating "ce texte original fantôme."[24] Chouraqui, Derrida argues, creates the position of translator as mediator, since his translation differs from traditional versions in that it discovers under the Greek text its historic context (he cites Chouraqui: "La traduction que je publie, nourrie par l'apport des versions traditionelles, a pour vocation de rechercher sous le texte grec son contexte historique").[25] The moment when Bloomsbury writers were unable or unwilling to employ the term *homosexual* in the public language provides the occasion for *Sodome et Gomorrhe* to become the phantom text of *Orlando*. In my argument, Proust's work gave Woolf the opportunity to recover the complexity and contradictions of history, so that when a term becomes untranslatable, it invites the role of translator-as-mediator.

Translation in a postcolonial context significantly reorients the role of the reader, by suggesting unsettling questions about the relationship to his native language. Lewis introduces his essay, addressed to an Anglo-American reader, with an acknowledgement that he is translating a talk given in French, and that his key phrase, the *abusive* translation, contains an adjective that in English does not include the French cognates "false, deceptive, misleading."[26] He argues for a translation that exploits the contradictory aims of making both a readable text and a masterful interpretation of the original. Building on Derrida's "Une bonne traduction doit toujours abuser" ("a good translation must always commit abuses"),[27] he

---

[23] Jacques Derrida, "D'un ton apocalyptique adopté naguère en philosophie," *Les fins de l'homme: à partir du travail de Jacques Derrida* (Paris: Éditions Galilée, 1981), 471.
[24] *Ibid.*, p. 478.   [25] *Ibid.*, pp. 478–9.
[26] Philip Lewis, "The Measure of Translation Effects," *Difference in Translation*, ed. Joseph P. Graham (Ithaca, N.Y.: Cornell University Press, 1985), 33.
[27] Jacques Derrida, "The *Retrait* of Metaphor," *Enclitic* 2:2 (1978), 22.

sets aside the translation that emphasizes content and the stable sign for one that focuses on "productive differences," while admitting the problem of "sacrificing rigor to facility."[28] Such a translation "will have a dual function – on the one hand, that of forcing the linguistic and conceptual system of which it is a dependent, and on the other hand, of directing a critical thrust back toward the text that it translates and in relation to which it becomes a kind of unsettling aftermath (it is as if the translation sought to occupy the original's already unsettled home, and thereby, far from 'domesticating' it, to turn it into a place still more foreign to itself)." While acknowledging "the staying power of classical concepts of translation" that domesticate a foreign work in the language of common usage, he urges a translation, based on "insightful reading," that preserves "the vital status of contrapuntal writing in the original."[29] In Woolf's hands several texts, notably *Antigone*, *War and Peace*, and *Sodome et Gomorrhe* became contrapuntal discourses, in the sense that they raise questions about her native language.

The word that is untranslatable in Woolf's text is often the site of a still unrecognized feeling that enters consciousness at the moment of awakening. After some years of detailing in her diary and her early fiction the difficulty of identifying personal feeling, she found in Proust a writer for whom, as she wrote in "Phases of Fiction," "everything that can be felt can be said" (*E*5: 67). She discovered in *À la recherche du temps perdu*, which she began to read in 1922, a model of the mind/body relationship in which feeling becomes a mode of thought capable of apprehending truth. Key passages in both writers focus on awakening as the moment in time and space when the mind commands both the conscious world of language and the unconscious body. Woolf shares with Proust the sense that the unconscious is a source of truth more profound than the intellect can apprehend, and that the narrator enjoys his greatest authority at the moment of awakening when language captures the experience of the dream. Lily Briscoe's awakening occurs at the end of "Time Passes," when she realizes that she cannot express what she feels about death. Like Proust's narrator's grief for his grandmother, her violent grief occurs suddenly, years after the death of Mrs. Ramsay. Involuntary memory affirms the continued and salutary presence of the dead that frees Lily to become a subject. In both novels involuntary memory opens the mind to the "truth in death" that is the condition both of the artist's subjectivity and the contingency of the sign.

---

[28] Lewis, "The Measure of Translation Effects," 39–41.   [29] *Ibid.*, pp. 59–60.

Writing *Mrs. Dalloway* Woolf wondered "whether this next lap will be influenced by Proust." As a reader of the C. K. Scott Moncrieff translation of the *Recherche*, she had been taking notes in which commentary is heavily dependent on her loose paraphrase of certain passages. An image from *The Pargiters* suggests the transition of Woolf as reader of Proust to Woolf as writer. There she sketched a program of contrapuntal writing in which she transformed the Proustian figure of the unconscious as an underwater terrain visited by the diver into an image of female writing about the body. *Orlando*, the most multilingual of Woolf's works, is the site of a truly *abusive* translation of *Sodome et Gomorrhe*. Written during a period when the trial of *The Well of Loneliness* reminded the public that in Britain homosexual acts were a crime, Woolf used the untranslatable word as a means to structure her novel, effectively shielding writing about lesbian experience from the law. The passage in which the gypsies refuse to translate *beauty* is heuristic: a culture that does not tolerate what is foreign forces the writer to flee, in order to create another world in the written language. *Sodome et Gomorrhe* pairs the homosexual and lesbian worlds, in which the dream world courts the contradictions that are inherent in seeing and hearing, a world that Proust figured as the home of an androgynous race where a man can turn into a woman.

Orlando directs a "critical thrust" back towards the *Recherche* in posing the visual image of the naked female body as a challenge to the question of sexual identity. At the historical moment when both Proust and Woolf could consign *gender* to the vocabularies of grammar and the law, Proust represented the contingency of sexual identity as a problem of visibility. The narrator who overhears without seeing Charlus and Jupien in the sexual act also fails to notice a woman's advanced pregnancy, as though sexual identity were a matter of visual perception. In the mirror scene Orlando undergoes a visual transformation in order to become a woman; subsequently although the language of her lawsuits accommodates a change in pronouns, her identity remains the same. By such means Woolf transforms the reality of female gender formation that is the occasion of prolonged suffering on the part of Proust's narrator into comedy.

By focusing the political implications of translation in a colonial context, diasporic writers fundamentally changed the way that translation is practiced and theorized. Their positions are anticipated by the figure of Louis in *The Waves*, who suggests that in a colonized society translation, owing to rituals of inheritance, is both urgent and impossible. His wish to translate a poem by Catullus "so that it is easily read" by clerks is hampered by assumptions of class and gender. Louis' project is riven by the tension between a reader whose taste has been degraded and his paralyzing sense that he cannot translate for such a reader. As an Australian his wish to inherit an armchair and a desk is given new meaning within a reading of the Tower of Babel that focuses on filiation. Derrida, an Algerian Jew who was expelled from a French school, reads the Tower of Babel as a scene of translation inscribed "within a scene of inheritance and in a space which is precisely that of the genealogy of proper names, of the family, the law, indebtedness."[30] It is the myth of a Semitic empire that wished to impose its tongue on the universe. Derrida reads Benjamin's emphasis on kinship as evidence that translation imposes responsibilities like those of "the marriage contract with the promise to produce a child whose seed will give rise to history and growth."[31] Benjamin, like Louis, and like himself, responds to a tradition that places them under the difficult obligations of the heir to keep the past alive. In *A Room of One's Own*, for instance, Woolf too saw men as "the natural inheritors of that civilization," and women as debarred from that position. There the figure of "J – H –" (Jane Harrison) suggests that although female subjects occupy a historical position, they lack a signifier outside the vocabulary of the law that determines inheritance (*RO*: 88). The reader of a translation enjoys the freedom of the outsider. Excluded from the traditions of university teaching he/she reads a foreign text without institutional support, a position that implicitly challenges the canon and the national language to which the educated male reader is heir.

In these circumstances Woolf asks under what conditions a work in Greek can be inscribed in a contemporary setting, and with what consequences for its significance and survival. *The Years* explores the question of *iterability*, which Derrida defines as the legibility of the sign in the absence of the sender or the receiver. In the novel the translation of *Antigone* is the key to a chain of events in which translation cements the connections between family lineage and colonial history. As a young student Edward Pargiter prepared a translation that qualified him for a place in the university where his father and grandfather had studied. As a don, he edits the text of *Antigone* that is read by his female cousin Sara as she lies in bed dreaming of love. She is an uneducated reader who embellishes the text, yet when she finishes reading composes her limbs in the position of the entombed Antigone, as though the imprint of the play on gender were independent

---

[30] Jacques Derrida, *The Ear of the Other: Otobiography, Transference, Translation*, trans. Peggy Kamuf, ed. Christie McDonald (Lincoln: University of Nebraska Press, 1985), p. 104.

[31] Derrida, "Des Tours de Babel," *Difference in Translation*, ed. Joseph P. Graham (Ithaca, N.Y.: Cornell University Press, 1985), 191.

of an attentive reading. The scene of translation during the family reunion in the final chapter attributes an untranslatable line to the interplay of family and colonial relations, when North asks his cousin Edward to translate a line from *Antigone*. North, who remembers enough schoolboy Latin to admire a line of Catullus, is a colonial who has returned from farming in Africa. When Edward recites in Greek Antigone's reply to Creon about love, which North asks him to translate, Edward refuses. And so does Woolf, who leaves the line in Greek in her text. Derrida's interpretation is that "a text lives only if it lives on, and it lives on only if it is at once translatable and untranslatable at the same time."[32] In Woolf's hands translation focuses the problem of *iterability* by embedding it in colonial politics. The line from *Antigone* is untranslatable only because those who can translate refuse, as though to deny that the iterability of *love* is a problem. That *Antigone* provokes such a conflicted response suggests that an imperial culture defends in the name of family lineage the very borders that translation is intended to cross, a history in which Woolf figures herself as well as her characters.

The reappearance of images and lines from Woolf's work in that of Assia Djebar again reorients the question of iterability, when an English text is translated by a Francophone novelist. Early in her career Djebar included Woolf in a course that she designed on European women writers whose work had been deepened by war. What in Woolf's world were taken to be the signs of mental illness, for instance hearing the voices of the dead, are heralded by the female writer in a culture with different spiritual traditions as the signs of her calling. Djebar's citations of Woolf's work suggest that she domesticated in Algerian culture the historical contingency of Woolf's language as a welcome alternative to French, the language of her education and of colonial institutions. Perhaps owing to her continual discomfort with French as the language of the occupier, Djebar wrote at length in *Ces voix qui m'assiègent* (1999), a Woolfian title, about the emergence of the subject among three languages – Berber, the mother language that she understands imperfectly, Arabic, both Koranic and the language of the street, and French, the "stepmother language," each of which to some extent both requires and evades translation. Faced with such complex choices she developed a version of the novel that couples personal with national history as "a place to think."[33] It is a curious testimony to Woolf's language that Djebar often

[32] Jacques Derrida, "Living On: Border Lines," trans. James Hulbert, *Deconstruction and Criticism*, by Harold Bloom, Paul de Man, Jacques Derrida, *et al.* (New York: Seabury Press, 1979), pp. 102–3.
[33] Assia Djebar, *Ces voix qui m'assiègent* (Paris: Albin Michel, 1999), p. 233.

seems more at home than Woolf in the position of the subject who resists colonization that a half-century after her death the diasporic writer could claim as her own.

L'amour, la fantasia (1985) reenacts the Antigone myth as French colonial history. Like Woolf's interpretation it focuses attention on the struggle between the state and patterns of kinship as Antigone understands them, and it spells out the horrors of live burial in more horrific terms than Woolf's suggestion of female interment in *The Years*. In Djebar's telling the play is a tale of hands, Antigone's hands, and the hands of the narrator outstretched towards an unidentified reader. *Vaste est la prison* (1995) opens and closes with an image familiar to readers of Woolf's description of writing the final page of *The Waves*, the hand that is driven across the page. Djebar poses the question that is central to the work of both: "The dead return to us; what do they desire in this sudden desert?"[34] It is Antigone's problem: in order to honor the dead the act of mourning must begin with a challenge to the language of the living.

The elusive connection between translation and mourning, which marks the furthest limits of this study of Woolf, is part of Djebar's feminist program. Her choice of a few lines from one of Woolf's early short stories, "A Haunted House" (1919), as preface to Part One of *Vaste est la prison* sheds light in both directions. There in a funeral scene female mourners hear a Berber lament that they cannot translate, while the narrator makes clear that to turn female mourning into history depends precisely on the willingness to translate the mother tongue into the hegemonic language, French. Djebar's connection between mourning and translation suggests a contrapuntal reading of Woolf's story, which was written towards the end of World War I. It concerns the voices of the dead that during sleep are heard below the level of recognition, like a heartbeat. The narrator divides the world between the ghostly couple who, seeking their joy, address their memories of each other, and the sleepers who overhear them: "Death was between us." The image of the male explorer and the empty house suggests a kind of historical tipping point, as in "Time Passes." Djebar cites the last lines, when the narrator awakens with a cry: "Oh, is this *your* buried treasure? The light in the heart" (*CSF*: 117). The narrator's enigmatic emphasis on *your* is broadly suggestive: the barrier between generations, the archeological reconstruction of a history that would include the wartime dead, and an unanswered semantic query about a border not to be crossed. Read in the context of *Antigone* as well as

---

[34] Assia Djebar, *So Vast the Prison*, trans. Betsy Wing (New York: Seven Stories Press, 1999), p. 346.

Vaste est la prison, it would seem that Woolf's story dramatizes the hegemonic voice that speaks to us at a level where it cannot be addressed, save by the mourning cry. To cross that border is the image that Djebar, as though responding to Woolf's linguistic hospitality, casts as the task of the translator.

CHAPTER I

Translation and ethnography in "On Not Knowing Greek"

The translator is the secret master of the difference of languages, not in order to abolish the difference but in order to use it to awaken in his own language, through the violent or subtle changes he brings to it, a presence of what is different, originally, in the original.

Maurice Blanchot, "Translating," *Friendship* (Stanford: Stanford University Press, 1997)

Woolf's essay "On Not Knowing Greek" in *The Common Reader* (1925) captures the historical moment when Victorian debates about the proper way to translate Greek were giving way to a broader interpretation of classical culture that linked it to events in the twentieth century. Together with "The Russian Point of View" and "Montaigne" it suggests the need to modify the perception of this volume of her essays as "meditations on English writers for English audiences."[1] Rather translation creates a reader whose position in the world is contingent on history and ethnology. Woolf prepared to write the essay by immersing herself for several months in rereading Greek tragedy and Plato, with the aim of drawing the common reader into an area that was governed by the university dons, in particular Matthew Arnold and Francis Newman, whom she does not name, and a poet, Shelley, whom she does. Moving back and forth between her citations in Greek and from R. C. Jebb's translations, Woolf blends Greek tragedy with an ethnographic sketch of Greek culture to create the sense that English is as foreign as Greek.

The title of the essay refers to the decades-long controversy about the teaching of Greek in British schools and universities that went on roughly from the 1870 debate on the Tripos at Cambridge until 1920, and deeply affected her understanding of the social significance of translation. Suzanne L. Marchand's densely factual study, *Down from Olympus: Archeology and*

---

[1] Laura Doyle, "Introduction: What's Between Us," *Modern Fiction Studies* 50 (2004), 5.

Philhellenism in Germany 1750–1970, studies the German precursors of the debate in England. She details the background of "rapturous Graecophilia" that she dates from the time of Schiller to the cultural revolutions of the 1960s and 1970s. Her study of *Altertumswissenschaft* begins with the shift in classical study in the eighteenth century from individual passion to institutional ideal. By the nineteenth century, study of the ancient world "was dominated by scholars trained in philology, the art of textual emendation and interpretation." Tracing the career of F. A. Wolf (1759–1824), she demonstrates that by the end of the eighteenth century Prussian classicism was dedicated to "the production of 'disinterested,' nonpopular, *historical* scholarship and contempt for comparative, ethnographic, and broadly philosophical questions."[2] The excavation of Olympia (1875–1881) began a series of grand-scale excavations that changed the history of Greek art to include pottery and the minor arts which in effect challenged the dominance of philology.[3]

Christopher Stray takes up the history of *Altertumswissenschaft* when it arrived in England, where, he points out, it helped to shift the orientation of the classics from liberal education to professionalism. Chronicling the change from amateur scholars to professional researchers, he summarizes the debate about classical scholarship: "the authority of the classics as an exemplar transcending change and relativity was severely eroded. Its claims to permanent value were eroded both by the brute fact of rapid and widespread social and cultural change, and by its having itself undergone change. Its claims to generality were eroded by the advance of specialization – both in the curricular field at large, and within classics itself."[4] By the end of the nineteenth century much of the philological work on Greek texts had been accomplished, and the excavations at Troy and Mycenae provided material support for interpreting Greek texts, with the result that those texts now invited a new kind of literary interpretation. The revision of the university Tripos at Cambridge had implications for gender, since it meant that women, who had no access to training in Greek composition in their early years, could now compete with men in the newly established fields of archeology and art criticism. Woolf lived through many of these changes, and was acquainted with several of the principal figures.

[2] Suzanne L. Marchand, *Down from Olympus: Archeology and Philhellenism in Germany 1750–1970* (Princeton: Princeton University Press, 1996), pp. 16–24.
[3] *Ibid.*, p. 112.
[4] Christopher Stray, *Classics Transformed: Schools, Universities, and Society in England, 1830–1960* (Oxford: Clarendon Press, 1998), p. 202.

Yet her design of *The Common Reader* shows her eager to avoid taking sides in the debates of an earlier generation. She wrote in her diary during 1922–23, "After all this stew, its odd how, as soon as I begin, a new aspect, never all this 2 or 3 years thought of, at once becomes clear; & gives the whole bundle a new proportion. To curtail, I shall really investigate literature with a view to answering certain questions about ourselves – Characters are to be merely views; personality must be avoided at all costs" (*D*2: 265). By this means she rejected quarrels about methods of translation, in favor of an interactive way of reading. In that vein she does not discuss the virtues of any particular translation or translator. Rather Woolf images Greek plays as sculpture performed: "their voices ring out clear and sharp; we see the hairy tawny bodies at play in the sunlight among the olive trees, not posed gracefully on granite plinths in the pale corridors of the British Museum" (*E*4: 42). The plays of Euripides although read "can be acted in the mind" (*E*4: 44).[5] As the member of an audience, the reader is called on to consider "the insoluble question of poetry and its nature," rather than to ponder questions of the relationship of Greek to English (*E*4: 43). Woolf worries about the untranslatable aspects of Greek texts: that we do not know how the actors sounded, whether we read Greek as it was written, and the impossibility of knowing when to laugh. These "questions about ourselves" concern reception. Read in its heuristic dimension "On Not Knowing Greek" diverts attention from the proper use of Greek texts to a sense that the reader may find twentieth-century problems performed in ancient plays.

The contradictions of the opening paragraph suggest the tone of the essay: "For it is vain and foolish to talk of knowing Greek, since in our ignorance we should be at the bottom of any class of schoolboys." The learned female narrator assumes the ignorance of a schoolboy, ironically a boy admitted to an exclusive educational system that was focused on the study of Greek. The essay deals with large questions of Greek character and culture while citing lines from Greek tragedy in Greek. In the essay Woolf is two persons. She is the Greek scholar, who does not always translate the line of poetry she cites, and opines that "It is useless, then, to read Greek in translations" (*E*4: 49). But she also reads Greek in a comparative context of culture and climate: a British schoolboy struggles to learn the language of speeches that were declaimed before an outdoor

---

[5] Yopie Prins writes of Woolf's translation of *Agamemnon* as "an imaginative restaging" of the play that opens up "a more mobile, more emotive" movement of thought. "OTOTOTOI: Virginia Woolf and 'The Naked Cry' of Cassandra," *"Agamemnon" in Performance 458 BC to AD 2004*, ed. Fiona Macintosh, Pantelis Michelakis, Edith Hall, and Oliver Taplin (Oxford: Oxford University Press, 2005), 172.

audience of thousands. Moving back and forth between these positions Woolf gives herself maximum flexibility, reaching backward to the vocabulary of the debate of an earlier generation over the correct way to translate Greek, at a time when the population of readers was expanding. The debate concerned whether a translation should seek to domesticate the foreign text by adapting it to the cultural expectations of its readers, or whether translation should aim to preserve a sense of the text's strangeness and difference. In Germany and England debate over these positions was derived from assumptions about the social status of the reader, whether he was unlearned, or a scholar.[6] In her essay Woolf revisited the debate between Matthew Arnold and Francis Newman over translations of Homer, and Shelley's translation of the *Symposium*, to argue the modernity of the Greeks as a people also "aware of their own standing in the shadow" (*E4*: 51). She agreed that translation is a reflection of the nation in Arnold's terms, while allying her position with Newman's "unlearned" reader. But her emphasis on "the tremendous breach of tradition" between Britain and ancient Greece enlarged the debate on purely linguistic issues: she stressed the otherness of Greek climate and culture, Shelley's contribution to our knowledge of ancient Greek sexual practice, the positions of the sender and receiver of a translation, and reading the Greeks as a way to satisfy postwar spiritual hunger (*E4*: 38).

Although Matthew Arnold as a "personality" is not named in the essay, the title mimics passages on knowing Greek in "Literature and Science" (1885). In his discussion of the appropriateness of literary study to students who might prefer an education in natural sciences, Arnold played on *knowing* in some thirty repetitions: "When I speak of knowing Greek and Roman antiquity, therefore, as a help to knowing ourselves and the world, I mean more than a knowledge of so much vocabulary, so much grammar, so many portions of authors in the Greek and Latin languages, I mean knowing the Greeks and Romans, and their life and genius, and what they were and did in the world ... when we talk of endeavouring to know Greek and Roman antiquity, as a help to knowing ourselves and the world, we mean endeavoring so to know them as to satisfy this ideal, however much we may still fall short of it."[7] Woolf's diary entry significantly

[6] In the nineteenth century Bohn's Classical Library was the most famous among several that reprinted existing translations of classical texts. In 1887 Bohn offered some ninety-eight volumes at five shillings apiece. Matthew Arnold disapproved of them. Kenneth Haynes, "Greek and Latin Literature: Introduction," *The Oxford History of Literary Translation in English*, vol. IV: *1790–1900*, ed. Peter France and Kenneth Haynes (Oxford: Oxford University Press, 2006), 165.
[7] Matthew Arnold, *Complete Prose Works of Matthew Arnold*, vol. X, ed. R. H. Super (Ann Arbor: University of Michigan Press, 1974), pp. 57–8.

rewrites Arnold's "knowing ourselves" as "answering certain questions about
ourselves," and her title problematizes one of Arnold's favorite words. The
first sentence challenges his position by reminding her reader that the university was closed to female students. Yet the essay shows her intimately
acquainted with Arnold's position, which she first acknowledges and then
rejects.[8]

In "On Translating Homer" (1861) Arnold attacked Francis Newman's
translation of the *Iliad*, ostensibly on the grounds of its awkward and archaic
diction. The Professor of Poetry at Oxford, while protesting that he had
"neither the time nor the courage" to translate Homer himself, laid down
the rules for translation in a series of negative and positive "counsels."[9] The
ideal translator's aim should be "to reproduce on the intelligent scholar, as
nearly as possible, the general effect of Homer," whereas "if his proper aim
were to help schoolboys to construe Homer," he might follow the example
of Newman.[10] Arnold was aware that "people speak as if there were two real
tribunals in this matter, – the scholar's tribunal, and that of the general
public."[11] In fact he addressed both audiences, the reader who would
recognize the well-known passages of the *Iliad* when cited in Greek, and
the reader hesitating among competing translations. Woolf's essay addresses
an audience split along similar lines, but by a shift of emphasis changes the
tone from one of fastidious rebuke to invitation. In her essay the *Odyssey*
receives brief mention, and she focuses on Greek tragedy in terms of
characters that face human dilemmas.

As Lawrence Venuti points out, the debate involved far more than Homer.
Newman (1805–97) was a classical scholar who taught at Manchester New
College and then University College, London. In addition to his work on
Greek and oriental languages, he wrote a number of religious works, and
essays on political issues including women's suffrage and the abolition of
slavery. His translation projects included material for students, and translations of Horace and the *Iliad* for "the *unlearned* English reader," who
read for amusement. In his view translation should magnify foreignness,
because "literature witnesses, and tends to uphold national diversity." As
he wrote in the preface to his *Iliad*, he "foreignized" the text as a way to
resist the tendency to standardize the English language. His method was to
introduce archaic words, *noisome* and *lief* for instance, so as to "attain a

---

[8] In a diary entry of January 1919 Woolf judged Arnold not to have "what I call an interesting mind"
    (*D*1: 238).
[9] Arnold, *Complete Prose Works*, vol. 1, ed. Super (Ann Arbor: University of Michigan Press, 1960),
    pp. 97–9.
[10] *Ibid.*, p. 118.   [11] *Ibid.*, p. 117.

plausible aspect of moderate antiquity, while remaining easily intelligible."[12] Arnold's aims were by contrast to impose the standards of a cultural elite. Venuti concludes, "Translation for Arnold was a means to empower an academic elite, to endow it with national cultural authority, but this empowerment involved an imposition of scholarly values on other cultural constituencies – including the diverse English-reading audience that Newman hoped to reach."[13] Their debate continued in a series of articles in British and American magazines. But in the end Newman fell into obscurity, while Arnold's reading "continues to be affiliated with the academy and with the dominant tradition of English-language translation, fluent domestication."[14]

Woolf appears to take both sides in the debate whether a translation should please the taste of the "unlearned" reader or the judgment of the scholar. She domesticates translation by her frequent comparisons with familiar British poets and novelists, but she also displays her knowledge of Greek when she quotes without translating several lines from *Agamemnon*. "It is useless, then, to read Greek in translation," introduces her Arnoldian attack on Professor Mackail for "'wan,'" a word that evokes William Morris, who had translated the *Odyssey* using archaisms (*E4*: 49). At the same time Woolf appealed to a wider "cultural constituency" when she shaped for herself a position more like that of an explorer than a university professor, by considering Greek literature from the perspective of comparative climate and geography – the English vs. the Greek village, and the context of oral delivery. Far from assuming authority over the text, she readily admits the likelihood of "reading wrongly . . . reading into Greek poetry not what they have but what we lack" (*E4*: 48). While giving full play to the difficulty of understanding a Greek text, she concludes that "even for the unlearned some certainties remain," for instance "the triumph of narrative" in the *Odyssey* (*E4*: 50). Here she would seem to echo Newman's plea for the "unlearned" reader, the "children and half-educated women" who cannot read the original.[15] But after discussions of beauty, humor, and language, the essay ends on an Arnoldian note of spiritual longing: "it is to the Greeks

[12] Lawrence Venuti, *The Translator's Invisibility: A History of Translation* (London and New York: Routledge, 1995), pp. 118–23.
[13] *Ibid.*, p. 132.   [14] *Ibid.*, p. 145.
[15] Francis Newman, "The Unlearned Public Is the Rightful Judge of Taste," *Homeric Translation in Theory and Practice* (1861), in *Western Translation Theory from Herodotus to Nietzsche*, ed. Douglas Robinson (Manchester and Northampton, Mass.: St. Jerome Publishing, 1997, second edition 2002), p. 257.

that we turn when we are sick of the vagueness, of the confusion, of the Christianity and its consolations, of our own age" (*E4*: 51).

Yet the unnamed professors do not have the last word, for near the end of Woolf's essay there is a brief unsettling reference to Shelley, in a passage where she writes of the danger of "reading into Greek poetry not what they have but what we lack."[16] It is an instance of Woolf's tendency to couple the interlingual translation of a foreign text with an intralingual reminder (what Jakobson calls a circumlocution) of the vexed history of a word that for the moment remains untranslatable. At issue is Shelley's translation of a line from *The Banquet*, the controversial translation of the *Symposium* left unpublished in his lifetime: "For everyone, even if before he were ever so undisciplined, becomes a poet as soon as he is touched by love" (*E4*: 48–9). How could the reference and the line fail to remind Woolf's reader that Shelley's translation, published posthumously by Mary Shelley, was his attempt "to explain to Mary and, if the translation were ever published, to the English world the subject of homosexuality, which formed a barrier to a true understanding of the Greek mind and prevented a true appreciation of Plato's genius."[17] With eventual publication in mind Shelley modified the language of certain passages, although, he wrote, "we are not exactly aware ... what the action was by which the Greeks expressed their passion." In his translation for instance the term for sexual gratification ($\chi\alpha\rho\acute{\iota}\sigma\alpha\alpha\theta\alpha\acute{\iota}$) was translated as "devotion."[18] After Shelley's death Mary Shelley worried about "the common reader" (her phrase as well as Woolf's) as she faced the difficult task of publishing her husband's work without further altering the text. She deleted a speech by Alcibiades, but fretted over changes in diction that emphasized friendship: "I have altered and omitted ... but I could not bring myself to leave the word *love* out entirely from a treatise on Love."[19] The expurgated version of *The Banquet* appeared in 1840, the full text not until 1931.[20]

---

[16] Rowena Fowler notes that Greek "was associated in Woolf's mind with forbidden knowledge and sexual violence and with a whole network of disturbing personal memories." "'On Not Knowing Greek': The Classics and the Woman of Letters," *Classical Journal* 78 (1982–3), 346.

[17] James A. Notopoulos, *The Platonism of Shelley: A Study of Platonism and the Poetic Mind* (Durham, N.C.: Duke University Press, 1949), p. 384.

[18] Cited in Jennifer Wallace, *Shelley and Greece: Rethinking Romantic Hellenism* (London: Macmillan, 1997), p. 106.

[19] Mary Shelley, *The Letters of Mary Shelley*, vol. II, ed. Frederick L. Jones (Norman: University of Oklahoma Press, 1944), [Letter 508, October, 1839], pp. 139–40.

[20] Praise of Shelley's translations in *Posthumous Poems* is summarized by Kenneth Haynes. "Translation and British Literary Culture," *The Oxford History of Literary Translation in English*, vol. IV: *1790–1900*, ed. Peter France and Kenneth Haynes (Oxford: Oxford University Press, 2006), 10.

Woolf read the *Symposium* in Greek, and more than once. Her seven pages of holograph notes date from her reading in 1908, and in 1920 she wrote to her former Greek tutor, Janet Case, "I am reading the Symposium – ah, if I could write like that" (*L2*: 446). It is one of several instances of Woolf's play of mind as she entertained the idea of measuring herself against a foreign writer. What might it have meant for Woolf to "write like that"? Was she thinking of an essay written like a Platonic dialogue? Did she hint at conversation with her readers about homosexuality? What role might desire play in the essay she did write? Woolf and Shelley had both as students fallen in love with the Greeks; both had studied a range of European languages (and Shelley had made a stab at Arabic); and translation was an important stimulus to their creative work.[21] Translation from the Greeks helped them to transcend the limits of the subject imposed by British law, under which homosexuality remained a crime until 1964, and to realize that outside public discourse same-sex love was associated with the highest achievements in poetry and philosophy. Woolf's interest in Proust and Gide is evidence of her continuing need to understand a full range of desire and its representation in language. Although she seems to chide Shelley for taking twenty-one words to translate thirteen of Plato's, the larger concern of the paragraph and the essay is that British readers may misunderstand "a vigour which pours out of olive-tree and temple and the bodies of the young" (*E4*: 48).

Melba Cuddy-Keane analyzes this essay as part of her portrait of Woolf as an intellectual fully engaged in the public issues of her time. Cuddy-Keane brings together historical and textual analysis to argue that "at a time of growing specialization and increasingly objective methodology in academic English studies, Woolf defended an amateur status and a wide-ranging and catholic reading practice."[22] In order to present a position that challenged the conventional rhetorical practices of patriarchal discourse, Woolf devised a "method" that she referred to in 1923 as "turn and turn about" (*D2*: 247). Cuddy-Keane adapts Woolf's phrase to the rhetorical strategy of shifting positions that gave her "an alternative to the authorial-authoritative dominance of patriarchal discourse."[23] The reader is challenged: "No longer situated as a spectator witnessing a debate, the reader undergoes repeated repositionings; it is as if the reader gets comfortable settled in one easy chair

---

[21] Timothy Webb discusses Shelley's motivations for translation in chapter one of *The Violet in the Crucible: Shelley and Translation* (Oxford: Clarendon Press, 1976).

[22] Melba Cuddy-Keane, *Virginia Woolf, the Intellectual, and the Public Sphere* (Cambridge: Cambridge University Press, 2003), p. 2.

[23] *Ibid.*, p. 142.

only to be told to shift to another facing the opposite way. The different chairs are all presented as viable ideological locations, including the chair made from the stuff of conventional assumptions, traditional thinking, and patriarchal attitudes."[24] By this means "Woolf both satisfies conventional scholarly expectations ... while, at the same time, she disempowers the authoritative stance by situating interpretation with an on-going process of provisionality and exploration."[25]

The diary entry in which Woolf introduced the term "turn and turn about" is a more complex sketch of the strategy by which she introduced *The Banquet*, insinuating desire by saying yes before she says no to the dominant discourse. It opens provocatively, "Nothing else of great importance has happened," and then traces the strange prompting of her desire in the setting of patriarchal culture. Her phrase is introduced under a negative sign: "Leo Myers, who is glazed with disillusionment & middle age, as tongues are glazed, said that my turn & turn about method is wrong. The Drs. say so" (*D2*: 247). Her "method" meets harsh judgment from a male speaker who represents other authoritative speakers, but his "glazed" tongue is the symptom of disease. The context is a discussion by Myers and Clive of their "dissipation" in the demi-monde that prompted Woolf to wonder, "I want – I want – But what do I want? Whatever I had, I should always say I want I want." When "Leo Myers said we all feel excluded," Woolf noted his sizable income and his freedom to travel, yet "it was I who got the romance by thinking this, not poor Leo, who is glazed like a tongue" (*D2*: 247). The passage suggests that this conversation among male heterosexuals prompted Woolf to acknowledge a desire so diffuse that it engenders a new meaning of "dissipation." The passage typifies a pattern of resistance that appears everywhere in Woolf's work. It begins in a setting of intellectual and socio-economic privilege, where for the purposes of conversation she entertains alien habits of mind, before coming at the end of the paragraph to a position quite opposite although perhaps unuttered. Whatever she might have meant by "romance," the term renames desire, which keeps her thought in the realm of possibility and so resists resentment as well as closure.[26]

"On Not Knowing Greek" lays claim to cultural capital, in John Guillory's sense of "linguistic capital, the means by which one attains to a

[24] *Ibid.*, p. 137.   [25] *Ibid.*, p. 141.
[26] Mary Jacobus sums up the argument by French feminists that deals with "the repression of women's desire by representation itself," in "The Difference of View," *Women Writing and Writing About Women*, ed. Mary Jacobus (London: Croom Helm, in association with Oxford University Women's Studies Committee, 1979), 12.

socially credentialed and therefore valued speech," and in so doing it traces a history that parallels the centuries-old arguments over translations of the *Aeneid*.[27] André Lefevere argues that at the time of Dryden's translation the audience was already divided between those who like his aristocratic patron might have been able to make a comparison with the original, and the bourgeois reader to whom he addressed the notes. The question whether a translation supplements or supplants the original divides the readership along lines of class and education. Reviewing the historical context of some fifteen translations Lefevere concludes that the needs of readers are "responsible for the existence, from the seventeenth century onwards, of a double lineage of Virgil translations into English: one, like Dryden's more concerned with emulating the original, without, however, neglecting to acquaint its reader at the same time with current discourse about that original; and another, with many translators now forgotten, who tried to make the cultural capital represented by both Virgil and the language he wrote in, accessible to as many readers as possible, in as many forms as were believed to be helpful for that purpose."[28] Given that Arnold's model still dominates translations from the Greek, Woolf's essay does not seem to have succeeded in any practical sense of turning attention to the needs of the common reader. Perhaps it is more significant that during her lifetime England achieved nearly total literacy, so that more readers without Greek sought translations.[29]

In the essay Woolf attempts to domesticate difficult works by pointing out the differences between Greek and English climate, and the similarities of life in small villages, in order to sketch the relationship of the text to its culture. In so doing she encountered the problematic use of translation in ethnography. Talal Asad's well-known observations about the power relations that obtain between the ethnographer and the culture that he represents theorize the rhetoric of "On Not Knowing Greek." Whereas the linguist – or the translator – deals with an existing discourse, the anthropologist "must construct the discourse as a cultural text in terms of meanings *implicit* in a range of practices. The construction of cultural discourse

---

[27] Cited by André Lefevere, "Translation Practice(s) and the Circulation of Cultural Capital: Some *Aeneids* in English," *Constructing Cultures: Essays on Literary Translation*, ed. Susan Bassnett and André Lefevere (Clevedon, Philadelphia, Toronto, Sydney, Johannesburg: Multilingual Matters, 1998), 43. The term was coined by Pierre Bourdieu.

[28] *Ibid.*, p. 51.

[29] Todd Avery and Patrick Brantlinger report that by 1900 England had achieved "almost universal literacy." "Reading and Modernism: 'Mind Hungers' Common and Uncommon," *A Concise Companion to Modernism*, ed. David Bradshaw (Oxford: Blackwell, 2003), 244. They note that Woolf "wrote about reading more often than any other modernist writer," 251.

and its translation thus seem to be facets of a single act."[30] When Woolf writes that among the Greeks, we encounter "the stable, the permanent, the original human being," or "the original man or woman," she denies Greeks their history (*E*4: 42). Her position is consistent with an ethnographic assumption of reality that blurs social distinctions in the society under study. Asad concludes: "My point is only that the process of 'cultural translation' is inevitably enmeshed in conditions of power – professional, national, international." The result is that "in the long run it is not the personal authority of the ethnographer, but the social authority of his ethnography that matters."[31]

The problematic nature of translation in this context complicates questions of reading and representation. The translation of an ancient text or of another culture starts from different assumptions: the former assumes the documented referentiality of language in texts that have been preserved for centuries, whereas translation by the ethnographer must take account of performance, in which meaning is derived in part from cultural context. The problem is particularly acute in Greece, as Michael Herzfeld argues: "If modern Greece holds up a looking-glass to the discipline that shares with it a history of elaborating the meaning of 'the West,' its language enshrines many of the most piquant paradoxes of its dual role as incarnation of Hellas and orientalized land of unredeemable marginality."[32] Herzfeld studies "the semantic instability" of the ethnographer's encounter, where performance is inevitably confused with intent. The assumption of an original text, and even the use of the classical alphabet, reinforce what he terms "the referential illusion . . . Thus the use of standardized translations and a classical mode of transliteration obliterates the play of actors' perhaps quite divergent intentions in favor of structural unity and images of social stability and equilibrium."[33] We can see the outlines of this problem emerging in the diary that Woolf kept during her trip to Greece in 1906. As a tourist she noted the differences among spoken Greek, the language of the newspaper, and the language of the classics. She reminded herself that "it is amusing to be able to abuse entirely," and so divided Greece between classical and contemporary: "The justice of that division has been provided

[30] Talal Asad, "The Concept of Cultural Translation in British Social Anthropology," *Writing Culture: The Poetics and Politics of Ethnography*, ed. James Clifford and George E. Marcus (Berkeley: University of California Press, 1986), 160.
[31] *Ibid.*, p. 163.
[32] Michael Herzfeld, "The Unspeakable in Pursuit of the Ineffable," *Translating Cultures: Perspectives on Translation and Anthropology*, ed. Paula G. Rubel and Abraham Rosman (Oxford and New York: Berg, 2003), 111.
[33] *Ibid.*, p. 115.

etymologically, & ethnologically."[34] Greece represented for Woolf the farthest reach of history and the civilization to which Britain was heir, but the Greece of 1906, as her language suggests, is an orientalized other. Woolf's rhyming pairs: etymology/ethnology and amuse/abuse suggest that a passage written to herself already shows colonial inflections, young as she was.[35]

Debates about Greek ethnology and "primitive" society were actively pursued among Leslie Stephen's associates. One influential book, *Ancient Law* (1861), which remains a classic of the literature, was written by Henry Sumner Maine (1822–88), a Cambridge graduate and a friend of Leslie Stephen's older brother, James Fitzjames Stephen (1829–94). In chapter five, "Primitive Society and Ancient Law" Maine cites Homer to support his argument that primitive society was an aggregation of patriarchal or family groups rather than a collection of individuals. The book brings together a version of ancient Greek history and law under the heading of "primitive jurisprudence."[36] "Primitive" was good currency among many Victorian anthropologists, as is apparent in numerous titles of the period, for instance Franz Boas' *The Mind of Primitive Man* (1929). As late as 1954, in a collection of broadcast talks, Godfrey Lienhardt wrote that "the problem of describing to others how members of a remote tribe think . . . begins to appear largely as one of translation, of making the coherence primitive thought has in the language it really lives in, as clear as possible in our own."[37]

The wide circulation of "primitive" in the context of ethnology and translation suggests how a single word might date an attitude that a generation before it was abandoned by ethnologists was used by Woolf to identify the mental habits of an older generation. The tourists who visit South America in *The Voyage Out* are oriented by the gaze to a notion of the *primitive*. Woolf used the word in her fiction only five times, three in this novel, where she portrays older characters who are committed to a view of

---

[34] Virginia Woolf, "Greece 1906" (*APA*: 340).
[35] But see Artemis Leontis, who reads Woolf's "A Dialogue on Mount Pentelicus" as opening "a chasm between the ancient Greek and the loyal British subject, once viewed as successive inhabitants on high culture's imaginary plane. The modern subject experiences the erosion of crucial links between himself and antiquity." *Topographies of Hellenism: Mapping the Homeland* (Ithaca, N.Y.: Cornell University Press, 1995), pp. 17–18.
[36] Henry Sumner Maine, *Ancient Law: Its Connection with the Early History of Society, and its Relation to Modern Ideas* (New York: Holt, 1864; reprint edition Tucson: University of Arizona Press, 1986), 109–65.
[37] Godfrey Lienhardt, "Modes of Thought," *The Institutions of Primitive Society: A Series of Broadcast Talks* (Oxford: Basil Blackwell, 1967), 96–7.

South American antiquities and society as "primitive." Mr. Pepper describes an outpost of the British Empire that is "bigger than Italy, and really nobler than Greece." The people are "strangely beautiful, very big in stature, dark, passionate, and quick to seize the knife," their art "primitive carvings coloured bright greens and blues" (*VO*: 90). Mr. Flushing lectures his wife that "before the dawn of European art he believed that the primitive huntsmen and priests had built temples of massive stone slabs, [and] there might be prehistoric towns, like those in Greece and Asia" (*VO*: 237).

The western tendency to view a foreign culture as unchanging and its art as primitive is borne out in the scene of visiting a South American village. The narrator emphasizes the strangeness of the encounter of British tourists with indigenous women, who are seen "plaiting straw or . . . kneading something in bowls" (*VO*: 284). Mark Wollager argues that the resemblance of the women to popular postcard images of native women is part of the vogue of primitivism in European art.[38] The British characters are travelers, not ethnographers, so the unequal power relation that is implicit in ethnographic discourse is expressed in the novel as a conflict of the gaze. The villagers "stare" as the travelers "peered into huts," until the visitors are absorbed into the scene. Whereas by western standards of decorum the tourists are making a tour of inspection, the villagers' stares are, ironically, rude intrusions on personal privacy.[39] The narrator writes of "the motionless inexpressive gaze of those removed from each other far, far beyond the plunge of speech" (*VO*: 284). Their unfamiliar utterance is represented as "some harsh unintelligible cry" (*VO*: 285). Although the tourists may seem to play an active role, Wollager concludes that Rachel and her companions are all "involuntary agents of the dominant powers to which Rachel typically feels subjected."[40]

In "On Not Knowing Greek" the word "primitive" characterizes Woolf's response to Antigone and Ajax, when they are "stirred by death, by betrayal, by some other primitive calamity" (*E4*: 42). Perhaps death is primitive. But elsewhere when she remarks "the nimbleness of wit and tongue peculiar to the Southern races," and the Greek village, where "life is simply sorted out into its main elements" (*E4*: 39), her position is consistent with ethnographic assumptions that efface the heterogeneity of the society under study.[41]

[38] Mark Wollager, "Woolf, Postcards, and the Elision of Race: Colonizing Women in *The Voyage Out*," *Modernism/Modernity* 8 (2001), 61.
[39] Andrea Lewis writes that "In this scene the private activities of the natives become a public spectacle for the English, a point of ethnographic interest for them." "The Visual Politics of Empire and Gender in Virginia Woolf's *The Voyage Out*," *Woolf Studies Annual* 1 (1995), 117.
[40] Wollager, "Woolf, Postcards, and the Elision of Race," 67.
[41] Tejaswini Niranjana, *Siting Translation: History, Post-Structuralism, and the Colonial Context* (Berkeley: University of California Press, 1992), p. 81.

Once Woolf has exploited the differences between translation in the hands of a don or a poet, the translator is no longer invisible, and the discourse shifts to the changing norms of translation. Theo Hermans explores the paradoxes of translation to argue that all translation involves interpretation: "What happens when we decide to pay sustained attention to translation, when we want to investigate both the practice and the discourse about translation across a wide cultural spectrum, historically and geographically, i.e. when we engage in the discipline called translation studies? What happens is that problems arise."[42] One fundamental difficulty is that since the translator like the historian makes statements on behalf of another, his role is hardly transparent. Since the problem is complex and there are no answers, the translator, he concludes, might well adopt the position of the ethnographer.[43] Claude Levi-Strauss, discussing the problems of representing a system of beliefs, wrote that "we force ourselves to *translate* into our language rules originally stated in a different code."[44] Since to seek a solution by creating a metalanguage leads to aporia, Hermans suggests that if no solution is available, at least one can "make explicit the position from which the analyst is speaking – even if . . . there can never be a stable, ultimate position to work from."[45] We can see Woolf working along similar lines when she starts by responding to Greek culture in the image of seeing the Greeks across "a chasm which the vast tide of European chatter can never succeed in crossing" (*E4*: 39). She reads a line by Sophocles by imagining "some village, in a remote part of the country, near the sea" (*E4*: 39). The image of an outdoor audience of "seventeen thousand people" is estranged by her comparison with the readers of a ball scene from *Emma*. Her reading of Platonic dialogue as conversation among friends gives philosophical dignity to the inherent fluidity of her position: "Truth, it seems, is various; Truth is to be pursued with all our faculties. Are we to rule out the amusements, the tendernesses, the frivolities of friendship because we love truth? Will truth be quicker found because we stop our ears to music and drink no wine, and sleep instead of talking through the long winter's night?" (*E4*: 47). Arnold and Newman may have given Woolf the terms of a debate between scholarly and unlearned readers, and Shelley

[42] Theo Hermans, "Paradoxes and Aporias in Translation and Translation Studies," *Translation Studies: Perspectives on an Emerging Discipline*, ed. Alessandra Riccardi (Cambridge: Cambridge University Press, 2002), 17.

[43] *Ibid.*, p. 20.   [44] Cited in Niranjana, *Siting Translation*, p. 68.

[45] Theo Hermans, "Paradoxes and Aporias in Translation and Translation Studies," *Translation Studies: Perspectives on an Emerging Discipline*, ed. Alessandra Riccardi (Cambridge: Cambridge University Press, 2002), 21.

the reminder of a subtext on homosexuality, but her attempts to visualize
Greek culture reoriented the debate towards her contemporaries. Her sense
that translation responds to historical changes in the population of readers
was acute: following the war the reader made new demands on poetry; the
sense of beauty changed; and the common reader sought in translations
from the Greek spiritual as well as aesthetic satisfaction.

As a result of her knowing some Greek Woolf was able to create for
herself a position between the Greek text and its translations. A study by
Cees Koster explores the implications of this position. The study of internal
linguistic features of the text, or of its external contextual factors leads to
different sets of questions, he argues, that require some theoretical consideration. Since "a translation is a representation of another text and *at the
same time* a text in its own right," the text has two "senders," two "messages," and two "addressees."[46] The translator is correspondingly in two
positions as sender and addressee, but the distance between the roles "entails
a disconnection of the writer's intention and the text's verbal meaning."[47]
Referring to Koster's distinctions we can see that Arnold and Woolf handled
the double function of the translator in different ways. By insisting on the
accuracy of representing verbal meaning Arnold in effect occluded the
ideology of his intentions sufficiently to have repressed Newman's position.
Woolf, although she rebukes Professor Mackail for "wan" and Shelley for
prolixity, names neither Arnold nor Newman. In the language of translation
studies she implies that since the addressee has changed, the reader's codes
are not those that Arnold relied on, and further that external historical
factors have led to a new set of questions. As for Woolf's "intentions" in
relation to "the text's verbal meaning," it can be seen that she silently
inhabits the authoritative positions of Arnold and Newman only to modify
or reject them.[48] Yet the act of resistance required in order to create the
space for her voice as a spokesperson for the "unlearned" created the
ethnographer's classic problem of translation.

The problem of representation is central to the work of a translator who
involved herself in ethnography as well as classical translation. Pamela

[46] Cees Koster, "The Translator in Between Texts: On the Textual Presence of the Translator as an Issue
in the Methodology of Comparative Translation Description," *Translation Studies: Perspectives on an
Emerging Discipline*, ed. Alessandra Riccardi (Cambridge: Cambridge University Press, 2002), 28.
[47] *Ibid.*, p. 31.
[48] What would Woolf have made of Newman's "An intelligent child is the second-best reader of
Homer. The best of all is a scholar of highly masculine taste; the worst of all is a fastidious and refined
man, to whom everything quaint seems ignoble and contemptible"? In Newman, "The Unlearned
Public is the Rightful Judge of Taste," *Western Translation Theory from Herodotus to Nietzsche*, ed.
Robinson, 258.

Caughie, after questioning "the assumptions bound up with the reference theory of meaning and a mimetic theory of representation" in Woolf's novels, turns to the essays, where she again questions the adequacy of representational theory.[49] Whereas an emphasis on mimetic representation might lead to the assumption that Woolf's "common reader" is "the average or literate reader," in a world of plural discourses, the reader "is not merely affirmed; rather, she is constructed through the very stories she reads."[50] Woolf too understood representation as a challenge to the reader. In "How Should One Read a Book?" (originally a talk to schoolgirls in 1926) she addressed the problem in connection with reading poetry: "Its power of make-believe, its representative power, is dispensed with in favour of its extremities and extravagances. The representation is often at a very far remove from the thing represented, so that we have to use all our energies of mind to grasp the relation between, for example, the song of a nightingale and the images and ideas which that song stirs in the mind" (*E4*: 395–6). In "On Not Knowing Greek" the poetry of Aeschylus is an example of representation, for he gives us "not the thing itself, but the reverberations and reflection which, taken into his mind, the thing has made" (*E4*: 45).

Although Woolf's comments suggest that representation may pose a problem for readers of poetry, they also reflect its use during this period in the wider context of a scientific revisioning of the world. Gillian Beer has written extensively about Woolf's acquaintance with the work of Eddington, Jeans, and other physicists, and her particular fascination with wave theory. "From the 1920s on at least, Woolf found in the new physics dizzying confirmation of her sense that the real and the substantial are not the same. As early as 1923 she had invented a word for what she wanted to do: to 'insubstantise.'"[51] Mark Hussey, investigating the vocabulary and perceptions that Woolf shared with the physicist David Bohm, notes that "Woolf marks in her fiction the new framework of representation ushered in by early twentieth century physics."[52] Michael Whitworth documents in detail Woolf's awareness of research in atomic structure and theories of

[49] Pamela Caughie, *Virginia Woolf & Postmodernism* (Urbana: University of Illinois Press, 1991), pp. 113 and 137.
[50] *Ibid.*, p. 188.
[51] Gillian Beer, "Physics, Sound, and Substance: Later Woolf," *Virginia Woolf: The Common Ground* (Ann Arbor: University of Michigan Press, 1996), p. 120.
[52] Mark Hussey, "*To the Lighthouse* and Physics: The Cosmology of David Bohm and Virginia Woolf," *New Essays on Virginia Woolf*, ed. H. Wussow (Dallas: Contemporary Research Press, 1995), 81.

electrical phenomena, while warning that assertions about the connection between the uncertainty principle and modernism risk anachronism.[53]

In questioning representation, does Woolf ask, with Derrida, whether translation is of the same order as representation, in the sense of representing "the same semantic content, by a different word of a different language," or whether translation "escapes the orbit of representation."[54] Following Heidegger, Derrida associates representation with visibility as characteristic of the modern field, especially "the gesture which consists of placing, of causing to stand before one, of installing in front of oneself as available, of localizing ready at hand," so that the idea becomes "a copy in the mind."[55] He historicizes representation by reminding us that the ancient Greeks had no word for it, although he discusses at length the manner in which Platonism was a distant premonition of representation: "it would have destined it without itself being subjected to it."[56] In more recent history, he cites Lacan's observation of the "calculable" aspect of representation that in its most dangerous manifestation leads to police files and concentration camps.

Woolf approaches Derrida's position most closely in the passage where while he acknowledges that the modern subject derives its authority from representation, he questions its adequacy and value: "All of post-Cartesian . . . if not in fact the whole of modern discourse, has recourse to this category to designate all the modifications of the subject in its relationship with an object. The Great question, the generative question, thus becomes, for this epoch, that of the *value* of representation, of its truth or its adequacy to what it represents."[57] Woolf's characterization of Mr. Ramsay in *To the Lighthouse* exhibits the problematic value of representation that is associated with the values of war and empire. He is the post-Cartesian subject, when in the privacy of his poetry recitation he summons the visible world merely to confirm the text at hand: "as one raises one's eyes from a page in an express train and sees a farm, a tree, a cluster of cottages as an illustration, a confirmation of something on the printed page to which one returns, fortified, and satisfied" (*TL*: 38). He is the subject who "believes it can offer itself representations, disposing them and disposing of them."[58] His trance-like recitations of the poetry of war reveal him as a subject of the state, although he is far too timid to question the adequacy or the

[53] Michael Whitworth, "Physics: 'A Strange Footprint,'" *A Concise Companion to Modernism*, ed. David Bradshaw (Oxford: Blackwell, 2003), 208–211.
[54] Jacques Derrida, "Sending: On Representation," *Social Research* 49 (1982), 297–8.
[55] *Ibid.*, p. 309.   [56] *Ibid.*, p. 313.   [57] *Ibid.*, p. 310.   [58] *Ibid.*, p. 309.

limitations of imperial subjectivity, merely repeating a line from Tennyson's "Charge of the Light Brigade": "someone had blundered." The narrator abstracts his position in an image of the alphabet, in which Mr. Ramsay, aware of Z, has reached only Q: "After Q there are a number of letters the last of which is scarcely visible to mortal eyes, but glimmers red in the distance" (*TL*: 39). The problem seems to be that the visible world that he assumes is his to command by his gaze from the window of the train alters when, from a different spatial position, he sees the red light in the distance as a reminder that he has been left behind. In some sense Woolf's characters are the left-behind, not only the philosopher but the mother, the lover, and cohorts of school friends: representation from this position suggests the cost when what had been visible is no longer. The narrator enjoys no greater freedom, confined within an alphabetic culture that is governed by linear sequence.[59]

Derrida's discussion of representation (which I read in an English translation) is itself caught up in the web of translation. He notes the ways in which translation diverts meanings in several languages towards *representation*, as when German *vorstellen* and *darstellen*, and French *phantasia* or *phantasma* (in a lexicon of Plato) are translated by a single English word. Whereas he asserts that in ordinary language when we read of labor delegates or parliamentary representatives, *representation* raises no significant problems, Woolf complicates the problem in "Solid Objects" (1920), which investigates the dual status of representation as *vorstellen* and *darstellen*. In the story John ignores the duty to represent his constituents, in favor of collecting fragments from the beach and the rubbish tip, on which his selection confers identity. His companion Charles speaks in a few conventional phrases, and uses language to "dismiss a foolish train of thought" (*CSF*: 97). The story does less to represent John and his friendship with the commonsensical Charles, than to make present the conditions in which an object like a meteorite or a piece of iron becomes visible and is collected, as a precondition to representation that narrows the meaning to *vorstellen*, while John significantly fails in the sense of *darstellen*. Although Woolf does not mention the German words, she experiments with Derrida's topic in a way that leaves me as her reader uncertain of the outcome of the actions that the story attempts to document. In the story

---

[59] Walter Mignolo writes on the exclusion of non-alphabetic cultures from critical discourse, for instance in "Globalization, Civilization Processes, and the Relocation of Languages and Cultures," *Cultures of Globalization*, ed. Fredric Jameson and Masao Miyoshi (Durham, N.C.: Duke University Press, 1998), 37–43.

Woolf deconstructs representation as a process that begins in the visual construction of the planet, when two men are perceived "moving upon the vast semicircle of the beach" (*CSF*: 96). The narrator's gaze initiates a narrative which disturbingly reenacts the narrative of John's gaze, as though the visible were a labyrinth from which there is no exit.

Derrida admits that "it is difficult to think beyond representation," especially since it assumes a visible world.[60] He finds a satisfying alternative in the *envoi*, the French title of his address, and also the lines that send the poem out into the world. They are an aid to "thinking altogether differently." I wish to return to Derrida's first query and rephrase the problem of "thinking differently," to ask how translation comments on the visible world and the culture of representation. *Soul* was a dimension of spirituality that drew Woolf in the 1920s both to Arnold and to the Russian novel. It is an "insubstantial" dimension that she found wanting in the "materialist" writers of her generation. Yet the narrative in both *Night and Day* and *Mrs. Dalloway* puts *soul* at a visible distance, that is occupying another room or the dream world. When Woolf was forced into the position of the ethnographer who visualizes the seen as a way to control representation, her position was riven by the very contradictions of the Victorian ideologies that she engaged so fruitfully in "On Not Knowing Greek." By refusing to participate in the debate over the right way to translate Greek Woolf has in one sense recused herself from representing the classical world. When she does translate she silently employs not her own but R. C. Jebb's translations.[61] When she does not her position is little different from that of Edward in *The Years*, who refuses to translate for his nephew a famous line from *Antigone*. Although refusing to translate might in some circumstances be justifiable, it also shows her in the grip of an ideology manifested in the ethnological control of discourse. In "Structure, Sign, and Play" Derrida observes that "the ethnologist accepts into his discourse the premises of ethnocentrism at the very moment when he denounces them," which is perhaps an indication of the near-impossibility of thinking outside the ideologies of one's culture.[62] In *The Years* Nicholas' philosophical reflection on the soul opens a world beyond – if not representation, beyond the closed world of syntax and book. Nicholas' incomplete sentence, completed by

---

[60] *Ibid.*, p. 312.

[61] Andrew McNeillie identifies Jebb's translations in *Virginia Woolf: The Common Reader: First Series* (New York: Harcourt Brace Jovanovich, 1984), pp. 244–5.

[62] Jacques Derrida, *Writing and Difference*, trans. Alan Bass (Chicago: University of Chicago Press, 1978), p. 282.

Eleanor, suggests a discourse improvised across lines of putative gender and national estrangement. In subsequent chapters I study the ways in which Woolf sought a position of alterity by means of which, outside the institutions of church or state, she might not only bypass the ethnographic model of translation but create an ethics of hospitality that might attract the wide readership of people outside the university, and outside Europe as well.

CHAPTER 2

Antigone *and the public language*

Is there no guidance nowadays for a reader who yields to none in
reverence for the dead, but is tormented by the suspicion that reverence for the dead is vitally connected with understanding the living?
Virginia Woolf, "How It Strikes a Contemporary" (1923), *The
Common Reader*

Virginia Woolf's analysis of the links between patriarchy and Fascism has
been the focus of most studies of *Three Guineas*, but another aspect of
German culture that is focused on the politics of translation shows how her
Antigone writes history by challenging the vocabulary of public discourse.
I read Woolf's figure of Antigone in the context of European classical
studies which sought to connect ancient Greek thought to events in
twentieth-century history. The grand scale of the problem is indicated by
the number of philosophers, poets, and classicists in Germany and France
whose study led them to new readings of Sophocles. George Steiner offers a
broad analytical survey from Hegel and Hölderlin to Benjamin and Sartre.[1]
Miriam Leonard has studied the role of classical scholars in the political
upheavals in France since 1945, when scholars "used classical figures to
explore the nature of the citizen/subject in relation to politics and ethics."[2]
Whereas translation in "On Not Knowing Greek" is a way of coming to
terms with mourning "the vast catastrophe of the European war," the
translation of *Antigone* read in the context of contemporary European
interpretations motivates the reader to rewrite history from the perspective
of that mourning.

Woolf's Antigone is the figure who interrogates the European institution
of dictatorship not only by the force of her will and character but by her
insistence on taking the fight to language. To abstract her from the play and

---

[1] George Steiner, *Antigones* (New York and Oxford: Oxford University Press, 1984).
[2] Miriam Leonard, *Athens in Paris: Ancient Greece and the Political in Post-War French Thought* (Oxford:
Oxford University Press, 2005), p. 11.

from the centuries of its interpretation results in moralizing her figure in order to mirror the twentieth-century reader's expectations that she become the girl who sacrificed her life to defy a dictator.[3] The humanist reading takes for granted that Antigone is a female figure. To do so, argues Olga Taxidou, is to "take the discursive construct of the human/female Antigone as a finished product that then stands in for their interpreted Antigone," a process that is based on the assumption of "the separability of watching/reading and doing" as well as on an "empathic reading of character."[4] By overlooking the conditions of performance a humanist reading of the play fails to grasp the centrality of a politicized mourning, or the challenge to the assumption of a "reconstructed line of hermeneutics from the Greeks straight to the twentieth century."[5]

Woolf read *Antigone* throughout her life and in three languages, in the process frequently noting her reservations about translation. She read the play with her first tutor, Clara Pater, between May and July 1900, and in 1901 wrote to her brother Thoby of the experience.[6] Sybil Oldfield stresses the importance to her reading of her second tutor, Janet Case, who was a socialist, pacifist, and feminist. Under her tutelage Woolf studied Greek grammar, and patterned her taste on Case's love of Aeschylus, and possibly on her feminism as well.[7] In 1919 Woolf read *Antigone* again, as her reading notes comment "in Greek." These five pages of notes are the most extensive, and they record some naive first impressions, clearly meant for her eyes alone: "This is very good drama. Shows the divisions in peoples minds," or "This is a very philosophical play."[8] Since she was reading in Greek, it seems natural that the notes also include her reservations about translation, that it

---

[3] Caroline Winterer writes that in the United States Greek tragedy was assimilated to the Protestant religion. Among other tragic heroines, "Antigone [became] the dutiful daughter and sister who dies for her convictions. These women became heroic when they acted out the conventions of mid-century Protestant feminine morality." *The Culture of Classicism: Ancient Greece and Rome in American Intellectual Life, 1780–1910* (Baltimore and London: Johns Hopkins University Press, 2002), p. 95. Page duBois writes that "Attempts to see Antigone as perfectly heroic, as the defender of personal values against the cruel state, as a feminist exemplar, seem to me to misread the extent to which she is bound up in the pollution of her family, and naively to see her as a 'real' person rather than as a figure in language, in the cultural and linguistic codes of the ancient city." "Antigone and the Feminist Critic," *Genre* 19 (1986), 376.
[4] Olga Taxidou, *Tragedy, Modernity and Mourning* (Edinburgh: Edinburgh University Press, 2004), p. 34.
[5] *Ibid.*
[6] Henry Malley, "A Rediscovered Eulogy: Virginia Woolf's 'Miss Janet Case: Classical Scholar and Teacher,'" *Twentieth Century Literature* 28 (1982), 290.
[7] Sybil Oldfield, "Virginia Woolf and Antigone – Thinking Against the Current," *South Carolina Review* 29 (1996), 49.
[8] Monks House Papers, Reel 6, B 2. Oldfield reproduces the first two pages: "Virginia Woolf and Antigone," 52–3.

gets important words wrong, and "[slips?] along insignificantly compared with the Greek."[9] But these notes clearly do not record her most considered response to the play.

Woolf next read *Antigone* as she prepared to write "On Not Knowing Greek," although as Brenda Silver warns, the notes on the Greeks are difficult to date exactly.[10] The notes on her reading several of Sophocles' plays sometime between 1922 and 1924 rely on the French prose translation of Leconte de Lisle, while remaining critical of translations in general.[11] In her notes on *Oedipus Coloneus* we find, "I suppose that Sophocles loses more in translation than most. He deals less in general reflections upon life," since he represents "the little changes in mood and language."[12] Yet Woolf used French translations on several occasions as a way of making European texts accessible in a language that she read with ease.

The final notes on *Antigone* are among those in a notebook that Silver dates 1931–9, and are keyed in the margin to the first 161 pages of the Jebb translation.[13] They suggest that from the start of composition the play was part of Woolf's plans for *Three Guineas*. In October 1934 she noted in her diary: "Reading Antigone. How powerful that spell is still – Greek. Thank heaven I learnt it young – an emotion different from any other" (*D4*: 257). And in 1937 she transcribed in her notes several lines from Jebb's translation.[14]

As the history of Woolf's reading suggests, *Antigone* became a familiar text that allowed her to range among Greek, French, and English versions. In *Three Guineas* she becomes the translator who mediates among languages and social groups to demonstrate an ethics that requires her to share the position of her others. Women in 1938 who are denied university education, Woolf writes, "can only read our own tongue and write our own language," and so are "in fact, members not of the intelligentsia but of the ignorantsia" (*TG*: 81). Foreign language training, she implies, opens the wider horizons of an intellectual life. As a woman the translator takes up her position not with the learned professors but as a member of the "ignorantsia." She speaks on behalf not only of women, but of the dead in Spain, who haunt the text in the sense that they figure in photographs which she alludes to but does

[9] Monks House Papers, Reel 6, B 2.
[10] Brenda Silver, *Virginia Woolf's Reading Notebooks* (Princeton: Princeton University Press, 1983), p. 101.
[11] Leconte De Lisle, *Sophocle: traduction nouvelle* (Paris: Alphonse Lemerre, 1877). Woolf owned a copy, as well as his *Iliade* and *Odysée* (*D1*: 178n.).
[12] Berg Collection, Reel 13, R. N. XIX.B.51.
[13] Silver, *Virginia Woolf's Reading Notebooks*, p. 67. Berg Collection, Reel 13, R. N. X.B.8.
[14] Monks House Papers, Reel 6, B 16.

not reproduce. And, most surprisingly, at the end of the essay she shares the position of the dictator: "we are ourselves that figure." Woolf's translator is a figure empowered to cross the borders of kinship and nation.

In *Three Guineas* we can take the measure of Woolf's most ambitious attempt to recreate the English sentence. Elizabeth Abel reads *Three Guineas* as Woolf's response to Freud and the infantile fixation on the father. As a result "male and female correspondents face each other across an abyss that can be negotiated only in the discourse of the father."[15] Diana Swanson writes that in the 1930s Woolf "was revising the Western tradition to develop a new world of altered relations between the sexes and a new language for communicating about it."[16] Natania Rosenfeld argues that in the 1930s satire must have seemed "an echo. Some new narrative, some entirely different voice, must be inserted between the Dictator's 'I' and the resultant universal wail of 'ay, ay, ay, ay'; the authoritarian's solipsism had to be disrupted."[17]

Although I am in agreement with these interpretations of Woolf's language, her reading of *Antigone* is part of a larger twentieth-century European criticism in which new approaches to the interpretation of classical texts criticized by implication Fascist policies. *Three Guineas* was written during the period when trends in German classical studies, *Altertumswissenschaft*, were being implemented in British schools and universities with implications that opened the field to fresh interpretation, and made possible for the first time the professional study of the classics by women. The use of translation, which had been the recourse of readers without a university education, became a facet of textual study in the bilingual edition, for instance in R. C. Jebb's edition of *Antigone* (1891), which Woolf used in "On Not Knowing Greek." She wrote at a moment when translation made the world larger: it opened the common reader's intellectual horizon backwards towards the Greeks, and it lowered the barriers of class and gender which in England were policed by the phrase, "knowing Greek." Perhaps because she lived through these changes and was acquainted with some of the actors, Woolf treated *Antigone* as a foundational text. In her interpretation it marks the furthest reach of western

---

[15] Elizabeth Abel, *Virginia Woolf and the Fictions of Psychoanalysis* (Chicago: University of Chicago Press, 1989), p. 107.

[16] Diana Swanson, "An Antigone Complex? The Political Psychology of *The Years* and *Three Guineas*," *Woolf Studies Annual* 3 (1997), 35.

[17] Natania Rosenfeld, "Monstrous Conjugations: Images of Dictatorship in the Anti-Fascist Writings of Virginia and Leonard Woolf," *Virginia Woolf and Fascism: Resisting the Dictator's Seduction*, ed. Merry M. Pawlowski (Basingstoke and New York: Palgrave Macmillan, 2001), 123.

history, and it reveals that the structures of gender under which she and her generation continued to live originated in ancient Greece and had survived across western Europe.

Antigone draws our attention to forms of mourning that differ significantly from the traditions of elegy which many readers of Woolf perceive to be at work in her fiction.[18] Whereas elegy seeks consolation in the face of loss, Antigone's mourning asks the quite different question, How is the world of the living to conduct itself towards the world of the dead? In *Three Guineas* Woolf responds to the question, "how are we to prevent war," which asks for money, by translating the request into the ethical question that the essay engages: "The question we put to you, lives of the dead, is how can we enter the professions and yet remain civilized human beings; human beings, that is, who wish to prevent war?" (*TG*: 70). In order to effect this translation Woolf finds it necessary to call in question both the semantics and syntax of the public language. The necessity for so doing is figured as the feminine subject that although lacking a signifier occupies a historical position.

The debate about the role of the classics in British education involved several Cambridge dons well known to Woolf. She read *Antigone* in the edition of R. C. Jebb, which combined a Greek text on the left page, with a reading translation on the right, and notes of a historical and philological character printed below. Woolf was sometimes critical of his taste as a translator: "he never risks anything in his guesses: his sense of language seems to me stiff, safe, prosaic and utterly impossible for any Greek to understand" (*L2*: 221). Yet in "On Not Knowing Greek" Woolf silently employed his translations. Jebb bridged the gap between linguistic and textual expertise, so that his famous edition of Sophocles remains comparable to German editions, and he promoted as well the study of archeology.[19]

Simon Goldhill gives a lively summary of the heated quarrel between two of Woolf's friends, Walter Headlam (1866–1908) and A. W. Verrall (1851–1912) about knowing Greek, which he terms "a paradigmatic moment."[20]

[18] Two important discussions of elegy are: Gillian Beer, "Hume, Stephen, and Elegy in *To the Lighthouse*," *Essays in Criticism* 34 (1984), 33–55, and Christine Froula's *Virginia Woolf and the Bloomsbury Avant-Garde: War/Civilization/Modernity* (New York: Columbia University Press, 2005). Consolation is the theme of Froula's interpretation of *Mrs. Dalloway* in chapter four. In chapter eight, she reads *Three Guineas* as Woolf's response to St. Paul's view of women: "This veiled St. Virginia challenges St. Paul's interpretation of the Gospels from the perspective of the scapegoat at the heart of Paul's Church," p. 262. Froula's discussion of Antigone, pp. 247–50, focuses on *The Years*.
[19] Stray, *Classics Transformed*, p. 142.
[20] Simon Goldhill, *Who Needs Greek? Contests in the Cultural History of Hellenism* (Cambridge: Cambridge University Press, 2002), p. 194.

It was begun by Headlam's attack, *On Editing Aeschylus: A Criticism* (1891), on Verrall's commentary on *Agamemnon* (1889) and *Seven Against Thebes* (1885). The issue was "knowing Greek," the phrase that Headlam used to defend the older standard of textual expertise. Headlam, who wrote poems to some of the girls of Newnham, carried on a brief flirtation with Virginia Woolf, sixteen years his junior.[21] Verrall was important to Woolf for different reasons. Verrall not only edited Aeschylus, but he was a gifted lecturer and worked to bring Greek drama to a wide audience. He served on the Cambridge Play Committee, which by staging Greek plays re-asserted their literary interest. His interests were broad; he lectured on French literature, and was the first appointment to the new English Professorship. Woolf's decision to base her translation of *Agamemnon* on his may reflect as well her appreciation of his welcoming attitude towards female students.

The career of Jane Harrison (1850–1928) evolved at the center of this controversy. The Hogarth Press published her *Reminiscences of a Student's Life* (1925), in which she noted that at Cambridge archeology was "barely recognized ... whether by classicists or historians," and as a result "all my archeology was taught me by the Germans."[22] If, as Marchand suggests, the history of the study of classics is a matter of "generational cohorts and their defining historical experiences,"[23] then it is significant that Harrison studied with two of the leading figures in Germany. She mentions Heinrich Brunn (d. 1894), who articulated a program in which archeology was independent of philology. Whereas, in his view, philology had become a "science of language," and no longer represented the whole of antiquity, archeology demanded a place in the curriculum.[24] In *Reminiscences* Harrison saluted Wilhelm Dörpfeld as "my most honoured master."[25] She worked with him at the excavations at Athens in 1888. Dörpfeld devised a means of prehistorical dating, and later became Schliemann's "scientific" excavator, who reasserted his claim to have rediscovered Troy.[26] (In 1925 Harrison could not have guessed that Dörpfeld would later welcome the Fascist seizure of power.) In the early years Harrison was forced to make her career outside the university, until in 1899 she was appointed a lecturer in classical archeology at Newnham. Her career illustrates the difficulty of

[21] *Ibid.*, p. 234. See my discussion of their relationship in *Virginia Woolf and the Visible World* (Cambridge: Cambridge University Press, 2001), pp. 45–6.
[22] Jane Harrison, *Reminiscences of a Student's Life* (London: Hogarth Press, 1925), p. 64.
[23] Marchand, *Down from Olympus*, p. 321.   [24] *Ibid.*, pp. 143–4.
[25] Harrison, *Reminiscences*, p. 64.   [26] Marchand, *Down from Olympus*, pp. 87 and 124.

accommodating work in myth and art history in a university that was still dominated by philology.[27]

In the draft version of *A Room of One's Own* the narrator glimpses "was it Mr. Verrall? Mr. Sedgwick? Jane Harrison? ... venerable – & perhaps lovable would be the better word – some such figure I saw in the rampant spring evening."[28] Harrison studied at Newnham and took the undivided classical Tripos. Mary Beard observes that "the distinctive combination of myth, ritual and the visual arts that we associate with (more than anyone else) Jane Harrison is a combination rooted in the history of the Tripos."[29] It is a history that as we have seen reflected German classical scholarship. Although the editor of Woolf's draft version, S. P. Rosenbaum, notes that "the situation of women at Oxbridge is unmentioned, and the anger of men unnoticed," the Fitzwilliam manuscript includes a passage that Woolf later crossed out, referring to "the sort of mocking derision which women [verb?], when they have ceased to be young, & yet have won a great name; as Jane Harrison had, & never spend a penny on the proper up keep of their name, for no one ever serves them."[30] Then follows the image of Harrison's "great <fore> head, her shabby clothes, dress." Rosenbaum notes that the allusion to Harrison "is fancifully extended back almost a generation to include the well-known dons Verrall and Sedgwick."[31] In fact Harrison thanks Verrall (along with R. C. Jebb) as examples of scholarship in her Introduction to *Prolegomena to the Study of Greek Religion* (1903), and Sedgwick for help in translating the *Bacchae*. The book is dedicated to the Verralls. In other words the draft version of *A Room of One's Own*, by situating Harrison among her supporters, suggests the political dimension of her career.

The printed version merely hints at this history, in the image of Harrison as among "phantoms, only, half guessed, half seen . . . could it be the famous scholar, could it be J – H – herself?"[32] Woolf's phantoms haunt the places where their history was made, an aspect of her work that as we shall see was central to Assia Djebar's reading of Woolf. Here the phantom signals the

[27] Claire Breay, "Women and the Classical Tripos 1869–1914," *Classics in 19th and 20th Century Cambridge* (Cambridge: Cambridge Philological Society, 1999), 60–2.
[28] Virginia Woolf, *Women & Fiction: The Manuscript Versions of "A Room of One's Own,"* ed. S. P. Rosenbaum (Oxford: Blackwell, 1992), p. 23.
[29] Mary Beard, "The Invention (and Re-Invention) of 'Group D': An Archeology of the Classical Tripos, 1879–1984," *Classics in 19th and 20th Century Cambridge* (Cambridge: Cambridge Philological Society, 1999), 123.
[30] Woolf, *Women & Fiction*, ed. Rosenbaum, p. 24.   [31] *Ibid.*, p. xxiv.
[32] Virginia Woolf, *"A Room of One's Own" and "Three Guineas,"* ed. Michèle Barrett (London: Penguin Books, 1993), p. 15. Subsequent passages from both essays are referenced in the text.

specific details of Harrison's career mentioned in the draft version while suppressing the signifiers. The text evacuates Harrison's name as well as her history. When we act on Brenda Silver's idea of "versioning," and read the two versions as complementary, the phantom suggests the double aspect of the subject.[33] A phantom marks the place where a female scholar has created history.

Woolf's notes on the chorus suggest the origins of her fictional narrator. They preserve the sense that as a reader she was content to accept and admire as well as criticize, as she shuttled back and forth between the roles of amateur and professional (*D2*: 247). The notes are legible, sometimes barely, comprised of both sentences and brief phrases; intended for her eyes, they can be difficult to read. As a reader Woolf was able to keep in suspension the elements of her response while deferring the need to establish a critical position. For instance in one group of three pages of notes she refers to "the Oedipus Coloneus passage, from the Chorus, which is descriptive & lyrical." She then copies the first lines of the chorus in *Antigone* on love: "Love, unconquered in the fight, Love, who makest havoc of wealth, who keepest thy vigil on the soft cheek of a maiden," and the opening of the Ode to Man: "Many things are admirable, but nothing more admirable than man." It is widely observed that the optimism of the two passages is reflected nowhere else in the play. Olga Taxidou singles them out as a pair: "the humanist sensibility proposed in one is mirrored and coupled with the . . . notion of *eros* presented in the other."[34] Together they represent the sensibility that Antigone rejects. Their lyricism left Woolf as reader puzzled, for she commented that for the purpose of argument, "It is difficult to see exactly what bearing a chorus has upon a play."[35]

As a reader Woolf often assumed a position from which as a writer she moved in exactly the opposite direction. Although as a reader she responded primarily to the lyricism of the chorus, in "On Not Knowing Greek" she implies a significant analogy between the role of the narrator in her work and the chorus: "the old men or women who take no active part in the drama, the undifferentiated voices who sing like birds in the pauses of the wind; who can comment, or sum up, or allow the poet to speak himself or supply, by contrast, another side to his conception" (*E4*: 43). By deferring the moment

---

[33] Brenda Silver, "Textual Criticism as Feminist Practice: Or, Who's Afraid of Virginia Woolf Part II," *Representing Modernist Texts: Editing as Interpretation*, ed. George Bornstein (Ann Arbor: University of Michigan Press, 1991), 193–222.
[34] Taxidou, *Tragedy, Modernity and Mourning*, pp. 26–7.   [35] Berg Collection, Reel 13, XIX.B.49.

of judgment, the notes make room for the role of the narrator who inhabits the space of the "undifferentiated voices." The phrase is consistent with Woolf's often expressed distaste for "I" and for action as intervention. It implies the connection, as in *The Waves*, between the world of the birds and the wind, and that of speech. It figures a connection between the sounds of the natural world and the structures of language that Woolf used to establish a speaking position for the cry of mourning that public language excludes. It enabled her to open to question by means of dialogue certain unilateral positions that might otherwise have barred her way.

Woolf was not alone in drawing connections between Creon and the dictators of contemporary Europe. In Germany classical scholars after World War I widened the focus of philological scholarship to include the archeological evidence gathered from the discoveries at Troy, Mycenae, and Olympia. The enlarged field of Greek studies made it possible to stress its connection to events in postwar Europe. A survey of twentieth-century trends in German classical scholarship emphasizes the work done in the 1920s and 1930s, which is characterized by "a self-conscious redefinition of the purpose and relevance of classical studies in reaction to contemporary historical and social conditions."[36] Werner Jaeger (1888–1961) stressed the relevance of the classics to contemporary Europe. His "Third Humanism" led to "his attempts to accommodate humanism to Hitler's regime, even acting as spokesperson for the Third Reich within the classics field."[37] Among those who reacted against Jaeger's views was Karl Reinhardt (1886–1958), one of the group of Jewish writers and artists, including Kafka and Freud, that flourished in Germany prior to the Nazi era. His view, that "the scholar must be aware of the historical conditions of the work's origin, but his goal must be to bring an immediate, direct appreciation of the inner form and essence of the work … altered the nature of classical studies in the thirties."[38] His *Sophocles* (1933; translated into English 1979) was published in the year that Hitler came to power. As Hugh Lloyd-Jones writes in the "Introduction to the English Edition," Reinhardt offered in protest to resign the chair he held at Frankfurt, but was persuaded to stay and help to keep the university running. In 1942 he moved to Leipzig, where he and his wife nearly died of starvation.[39] Working under the influence of

[36] Review by James P. Holoka of "Hellmut Flashar, *Altertumswissenschaft in den 20er Jahren: Neue Fragen und Impulse* (1995)," *Bryn Mawr Classical Review* 96 (1996), 504.
[37] Gifford Lecture at the University of Edinburgh, www.giffordlectures.org/Author.asp?AuthorID=86.
[38] Holoka, Review: Flashar, *Altertumswissenschaft in den 20er Jahren*, 506.
[39] Hugh Lloyd-Jones, "Introduction to the English Edition," in Karl Reinhardt, *Sophocles*, trans. Hazel Harvey and David Harvey (Oxford: Basil Blackwell, 1979), pp. xv–xvi.

Nietzsche and Stefan George, Reinhardt was less interested in philology than in interpreting the links between character and action.

In *Three Guineas* Woolf might have been tempted to take action by turning *Antigone* into propaganda: "It is impossible to judge any book from a translation"; yet even such a masterpiece as *Antigone* "could undoubtedly be made, if necessary, into anti-Fascist propaganda. Antigone herself could be transformed either into Mrs. Pankhurst, who broke a window and was imprisoned in Holloway; or into Frau Pommer [a Prussian woman who was tried for protesting against hatred]. Antigone's crime was of much the same nature" (*TG*: 154). The behavior of Creon "is typical of certain politicians in the past, and of Herr Hitler and Signor Mussolini in the present. But though it is easy to squeeze these characters into up-to-date dress, it is impossible to keep them there. They suggest too much . . . if we use art to propagate political opinions, we must force the artist to clip and cabin his gift to do us a cheap and passing service" (*TG*: 154). Woolf was always reluctant to write propaganda, perhaps because the easy equivalences among characters that she sketches and rejects preclude the study of language that is the task of the translator.

Woolf apparently did not own a copy of Reinhardt's *Sophocles*. But if we see it as a contemporary example of opposing Fascism by attention to the poetics of Greek tragedy, in particular to the transformation of vocabulary for political ends, we can better grasp the significance of the linguistic reforms suggested in *Three Guineas*. Reinhardt's chapter on *Antigone* interprets her character not by moralizing but by analyzing her dialogue with Creon. He starts by dismissing Hegel, who had argued in *Lectures on the Philosophy of Religion* that

familial love, the holy, the inward, belonging to an inner feeling, and therefore known also as the law of the nether gods, collides with the right of the state. Creon is not a tyrant, but actually an ethical power. Creon is not in the wrong. He maintains that the law of the state, the authority of government, must be held in respect, and that infraction of the law must be followed by punishment. Each of these two sides actualizes only one of the ethical powers, and has only one as its content. This is their one-sidedness.[40]

Reinhardt counters that

such a struggle since the time of Hegel to penetrate to the true nature of the *Antigone* – the victorious and the defeated cause, plot and counterplot, right against right, idea against idea, family against the state, tragic guilt and atonement, freedom

---

[40] Translated in Steiner, *Antigones*, p. 37.

of the individual and fate, individual and society . . . all these are borrowed from the aesthetics of the late eighteenth or early nineteenth century, and they are either so general that they are just as applicable to German drama – which means that they are too vague; or they seem to fit the *Antigone* but then do not fit any other of the surviving tragedies of Sophocles – which means that they are too precise.[41]

Seeking to avoid "the Hegelian thirst for dialectic," he reads *Antigone* as "a drama of developments."[42] In their struggle both Creon and Antigone are "part of the divine setting which acts on human beings through the deed."[43] Unlike the chorus, which asks of Antigone's action in covering her brother's body "Isn't this action possibly a god's?" Antigone is motivated by "resistance on a different level, coming from a now unattainable region."[44] She says of the unwritten laws of the gods: "no one knows their origin in time."[45] The development of the play depends neither on a series of conscious actions nor on characters who are the mouthpieces of the gods. *Antigone* is a drama in which character and action are developed in terms of each other, and although the viewer may ultimately take away a sense of dialectic, it cannot simply be assumed.

Reinhardt writes of the exchange of one-liners (*stichomythia*) between Antigone and Creon, that they share a vocabulary to which they assign different meanings, so that "though outwardly they echo each other, the contrast of the different meanings tears the two spheres all the more sharply asunder."[46] Jebb's translation preserves the sense of their common vocabulary:

An: In thy discourse there is nought that pleases me, never may there be! – and so my words must needs be unpleasing to thee.[47]

Creon replies that she differs from the Thebans:

Cr: And art thou not ashamed to act apart from them?
An: No; there is nothing shameful in piety to a brother.
Cr: Was it not a brother, too, that died in the opposite cause?
An: Brother by the same mother and the same sire.
Cr: Why then, dost thou render a grace that is impious in his sight?
An: The dead man will not say that he so deems it.
Cr: Yea, if thou makest him but equal in honour with the wicked.
An: It was his brother, not his slave, that perished.
Cr: Wasting this land; while *he* fell as its champion.

[41] Reinhardt, *Sophocles*, pp. 64–5.   [42] *Ibid.*, pp. 65–6.   [43] *Ibid.*, p. 73.
[44] *Ibid.*, p. 75.   [45] *Ibid.*, p. 75.   [46] *Ibid.*, p. 79.
[47] R. C. Jebb, *Sophocles: The Plays and Fragments, Part III: The Antigone* (Cambridge: Cambridge University Press, 1891), lines 500–1. Subsequent references to lines from this edition appear in the text.

An: Nevertheless, Hades desires these rites.
Cr: But the good desires not a like portion with the evil.
An: Who knows but this seems blameless in the world below?
Cr: A foe is never a friend – not even in death.
An: 'Tis not my nature to join in hating, but in loving.
Cr: Pass then, to the world of the dead, and, if thou must needs love, love them. While I live, no woman shall rule me.   (lines 511–25)

Even in translation semantic differences are apparent in the meaning of *shame, piety, honor, desire, love,* and especially the meaning assigned to *brother.* To Creon Polyneices is a traitor deserving punishment; to Antigone a family member deserving the rites of burial.[48]

The rhetoric of *Three Guineas* achieves what has always seemed to me its claustrophobic quality from the fact that the writer feels compelled to respond to her correspondent in the question/answer format of a shared vocabulary that only emphasizes their semantic differences.[49] In order to understand how to prevent war it is necessary to explore the meaning of "patriotism," what it means to the educated man, and to his sister, whose "interpretation of the word 'patriotism' may well differ from his" (*TG*: 9). The entire argument is suffused with Woolf's semantic mission: "By poverty is meant enough money to live upon . . . By chastity is meant that when you have made enough to live on by your profession you must refuse to sell your brain for the sake of money" (*TG*: 75). In order to "find new words" to replace "dead words . . . corrupt words" (*TG*: 93), Woolf examines and redefines a number of terms: "influence," "outsider," "foreigner," "freedom," "society," "feminist," "profession," "culture and intellectual liberty," and "dictator." Her attack on the vocabulary of the public language that in another work might circulate as a subtext has become the focus of her rhetorical strategy.

Woolf's argument is designed to challenge old vocabularies and replace them with new.[50] The semantic problem of the play is implicitly modeled on what Woolf terms "Antigone's distinction between the laws and the

---

[48] Reinhardt's observation is now widely shared: "On the lips of different characters the same words take on different or opposed meanings because their semantic significance is not the same in religious, legal, political, and common parlance." Jean-Pierre Vernant, "Ambiguity and Reversal: On the Enigmatic Structure of *Oedipus Rex," Myth and Tragedy in Ancient Greece,* by Vernant with Pierre Vidal-Naquet, trans. Janet Lloyd (New York: Zone Books, 1988), 113.

[49] In January 1936 Woolf had considered titling the essay "Answers to Correspondents" (*D5*: 3).

[50] Cuddy-Keane notes an earlier instance of this tendency when Woolf questioned the terms of an argument in a 1932 BBC broadcast on the differences among high, middle, and lowbrow, and the attempt to link the terms to class distinctions. Her "Letter to the Editor" was never sent, although she had plans to rewrite it as an essay. *Virginia Woolf, the Intellectual, and the Public Sphere,* pp. 24–34.

Law," the laws of the state and the unwritten Law of the gods, which are manifest in another language, or in other words one signifier with two signifieds (*TG*: 76). Reinhardt might well have been writing of *Three Guineas* as well when he argued that in *Antigone* "the opposition is between two *realms*: word for word, and meaning for meaning, they *separate* from each other."[51] Although in Hegel's *Lectures* neither Creon nor Antigone is wholly right or wrong, in Reinhardt's argument that interpretation can emerge only when the reader comes to understand how Sophocles used the language of the characters to explore a problem of ethics and justice.

Certain vocabularies lend themselves to the development of a history that may be interpreted in terms of semantic change. Reinhart Koselleck analyzes the temporal structure of some words that have had the force to write the future. The meaning of certain key words, for instance *revolution*, *emancipation*, and *dictatorship*, have shifted over the centuries. *Revolution*, for instance, lost its earlier sense of an "epochal point of upheaval," to become a word that "increasingly registered the prevailing process of constant change."[52] *Emancipation*, which once meant a specific ceremony, now signifies an irreversible process. The word *dictatorship*, which comes from Roman legal language, was extended from the sphere of law to the entire society. Whereas earlier its meaning was "associated with the legal establishment of a time limit within which a dictatorship has to reconstruct the older order," after Napoleon I dictatorship creates itself and "provides its own historical legitimation."[53] Like *revolution* it suggests "an irreversible temporal process, loading its agents with responsibility while simultaneously relieving them of it, for the process of self-creation is included within the properties of the prospective future ... Like the historical circumstances they are to register, concepts themselves have an internal temporal structure."[54] Since the eighteenth century the group of those who were able to effect such changes has widened to extend beyond nobles and scholars to include all those who have learned to manipulate language.[55]

Translation gave Woolf the freedom to rewrite the history of *dictator* as well as *emancipation*. Creon is a dictator: "He is called in German and Italian Führer or Duce; in our own language Tyrant or Dictator" (*TG*: 129). The translator writes history by domesticating in English a term usually reserved for the history of foreign nations. Choosing a term from the

---

[51] *Ibid.*, p. 78.
[52] Reinhart Koselleck, *Futures Past: On the Semantics of Historical Time*, trans. Keith Tribe (Cambridge, Mass.: MIT Press, 1985, reprint New York: Columbia University Press, 2004), p. 250.
[53] *Ibid.*, p. 251.   [54] *Ibid.*, p. 251.   [55] *Ibid.*, p. 252.

vocabulary of psychoanalysis, Woolf characterized dictators in any language as suffering from "infantile fixation." Perhaps in order to deflect a sense that her argument was simply reactive, and to preserve balance, she expunged "the old names [that] we have seen are futile and false. 'Feminism' we have had to destroy. 'The emancipation of women' is equally inexpressive and corrupt" (*TG*: 125).

Disputed words in *Three Guineas* may also be understood in terms of Derrida's idea of translation within a language: "This border of translation does not pass among various languages. It separates translation from itself, it separates translatability within one and the same language ... Babelization does not therefore wait for the multiplicity of languages. The identity of a language can only affirm itself as identity to itself by opening itself to the hospitality of a difference from itself or of a difference with itself."[56] In *Three Guineas* the house, the traditional site of hospitality, has two faces. It is "the ruined house" of war-torn Spain, and a prison where English women are "locked in the private house" (*TG*: 96–7). Since they become foreign when they marry foreigners (*TG*: 99), the nation is a prison as well. The house as imaging "a difference from itself" articulates Woolf's main theme, the anomaly of the identity of patriarchal culture expressed in multiple languages.

Translation within the national language was a powerful tool of the Fascist state. At the time when Woolf was writing, the Nazis had appropriated the common language in order to fashion a public discourse that could disguise its murderous activities and stifle dissent. A Jew who had been deported was "taken into protective custody." "Freedom," on Woolf's list as well, was redefined by the Nazis to mean not the absence of restraints on the individual, but the absence of restraints on the state. The invasion of Poland was "a police action."[57] The most powerful rhetoric of the state was not, according to Victor Klemperer, addressed to the conscious mind: "Instead Nazism permeated the flesh and blood of the people through single words, idioms and sentence structures which were imposed on them in a million repetitions and taken on board mechanically and unconsciously."[58]

---

[56] Jacques Derrida, *Aporias*, trans. Thomas Dutoit (Stanford: Stanford University Press, 1993), p. 10.
[57] John Wesley Young, *Orwell's Newspeak and Totalitarian Language: Its Nazi and Communist Antecedents* (Charlottesville and London: University of Virginia Press, 1991), pp. 106–7.
[58] Victor Klemperer, *The Language of the Third Reich: LTI – Lingua Tertii Imperii: A Philologist's Notebook*, trans. Martin Brady (London and New Brunswick, N.J.: The Athlone Press, 2000), p. 15. Rowena Fowler in her study of Woolf and dictionaries notes that Woolf wrote during the era of Nazi book-burning. "Virginia Woolf: Lexicographer," *English Language Notes* 39 (2002). Jeanette McVicker argues that Woolf "contributed to a transformation of the British intellectual public

The argument of *Three Guineas* that is implicit in its pronouns suggests a correspondent modeled on Antigone, face to face with her antagonist. The writer begins by constructing "a sketch of the person to whom the letter is addressed," an educated man of her class (*TG*: 3). He is middle-aged, a member of the Bar, and politically active. Woolf's provisional title, "Letter to an Englishman" (March 1936 in *D5*: 18), suggests a character at home in a Greek tragedy, where character is defined in terms of qualities of mind. His attitudes may be inferred from the language of his question, "how to prevent war." One strand of Woolf's argument is the respondent's struggle over pronouns. The educated man is constantly addressed as "you," and individual paragraphs are structured by "your world," and "your clothes," contrasted with the pronouns that designate the daughters of educated men as "we" and "us": "How then are we to understand your problem, and if we cannot, how can we answer your question, how to prevent war? The answer based upon our experience and our psychology – Why fight? – is not an answer of any value" (*TG*: 6). The tone of the second guinea, which is addressed to a woman, is cooler, although in passages where the correspondent becomes an agent who enforces gender stereotypes, the hammering "you" reappears: "But, you will object, you have no time to think; you have your battles to fight, your rent to pay, your bazaars to organize" (*TG*: 59). We/you effectively divides the world into an acquiescent "you" that may include women, and a "we" as its other.[59]

Woolf's essay, "Women and Fiction" (1929), foresees an English woman who is no longer "condemned . . . to squint askance at things through the eyes or through the interests of husband or brother" (*E5*: 34) and will therefore demand a new sentence, to replace the sentence that men have designed, which is "too loose, too heavy, too pompous for a woman's use" (*E5*: 32).[60] *Three Guineas* carries the process a step further. The we/you rhetorical pattern, which is marked throughout the first and second guinea, dramatizes the argument. The rhythm of the prose alternates passages of you/we with passages in the third person that describe the photographs of

sphere . . . [as] evidenced by certain discursive strategies through which she both overtly identifies herself with the public sphere and the dominant culture that controls it while at the same time providing a brilliant critique of that dominant culture, one that would go so far as to suggest an alternative hegemony in *Three Guineas* and later works." "Woolf in the Context of Fascism: Ideology, Hegemony and the Public Sphere," *Virginia Woolf: Texts and Contexts: Selected Papers from the Fifth Annual Conference on Virginia Woolf*, ed. Beth Rigel Daugherty and Eileen Barrett (New York: Pace University Press, 1996), 30–1.

[59] Professor Stephen Scully of Boston University has pointed out that Antigone usually says "I," and resists "we."

[60] In "Men and Women" (1920) Woolf quoted *Far From the Madding Crowd* Bathsheba's "I have the feelings of a woman, but I have only the language of men" (*E3*: 195).

"dead bodies and ruined houses," the investigation of the term "influence," or the price of education, but the base line continues to be you/we: "'we' – meaning by 'we' a whole made up of body, brain and spirit, influenced by memory and tradition – must still differ in some essential respects from 'you,' whose body, brain and spirit have been so differently trained and are so differently influenced by memory and tradition" (*TG*: 16). The you/we pattern suggests that the woman who employs the language of her husband or brother has reached an impasse in relations with the other, while the essay makes urgent the question of its resolution.

The urgency of the question is apparent in Antigone's interview with Creon when it is read as a scene of interpellation, that is the first step by which the subject is enacted into history. In Althusser's well-known essay "Ideology and Ideological State Apparatuses," the subject is initiated when he feels himself hailed as by a policeman, "Hey, you there!"[61] The subject is called to respond in the language of the one who hails. Although discussion of the subject is peculiar to capitalist culture, "the category of the subject (which may function under other names: e.g., as the soul in Plato, as god, etc.) is the constitutive category of all ideology, whatever its determination (regional or class) and whatever its historical date – since ideology has no history."[62] Judith Butler asks of this construction, how "the longing for subjection, based on a longing for social existence, recalling and exploiting primary dependencies, emerges as an instrument and effect of the power of subjection."[63] The problem is to identify the change that turns Althusser's socially subjected individual into Butler's subject as a "linguistic category."[64] The strophe under discussion illustrates the nature of the difficulty, when the subject seeks, in Butler's terms, "recognition of its own existence in categories, terms, and names that are not of its own making ... in a discourse that is at once dominant and indifferent."[65]

By identifying gender as a trans-historical condition of the subject and its interpellation, the language of *Three Guineas* extends the usefulness of Althusser's classic formulation. For Woolf's narrator, as for Antigone, the struggle over control of the public language is the first step in reorganizing language so as to make a place for the feminine subject. Antigone has been hailed in the name of a law that she does not accept, by a sentry who is an emissary of the King of Thebes. Antigone is prevented by her relationship to

---

[61] Louis Althusser, "Ideology and Ideological State Apparatuses," *"Lenin and Philosophy" and Other Essays*, trans. Ben Brewster (New York: Monthly Review Press, 1971), p. 174.
[62] *Ibid.*, p. 171.
[63] Judith Butler, *The Psychic Life of Power* (Stanford: Stanford University Press, 1997), p. 20.
[64] *Ibid.*, p. 10.   [65] *Ibid.*, p. 20.

both Creon and her brother from becoming a speaking subject. Access to the language of Creon would mean persuading him to listen, and as Haemon says in his exchange with his father, "Thou wouldest speak, and then hear no reply?" (line 757). The more difficult problem of the brother emerges when Antigone addresses the chorus in a less confrontational tone. Their dialogue leads her to confront the history of her family, "my bitterest thought" (line 856). She laments the marriage of her mother, who slept with her own son, and concludes: "Brother, it was a luckless marriage you made" (line 871).

In this setting follows the most vexed passage in the play, in which Antigone mourns the death of Polyneices while linking him to the deprivation of her kinship rights to marriage and maternity. The passage offers such a stumbling block that Goethe, and some scholars, Jebb among them, believe it to be spurious. Yet it is central to reading Woolf's image of the brother. In the speech Creon condemns Antigone to a living tomb, a punishment that deprives her of husband and children. Antigone's reply focuses on her female role:

Never, had I been a mother of children, or if a husband had been mouldering in death, would I have taken this task upon me in the city's despite. What law, ye ask, is my warrant for that word? The husband lost, another might have been found, and child from another, to replace the first-born; but, father and mother hidden with Hades, no brother's life could ever bloom for me again. Such was the law whereby I held thee first in honour; but Creon deemed me guilty of error therein, and of outrage, ah brother mine! And now he leads me thus, a captive in his hands; no bridal bed, no bridal song hath been mine, no joy of marriage, no portion in the nurture of children; but thus, forlorn of friends, unhappy one, I go living to the vaults of death. (lines 905–19)

The passage, which is often read as Antigone's justification of her action, emphasizes her exclusion from the "law" that determines kinship. The problem is that she couples her sense of the deprivation of her reproductive rights with an enhanced erotic feeling for Polyneices. In Derrida's phrase, "there is something in the concept of the family that both repeats the system and renders its entire field problematic."[66] The scene of mourning has become a contested site.

Polyneices' marriage to the daughter of the Argive king Adrastus was, notes Jebb, "the seal of the armed alliance against Thebes, and thus the prime cause of Antigone's death ... as the doom of the whole race is in question, the brother is fitly mentioned" (p. 159). Antigone mourns in a way

---

[66] Cited in Miriam Leonard, *Athens in Paris*, p. 137.

that blends forgiveness of Polyneices with rage at the entire family. At one moment she is a forgiving sister: "I shall rest, a loved one with him whom I have loved, sinless in my crime; for I owe a longer allegiance to the dead than to the living: in that world I shall bide forever" (lines 71–5). Yet she angrily ascribes her fate to her family's sexual choices: "Alas for the horrors of the mother's bed! Alas for the wretched mother's slumber at the side of her own son, – and my sire! From what manner of parents did I take my miserable being! And to them I go thus, accursed, unwed, to share their home. Alas, my brother, ill-starred in thy marriage, in thy death thou hast undone my life!" (lines 861–71). Antigone's position is split between loyalty to the dead whose sexual choices have doomed the family and led to her death, and a sense of grief that is directed as well to her position as an outsider.

These rituals of kinship give rise to a mourning that combines grief for the dead brother with resentment of his social position. Before turning back to *Three Guineas* we might note the image that Woolf paints of her brother Thoby in "A Sketch of the Past." As a child Thoby although not "clever," was "dominant." She describes Thoby and his father as "naturally attracted to each other . . . I was a year and a half younger; and a girl."[67] From Thoby she first learned of the ancient Greeks, a fascination tinged with desire that lasted all her life. In a curious passage she describes a childhood fist fight, during which she suddenly dropped her fists: "It was a feeling of hopeless sadness. It was as if I became aware of something terrible; and of my own powerlessness" (*MB*: 71). Woolf's feeling of powerlessness against her brother must surely have been connected as well to "father's extraordinary demonstrative love for him" (*MB*: 126). Yet although the mixture of attraction and powerlessness might have led to an impasse, in Butler's phrase a "social deformation," when "symbolic positions have become incoherent," Thoby's premature death at twenty-six severed the tie between the social and the symbolic brother. His death and Woolf's mourning freed her to write *The Waves*, in which he assumes the ideality of a symbolic position.

Kinship assures intelligibility. In Butler's argument intelligibility is what makes life livable: "Antigone figures the limits of intelligibility exposed at the limits of kinship . . . Her fate is not to have a life to live, to be condemned to death prior to any possibility of life. This raises the question of how it is that kinship secures the conditions of intelligibility by which life

[67] Virginia Woolf, *Moments of Being*, ed. Jeanne Schulkind (New York: Harcourt Brace Jovanovich, 1985), p. 138. Subsequent references appear in the text.

becomes livable, by which life also becomes condemned and foreclosed."[68] Sally Pargiter in *The Years* (1937), spending an evening at home in bed while others attend a dance, opens a copy of *Antigone* that her cousin has translated into English verse. In a reading that is "random" and "inaccurate" she focuses on two related scenes of horror, the sight of the unburied corpse, surrounded by the vultures that she imagines, and the interment alive of Antigone. "She was buried alive. The tomb was a brick mound. There was just room for her to lie straight out" (*Y*: 131). Sally's response to two deformations of the rituals of kinship, the corpse unburied and the living girl buried, is to position her own body like Antigone's: "She laid herself out, under the cold smooth sheets" (*Y*: 131). Sally's action makes intelligible to the reader the deathlike life of a female in the Victorian family, surrounded by vultures.

In *Three Guineas* Woolf's consideration of intelligibility as the livable life is focused on the brother in whose name the daughter is denied formal education by the father. "Arthur's Education Fund," which is funded by the sacrifices of his sisters, admits a man to the university and then to public life, while his sisters remain cloistered in the private house. As in *Antigone* the laws of the *polis* confine the female within the house as a means of preventing her interference in the masculine world. Woolf's language is occasionally ironic: "There they go, our brothers who have been educated at public schools and universities" (*TG*: 57). But following the consideration in the second guinea of "Creon's claim to absolute rule over his subjects," her tone darkens as the narrator sketches the role of the brother in the future: "Then we can scarcely doubt that our brothers will provide us for many centuries to come ... that is to say [with] ridicule, censure, and contempt" (*TG*: 76). The high price of intelligibility is suggested in the image of the brother whose contempt for his sister makes dialogue impossible.

Nothing better illustrates the need for the feminine subject than Woolf's analysis of the conditions under which the brother's education becomes the apparatus that maintains the ideology of gender. Butler writes that Antigone "draws into crisis ... the representative function itself, the very horizon of intelligibility in which she operates and according to which she remains somewhat unthinkable."[69] In *Three Guineas* public correspondence figures the representative function of question and answer at an impasse. The

---

[68] Judith Butler, *Antigone's Claim: Kinship between Life & Death* (New York: Columbia University Press, 2000), p. 23.
[69] Butler, *Antigone's Claim*, p. 22.

narrator represents the letters she has received, quoting only the occasional phrase, and ends the third guinea with a refusal to sign the form that has been sent. In the context of a question that demands an answer the narrator takes up a position "outside your society," from which she seeks "new words."

Perhaps as the result of an impasse in question and answer, in *Three Guineas* the representative function is figured in terms of translation, as though the translator sought resolution in some foreign tongue. Woolf illustrates the likelihood of a woman's being asked for an opinion with an anecdote in which she supposes that the Duke of Devonshire asks the maid who was peeling potatoes in the kitchen for help construing a passage of Pindar, to which she responds with a shriek. "That, or something like it, is the cry that rises to our lips when the sons of educated men ask us, their sisters, to protect intellectual liberty and culture. But let us try to translate the kitchenmaid's cry into the language of educated people" (*TG*: 79–80).[70] Translation of a Greek poet dedicated to eulogizing men and communities reveals the way in which the British educational system maintains barriers of gender and class that require another kind of translation. War and violence, the "dead bodies and ruined houses" in Spain, have made translation urgent, yet the passage underscores its immediate difficulty. Woolf's humorous image of the servant who when asked about Greek shrieks "Lawks Louie, Master must be mad!" (*TG*: 79) hints at the association of Greek with madness that haunted her own life. In *Three Guineas* translation marks the place where the socially disempowered subject encounters a history that she cannot read. While omitting to translate Pindar, Woolf's narrative instead translates the shriek into language designed "to break the circle, the vicious circle of prostituted culture" (*TG*: 92).

If the kitchenmaid's cry opens the third guinea, it may be said to close with "the ancient cry" of "the black night that now covers Europe" (*TG*: 128). When Woolf's text associates the cry with the radio it focuses on *Antigone* and *Three Guineas* the problems of representation and translation that are associated with female mourning. Antigone's mourning is related to her ability to act, which the language of the play throws in doubt. Nicole Loraux analyzes the vocabulary of hands in *Antigone*, starting from Sophocles' predeliction for compounds using *auto*. Its most frequent

---

[70] Charles Segal writes of the twelfth Pythian Ode as the transformation of a female mourning wail into flute-song. "The Gorgon and the Nightingale: The Voice of Female Lament and Pindar's Twelfth Pythian Ode," *Embodied Voices: Representing Female Vocality in Western Culture*, ed. Leslie C. Dunn and Nancy A. Jones (Cambridge: Cambridge University Press, 1994), 17–34.

meaning is oneself, or referring to one's will ("de toi-même, de ta propre volonté . . . son sens le plus fréquent"), equally at home in the language of the law or of reflection.[71] It appears in this primary sense in the opening scene of the play, when Antigone asks of Ismene, "Wilt thou aid this hand to lift the dead?" (line 43). Ismene replies, speaking of Oedipus' "self-blinding hand" (line 53) and of the deaths of her brothers, "wrought out with mutual hands" (line 57). Loraux, noting the frequent use of *auto* in several compounds, asks why the term is not applied to Antigone's death, as it is to the deaths of Haemon and Eurydice. Although in Greek society the hand of a suicide was severed, we hear only of Creon's hands around his dead son, but not of Antigone's. Nothing in the text says explicitly that she has died by her hand. Since she shed no blood, hers is a death "sans main."[72] Like the deaths for instance of Phèdre and Leda, that of Antigone is placed under the sign of a lack, a death that is not an action, rather a veiling.[73]

The double burial of Polyneices raises the question of the deed that is linked to a hand by the language of the sentry. The cry that Antigone utters over the body of Polyneices occurs offstage and is communicated to Creon by the sentry in his language. His representation of her cry suggests a semiotic distinction between Antigone's first and second attempts to cover her brother's body. At first Antigone speaks as though she were planning the burial in the future: "I, then, will go to heap the earth above the brother whom I love" (line 181). Only when the sentry reports to Creon do we realize that the deed appears already to have been accomplished.[74] Despite the sentry's narrative control of tense he is uneasy. Out of fear he makes every effort to isolate himself from the deed: "I wish to tell thee first about myself – I did not do the deed – I did not see the doer – it were not right that I should come to any harm" (lines 238–9). Seth Benardete remarks that the first report "is so circumstantial – it reads like a detective story's presentation of a clueless crime."[75] Creon is enraged when the chorus suggests that a deed without a visible agent might be the work of the gods. Following the famous Ode to Man, Antigone is led in by the sentry,

---

[71] Nicole Loraux, "La Main d'Antigone," *Metis* 1 (1986), 170.   [72] *Ibid.*, p. 191.

[73] Jean-Pierre Vernant uses Marx's discussion of the hand and work to reach a conclusion that takes no account of gender: "In art, production produces not only an 'object for the subject' but also 'a subject for the object' – for the new object just created," a change comparable to that effected by the work of Euclid or Plato. Jean-Pierre Vernant with Pierre Vidal-Naquet, *Myth and Tragedy in Ancient Greece*, trans. Janet Lloyd (New York: Zone Books, 1988), pp. 240–2.

[74] Woolf noted a similar moment when the sentry reports Antigone's funeral in advance of the event, in "On Re-reading Novels" (*M*: 162).

[75] Seth Benardete, *Sacred Transgressions: A Reading of Sophocles' "Antigone"* (South Bend, Ind.: St. Augustine's Press, 1999), p. 32.

who is relieved to have satisfied Creon by capturing her: "I saw her burying the corpse that thou hast forbidden to bury. Is that plain and clear?" (lines 404–5). Since the law of the *polis* as Creon proclaims it demands that this deed be performed by a hand, it would seem that the sentry's visual identification confirms as human an agent that would otherwise be ambiguously situated between the domains of god and man. I wonder whether the novelty of the sentry's characterization, which seems to resemble that of Shakespeare's clowns, does not in effect draw attention to the almost academic exercise that he performs. His speech serves to define the semiotic conditions of hand and deed, to make of the deed an act that language assigns; as a speaker he is careful to sequester representation from agency.

Discussion of the double burial focuses on the possibility that during the night the gods have intervened in the first burial, a matter that the sentry would naturally fail to grasp.[76] The second time that Antigone scatters dust on the corpse she has been seen and heard. The sentry reports to Creon that "a whirlwind lifted from the earth a storm of dust, a trouble in the sky, and filled the plain, marring all the leafage of its woods" (lines 416–18). Part of his account concerns Antigone's "wailing ... and curses" as she strewed the dust, which he chooses to represent in an analogy with the natural world: "And when, after a long while, this storm had passed, the maid was seen; and she cried aloud with the sharp cry of a bird in its bitterness, – even as when, within the empty nest, it sees the bed stripped of its nestlings" (lines 421–5). The image is, writes Marsh McCall, "beautiful and moving, but it is not evidence for what has actually happened, since for the second time the guard's own interpretation of events is decisive in his choice of language."[77] Rather the bird cries are, as Ulrike Dünkelsbühler points out, signals which the sentry translates into language, an image of translation at the limit between concept and metaphor.[78]

After the second burial Antigone is brought before Creon: when he asks her, "dost thou avow, or disavow, this deed" and she answers "I avow it; I make no denial," her reply merely echoes his words (lines 442–3). What might be considered proof of Antigone's agency is in fact an act of ventriloquism. As an act of language the cry, accompanied by groans and curses, suggests an alternative to both the sentry's representation and the ventriloquism enforced by Creon. The site of the brother's grave appears to be the

---

[76] Marsh McCall, "Divine and Human Action in Sophocles: The Two Burials of the *Antigone*," *Yale Classical Studies* 22 (1972), 111–12.

[77] *Ibid.*, p. 115.

[78] Ulrike Dünkelsbühler, *Reframing the Frame of Reason: Trans-lation In and Beyond Kant and Derrida*, trans. Max Statkiewicz (Amherst, N.Y.: Humanity Books, 2002), pp. 209–10.

place where female mourning gains authority independent of public language. Although Antigone's cry has been associated with the laments of Haemon and Creon at the end of the play, it differs in that it is uttered in circumstances where the female mourning voice exceeds the limits of language and becomes untranslatable.

Lacan associates the cry with a particular form of solitude which he finds articulated in Reinhardt's *Sophocles*. It is "the special solitude of Sophoclean heroes [who find] themselves at a limit that is not accounted for by their solitude relative to others . . . beyond established limits."[79] Lacan's central term in discussing this solitude is *Atè*: it is something stronger than "misfortune"; it is "the limit that human life can only briefly cross."[80] The limit is marked in the play by the dimension of visibility. Thus the first burial of Polyneices is unseen. During the second burial the bird-like cries that the sentry attributes to Antigone put her at another limit of the visible – metamorphosis.[81] The limit is expressed in language by an evasion of the signifier. Thus Antigone opposes to Creon's laws an order of law that "is not developed in any signifying chain or in anything else," in other words incommunicable.[82] Antigone defends her brother from a point beyond the horizon of language, "the moment when the emergent signifier freezes it like a fixed object."[83] Only when Antigone has "crossed the entrance to the zone between life and death" does her lamentation begin, which suggests that true lamentation is a non-linguistic utterance.

Charles Segal writes of the female voice in texts from Homer to Greek tragedy as possessing "a magical, and hence terrifying, power to cross the barrier between life and death."[84] He surveys the female lament in Homer, Hesiod, and Sophocles, noting that its intensity "risks crossing over into the non-human."[85] Whereas in Homer "the female lament is an essential part of the rituals within the city and so can express the whole community's sorrow . . . in fifth-century Athens, the division between male and female experience is much sharper, and the voice of the women is no longer assumed to be the voice of the community."[86] Whereas the lyrical voice that opens enigmatically onto the natural world is apparent in the interchapters of *The Waves*, in *Three Guineas* the "infantile fixation" of dictators

---

[79] Jacques Lacan, *The Seminar of Jacques Lacan: Book VII: The Ethics of Psychoanalysis 1959–1960*, trans. Dennis Porter, ed. Jacques-Alain Miller (New York and London: W. W. Norton, 1992), pp. 271–2.

[80] *Ibid.*, pp. 262–3.   [81] *Ibid.*, p. 265.   [82] *Ibid.*, p. 278.   [83] *Ibid.*, p. 279.

[84] Charles Segal, "The Female Voice and its Contradictions: From Homer to Tragedy," *Religio Graeco-Romana: Festschrift für Walter Pötscher*, ed. Joachim Dalfen, Gerhard Petersmann, and Franz Ferdinand Schwarz (Horn/Graz: Berger, 1993), 60.

[85] *Ibid.*, p. 72.   [86] *Ibid.*, p. 73.

has created the cry of the infant "with no language but a cry" (*TG*: 128). Woolf's play on infant/infantile, that stresses children and childish fathers, suggests that the feminine voice has been effectively elided.

Nicole Loraux discusses female lament in the context of her assertion that "every [Greek] tragedy deals with the staging of mourning."[87] After some earlier Greek plays had dealt with the defeat of Athens, Greek dramatists were forbidden to write of recent history, and turned their attention instead to myth. Lamentation in her argument became a means to question the policies of the contemporary city-state in the context of myth. Political life is characterized not by consensus, as we might like to imagine, but is "essentially conflictual, with the conflict almost always repressed ... [so that] any behavior that rejects the ordinary functioning of the city-state is antipolitical ... in an oppositional mode, one policy as opposed to another."[88] Greek tragedy represents this historical opposition as lamentation. Loraux might well be writing of *Three Guineas* as well when she argues that two related words, the cry *aiai*, and the word for *always*, *aei*, are occasioned when "some temporal break has occurred in the life of a city-state," in a manner that threatens the view of its unchanging nature.[89] The cry *aiai*, as it appears in a list of works by Aeschylus, Sophocles, and Euripides, always expresses lamentation, affecting even Creon himself by the end of *Antigone*. The cry also marks the stages of the action, "because at every turning point in a tragedy, it shifts, changing its voice as the tragic element touches different characters."[90]

The political content of women's lamentation is hardly a matter of Greek tragedy only. Margaret Alexiou describes an ancient Greek tradition of women's utterances that were considered threatening to men and to public discourse. Plutarch in his *Life of Solon* describes the decree from the sixth century BC which forbade "everything disorderly and excessive in women's festivals, processions and funeral rites," in an attempt to turn what had been a public ceremony held outside into a private affair that attracted as little attention as possible.[91] The threat posed by lamentation persists in contemporary rural Greece. A. Caravelli's study of the "lament performers" reveals that the lament continues to define an exclusively female world of shared grief that maintains communication with the dead, and is not accessible to outsiders. In the villages that she studied, the lament can be

[87] Nicole Loraux, *The Mourning Voice: An Essay on Greek Tragedy*, trans. Elizabeth Trapnell Rawlings (Ithaca, N.Y.: Cornell University Press, 2002), p. 48.
[88] *Ibid.*, p. 27.   [89] *Ibid.*, p. 29.   [90] *Ibid.*, p. 38.
[91] Margaret Alexiou, *The Ritual Lament in Greek Tradition* (Cambridge: Cambridge University Press, 1974), p. 15.

delivered only when the performer is "in pain," and so can achieve the
special state of consciousness in which the singer wails and tears her hair, a
style of delivery that is as important as the words. The lament also becomes
an instrument of feminine protest, for instance against medical procedures
which have failed, or against war.[92]

Nor, according to Alexiou, was the lament in ancient Greece entirely a
matter of expressing sorrow, since "the right to inherit was directly linked to
the right to mourn." Male descendants became heirs. "If a man died without heirs, his estate passed to collaterals and their descendants. An extinct
household therefore passed to the next of kin, who absorbed the property
into their own." Solon's legislation by reducing the role of women at
funerals reduced their influence over property decisions: "If the family,
based on father-right, was to be established as the basic unit of society, then
the power of women in religious and family affairs must be stopped, and
they must be made to play a more secondary role at funerals."[93] In lament-
ing that she will never become a wife or mother, Antigone laments as well
the extinction of her family. She stages her departure, argues Helen P. Foley,
as an "assertive public lamentation for herself," in contrast to Eurydice, who
moved into her house to mourn the death of Haemon. What was forbidden
in society is permitted in tragedy; it is a paradox "that tragedy permits male
choruses and actors not only to imitate female behavior but to imitate
female behavior forbidden to contemporary women in a public context."[94]

In the third guinea the cry circumvents the wireless, which by broad-
casting in a national language stressed national identity. Woolf's passage on
lamentation introduces the lines in which Creon condemns Antigone to
living death. As the narrator listens to the radio voice intone, "Homes are
the real places of the women," she seems to hear an ancient cry, "Ay, ay, ay,
ay . . . But it is not a new cry, it is a very old cry. Let us shut off the wireless
and listen to the past" (*TG*: 128–9). Woolf hears the radio voices as
indoctrination: "the clamour, the uproar . . . such that we can hardly hear
ourselves speak; it takes the words out of our mouths; it makes us say what
we have not said" (*TG*: 129). She alludes to Hitler, whose rapid rise to power
was facilitated by the radio, which fostered a mass listening public.[95] In a

---

[92] A. Caravelli, "The Bitter Wounding: The Lament as Social Protest in Rural Greece," *Gender and Power in Rural Greece*, ed. J. Dubisch (Princeton: Princeton University Press, 1986), 185.

[93] Alexiou, *The Ritual Lament*, pp. 20–1.

[94] Helen P. Foley, "The Politics of Tragic Lamentation," *Tragedy, Comedy and the Polis: Papers from the Greek Drama Conference, Nottingham, 18–20 July 1990*, ed. Alan H. Sommerstein, Stephen Halliwell, Jeffrey Henderson, and Bernhard Zimmerman (Bari: Levante Editori, 1990), 138.

[95] Alice Yaeger Kaplan, *Reproductions of Banality: Fascism, Literature, and French Intellectual Life* (Minneapolis: University of Minnesota Press, 1986), pp. 134–9.

wartime monologue Hitler recognized the advantage for him of a citizenry that did not read: "The ideal solution would be to teach this people an elementary kind of mimicry ... No special books for them! The radio will be enough to give them the essential information."[96] In the face of a breakdown of communication that is marked by cries and ellipses, Woolf expands the time frame to ancient Greece, where the cry recalls the world of women who are shut away in the house. Whereas the wireless imitates the effect of Creon's speech to Antigone, the mechanical reproduction of the voice that prompts ventriloquism and obedience, the cry transcends the barriers of language.

Hitler's "elementary kind of mimicry" would seem to be Woolf's image of the ideology of gender, in which ventriloquism evades the conscious recognition of the actors. In *The Voyage Out* the engagement of Rachel and Terence is represented as an act of ventriloquism: "'We love each other,' Terence said. 'We love each other,' she repeated" (*VO*: 271). In *Night and Day* a telephone conversation shows Katherine and Ralph in the same position as he explains to her that he has torn up his letter: "'I shall tear up everything too.' 'I shall come.' 'Yes. Come to-day.' 'I must explain to you ...' 'Yes. We must explain'" (*ND*: 458). In *To the Lighthouse* Lily, although she does not utter, recalls several times the words of Mr. Tansley: "Women can't write, women can't paint" (*TL*: 94). At the conclusion of *Between the Acts* Miss La Trobe experiences a moment of freedom from coerced speech; when she imagines "Words without meaning – wonderful words" she sacrifices representation to babble (*BA*: 212). In *Three Guineas* Woolf breaks the pattern of ventriloquism by translating the request for a guinea: "we can best help you to prevent war not by repeating your words and following your methods but by finding new words and creating new methods" (*TG*: 131).

Before the Nazi era German radio had experimented with a medium in which a newly imagined orientation of sound compensated the listener for the loss of visibility.[97] The reader who wonders at the speed of Woolf's transition from Hitler to Creon – "We are in Greece now" – has encountered what Rudolf Arnheim terms "an acoustic bridge" between two periods of European history. In *Radio: The Art of Sound* (1936) he explains: "By the

---

[96] Young, *Orwell's Newspeak*, p. 69. At several points Woolf notes that she heard Hitler's voice on the radio: in *D5*, and in "The Leaning Tower" (*M*: 131).

[97] Melba Cuddy-Keane studies the effects of the sounds of the phonograph and radio in Woolf's novels in "Virginia Woolf, Sound Technologies, and the New Aurality," *Virginia Woolf in the Age of Mechanical Reproduction*, ed. Pamela L. Caughie (New York and London: Garland Publishing, 2000), 69–96.

disappearance of the visual, an acoustic bridge arises between all sounds: voices, whether connected with a stage scene or not, are now of the same flesh as recitation, discussion, song and music. What hitherto could exist only separately now fits organically together: the human being in the corporeal world talks with disembodied spirits, music meets speech on equal terms."[98] So in *Three Guineas* Creon has become a speaking ghost and reading is supplanted by a spectral experience. What is at stake seems in the context of this argument an alternative to syntax with its rigid laws of exclusion. The bridge that connects all sounds whether intelligible or not includes the cry as a kind of music that "meets speech on equal terms." The radio as Woolf represents it both echoes the rituals of public speech that occur in *Antigone*, and figures a mechanical context that disseminates the cry echoing in "the black night that now covers Europe," without translating it into a semantic and syntactic field. Woolf's "Let us shut off the wireless and listen to the past" frees her from the broadcast in a national language and the need to translate, since the cry allied to music is not specifically Greek, German, or English.

In my argument Woolf's feminine subject is not an abstraction, a discursive construction of interest mainly to psychoanalytic criticism. Situated between languages, Woolf's subject cannot be identified with a particular pronoun or signifier, but may be figured in a historical context. In *Three Guineas* the subject is figured as Antigone. She is not simply Antigone, the brave and self-destructive girl, loyal to her brother, who shows Creon the superiority of the gods of love. Rather, in Neville's phrase from *The Waves*, the subject "coasts round the purlieus of the house" (*W*: 24). That is, it enjoys the freedom of a liminal space: "a place where one has the right to range at large; a haunt" (*Shorter OED*). Readers can find the places where the subject has been. Some sites are historical: Jane Harrison's college at Cambridge, the symbolic site of the brother's burial, or the house as it is figured in "Time Passes." Assia Djebar, as we shall see, identifies such a site in "A Haunted House." To shut off the wireless suggests an acoustic site where history has been for the moment abrogated in order to free the

---

[98] Rudolf Arnheim, *Radio: The Art of Sound*, trans. Margaret Ludwig and Herbert Read (London: Faber and Faber, 1936), p. 195. Cited in Mark E. Cory, "Soundplay: The Polyphonous Tradition of German Radio," *Wireless Imagination: Sound, Radio, and the Avant-Garde*, ed. Douglas Kahn and Gregory Whitehead (Cambridge, Mass.: MIT Press, 1992), 335. Gillian Beer writes that "expansion of *voice* divorced from sight is the characteristic new experience of the 1930s." "'Wireless': Popular Physics, Radio and Modernism," *Cultural Babbage: Technology, Time and Invention*, ed. Francis Spufford and Jenny Uglow (London and Boston: Faber and Faber, 1996), 166.

feminine cry of mourning from the constraints of public and national language.

In her study of *Agamemnon* Yopie Prins argues that Woolf's conception of the play preserves the sense of the sound of Greek. Her translation is "enacted somewhere between the page and the stage, in the interplay between theatrical and textual performances of translation."[99] As someone who had seen Greek plays performed, Woolf "made sense of Greek in a different way, not to reclaim a living language that could be pronounced but to proclaim the experience of reading Greek as a dead language, no longer spoken."[100] The untranslatability of Greek left Woolf free "to perform 'not knowing' [Greek] as a movement of thought more mobile, more emotive, or as she phrased it, 'an emotion different from any other.'"[101] So in the third guinea the cry that literally translates the narrator back to classical Greece is located between a text to be read and a wireless performance.

The cry eludes both sign and syntax. In *Antigone* and *Three Guineas*, where it is haunted by representation and agency, it is located at an impasse. Perhaps that is one meaning of an elusive passage from Woolf's diary entry of March 7, 1937, her sense that "the book may be damned, with faint praise; but the point is that I myself know why it is a failure, & that its failure is deliberate. I also know that I have reached my point of view, as writer, as being" (*D3*: 65). Insofar as the passage concerns her place in history, her fame, she will be content "to hold myself aloof." I want to suggest that the passage redefines "deliberate" failure as the recognition that the feminine subject could not speak the public language as it currently existed. One of the problems with discussions of feminine subjectivity is that it so often sounds like defeat: Lily Briscoe does not complete her painting; she has her vision. Many passages in Woolf's diaries attest to the strain in daily life of reconciling the positions of writer and speaker of the common language. The position of correspondent in *Three Guineas* encompasses both roles, but reconciles nothing. Rather it exacerbates oppositions: we and you, semantic differences occasioned by gender, and most importantly the public language and the sentence undergoing revision to accommodate women's writing. The subject of *Three Guineas* does not attempt to reconcile these positions. Woolf wrote

---

[99] Prins, "OTOTOTOI: Virginia Woolf and 'The Naked Cry' of Cassandra," *"Agamemnon" in Performance*, ed. Macintosh *et al.* (Oxford: Oxford University Press, 2005), 167.

[100] *Ibid.*, p. 172.

[101] *Ibid.* Vassiliki Kolocotroni writes of Greek in the work of Woolf, that "Greek words, Greek names are signposts and gates, both suggesting and barring access into a world of strangeness." "Greek Lessons in Early Virginia Woolf," *Modern Language Review* 100 (2005), 315.

of its "horrid anticlimax" (*D5*: 133). The essay ends with the correspondent in several positions: pledging herself to "find new words," refusing to sign the form, and apologizing "for writing at all." The final sentence delights in the impasse of question and answer: "The blame for that however rests upon you, for this letter would never have been written had you not asked for an answer to your own" (*TG*: 131).

Although there is agreement that the rhetoric of *Three Guineas* is meant to unsettle the reader, its contradictions and the extensive notes continue to be problematic. Some attempts to sound Woolf's motivation are suggestive. Alex Zwerdling writes at length about the struggle between Woolf's anger and her art as she became "increasingly aware of the concessions her writing involved and increasingly unwilling to make them."[102] Jane Marcus, while defending Woolf's anger, finds it held in check by the letter form and the footnotes.[103] Pamela Caughie engages the central question of the reader's active response when she criticizes Marcus' support of Woolf's Outsiders Society: "Woolf reveals in *Three Guineas* that there is no real choice for outsiders within the social-economic system *as it now functions*, for the system continually circles back on itself, reinforcing and endlessly reproducing its own forms of production."[104] In such a climate, *Three Guineas* "is socially responsible ... in its very use of rhetoric as a training in language and politics."[105]

By the end of *Three Guineas* we glimpse a new role for the translator as a mediator among languages, although British printing conventions made it difficult to articulate that position. Some fifty years later in *Glas* (1986) Derrida raised the question of mourning and Antigone on a page whose design does away with notes and represents translation from Greek and German in the context of semantic change. Parallel columns display Derrida's reading of Hegel's interpretation of *Antigone* alongside his reading of Genet. A third column notes including sources in several languages as well as etymologies of important words: "The text therefore presents itself as the commentary on the absent word that it delimits, envelops, serves, surrounds with its care. The text presents itself as the metalanguage of the language that does

---

[102] Alex Zwerdling, *Virginia Woolf and the Real World* (Berkeley: University of California Press, 1986), p. 269.
[103] Jane Marcus, *Art and Anger: Reading Like a Woman* (Columbus: Ohio State University Press, 1988). Mark Hussey summarizes some of these responses in *Virginia Woolf A–Z* (Oxford: Oxford University Press, 1995), p. 298.
[104] Pamela Caughie, *Virginia Woolf & Postmodernism: Literature in Quest & Question of Itself* (Urbana: University of Illinois Press, 1991), p. 117.
[105] *Ibid.*, p. 118.

not present itself."[106] Woolf's mediation is expressed in a more conventional page layout that relegates some of her reading of Antigone to footnotes, while at the same time she protests against "the vulgarity of the notes" (*D5*: 134).[107] Woolf had earlier in 1920 assisted in the printing of Hope Mirrlees' *Paris*, a poem which was modeled on Mallarmé's *Un coup de dés jamais d'abolira le hazard* (1897, reprinted 1914), as well as on contemporary work by Jean Cocteau and Pierre Reverdy. Its unusual typographical difficulties challenged Woolf's abilities as a printer.[108] Yet her experience did not carry over into the printing of *Three Guineas*, where a different layout might have made it clearer that to resist propaganda it is necessary to read not only several newspapers, but several languages. I wonder if the long and sometimes overloaded paragraphs of *Three Guineas* do not reveal the strain of the upstairs/downstairs system of text plus notes, whereas a redesign of the page might more clearly have drawn the reader's attention to the position of the translator who protects "the language that does not present itself" by mediating between ancient and contemporary texts from the perspective of semantic change.

In a later essay/talk Derrida used his position as speaker to mark the difference between "law" and "justice." There he engages more directly the position of the translator who brings ancient texts to bear on contemporary ethics. In "Force of Law: The 'Mystical Foundation of Authority,'" a talk delivered at a symposium *Deconstruction and the Possibility of Justice* (1989), he defends deconstruction against the hostile claim that it has disregarded the violence of history: "As to the legacy we have received under the name of justice, and in more than one language, the task of a historical and interpretive memory is at the heart of deconstruction."[109] It would seem that the

---

[106] Jacques Derrida, *Glas*, trans. John P. Leavey, Jr. and Richard Rand (Lincoln: University of Nebraska Press, 1986), p. 129. Derrida said of *Glas*, "I am trying to produce new forms of catachresis, another kind of writing, a violent writing which stakes out the faults (*failles*) and deviations of language, so that the text produces a language of its own, in itself, which, while continuing to work through tradition, emerges at a given moment as a *monster*, a monstrous mutation without tradition or normative precedent." Derrida, "Deconstruction and the Other," *Debates in Continental Philosophy: Conversations with Contemporary Thinkers*, ed. Richard Kearney (New York: Fordham University Press, 2004), 154.

[107] Vara Neverow and Merry Pawlowski have organized her 124 notes into a chart that fills in missing information. "A Preliminary Bibliographic Guide to the Footnotes of *Three Guineas*," *Woolf Studies Annual* 3 (1997), 170–210.

[108] Julia Briggs, *Reading Virginia Woolf* (Edinburgh: Edinburgh University Press, 2006), p. 84. The full text of *Paris: A Poem* appears in *Gender in Modernism: New Geographies, Complex Intersections*, ed. Bonnie Kime Scott (Urbana: University of Illinois Press, 2007), pp. 271–86.

[109] Jacques Derrida, *Deconstruction and the Possibility of Justice*, ed. Drucilla Cornell, Michel Rosenfeld, and David Gray Carlson (New York and London: Routledge, 1992), p. 19.

translator as well as the philosopher has a role to play in the transnational question of justice. Questions of translation are implicit as well in the defense of his speaking position as a particular problem of engaging with the theme of the colloquium. The translation of the English phrase, "to enforce the law," which has no equivalent in French ("appliquer la loi ... loses the allusion to force"), led him back to discussions of justice by Pascal and Montaigne that introduce the idea of "the mystical foundation of authority."[110] An untranslatable phrase, far from being a handicap, is turned into an opportunity to construct an argument based on etymology and the history of French thought.

It seems clear that the imminence of war with Germany during much of Woolf's lifetime created the circumstances in which mourning was in conflict with the public language. From its traditions of classical scholarship to the mechanical reproduction of the voice a certain aspect of German culture was imprinted on Woolf's understanding of the relationship of representation to history. Like classical scholars in Germany she seized the occasion of translation to challenge the public vocabulary and to reconstruct the sign. Once signifier and signified are uncoupled, the possibility of semantic change is no longer confined to the relationship between the foreign and the English text. In a linguistic situation that allows for choice, ventriloquism comes to seem ethically suspect, the high price of gender intelligibility. Only the mourning cry is seen to breach the barriers of kinship and nation. Whereas the untranslatable phrase led Derrida to examine discussions of justice in French history, Woolf's treatment of the untranslatable is related to the emergence of the feminine subject from her unwritten history. Confined within her own language, or in the phrase that Woolf takes from *Macbeth*, "cribb'd, cabin'd and confin'd," the subject seizes upon the untranslatable as a signal to bring her history to light (III:iv:24). Interlingual translation of a foreign text marks the place where the feminine subject is sent into hiding under the aegis of "not knowing Greek," only to emerge in the act of intralingual translation.

[110] *Ibid.*, p. 14.

CHAPTER 3

Tolstoy, Dostoyevsky, and the Russian soul

> Of all those who feasted upon Tolstoy, Dostoyevsky, and Tchekhov
> during the past twenty years, not more than one or two perhaps have
> been able to read them in Russian. Our estimate of their qualities has
> been formed by critics who have never read a word of Russian, or seen
> Russia, or even heard the language spoken by natives; who have had to
> depend, blindly and implicitly, upon the work of translators.
>
> (*E4*: 182)

Woolf's reading of Tolstoy as a novelist/historian enabled the revisionist view of history that is apparent in the structure of *Mrs. Dalloway* and *The Years*. Her interest in the Russian "soul" on the other hand, in the works of Dostoyevsky and Chekhov, is manifested throughout her stories and novels, and the study of *soul* in the diaries poignantly records her spiritual hunger. During the period 1912–25 Woolf learned some Russian, collaborated on a translation, and as a publisher and essayist helped to promote the sales of Russian works. Whereas most members of Woolf's class read French and were familiar with other western European languages, the sudden popularity of Russian fiction in the translations of Constance Garnett opened new paths of circulation in a language that was totally foreign to most English readers. Woolf began reading the Russian novel in 1912 on her honeymoon, when on the recommendation of Lytton Strachey she read a French translation of *Crime and Punishment*, *Le crime et le châtiment*. As Garnett's translations gradually became available, Woolf broadened her reading list to include not only Dostoyevsky, but Tolstoy, Turgenev, and Chekhov, and she read as well some lesser-known writers, Aksakov and Bunin. Leonard gave her a copy of Garnett's translation of *The Brothers Karamazov* in 1912; she presented him with *The Idiot* in 1913, and *The Insulted and the Injured* in 1915.

Russian literature boosted the fortunes of the Hogarth Press during the period 1920–3. Sales of Russian writers overshadowed all previous publications save those by T. S. Eliot and Virginia. Laura Marcus in her analysis of the activities of the Press stressed the heterogeneity of its publications. Although many small presses sprang up in England in the 1920s, most lasted only a few years.[1] That the Hogarth Press survived, and so freed Woolf from the conventional taste of commercial publishers, was owing in part, according to Leonard, to broadening their list, so that in addition to publishing the work of their friends, they began to include translations. Leonard and Virginia were tutored in Russian by S. S. Koteliansky, who brought Russian works to the Press, and they learned enough to collaborate with him on seven Hogarth translations.[2] After the Russian Revolution, sales of Tolstoy's work outstripped those of other Russians, and the Hogarth Press published four works by and about Tolstoy. Leonard wrote of the translation of Gorky's *Reminiscences of Tolstoy* (1920) "that the success of Gorky's book was really the turning point for the future of the Press and for our future."[3] In fact eight of the twenty-seven publications of the Press from its founding to 1923 were Russian translations. They together with *Kew Gardens* decided them "to allow the Press to expand and become professional, respectable, and commercial."[4] As a book reviewer Woolf contributed to this success. Her reviews of books by and about Tolstoy, Dostoyevsky, and Turgenev, from 1912–25, helped to create an audience for Russian literature.[5] It is significant that these works of translation were outside the purview of the university dons who had so vexed the problem of translating classical texts.

Perhaps because Woolf knew only a little Russian, and the literature did not provoke the ideological furor of Greek study, her positions as reader, translator, and critic were at first more narrowly focused than they had been in "On Not Knowing Greek." Natalya Reinhold, in a survey of Woolf's seventeen essays on Russian literature, notes her emphasis on differences of cultural identity, examines Woolf's motives for reading Russian writers, and after 1933 "her growing disappointment with Russian literature." Reinhold

[1] Laura Marcus, "Virginia Woolf and the Hogarth Press," *Modernist Writers and the Marketplace*, ed. Ian Willison, Warwick Gould, and Warren Cherniak (London: Macmillan, 1996), 128.
[2] In 1932 Woolf wrote that "I scarcely like to claim that I 'translated' the Russian books credited to me. I merely revised the English of a version made by S. Koteliansky" (*L5*: 91).
[3] Leonard Woolf, *Downhill All the Way* (London: Hogarth Press, 1967), pp. 67–8.
[4] Laura Marcus, "The European Dimensions of the Hogarth Press," *The Reception of Virginia Woolf in Europe*, ed. Mary Ann Caws and Nicola Luckhurst (London: Continuum, 2002), 348. A brief study of the Press and Russian writers appears in Marcus' "Introduction" to *Translations from the Russian by Virginia Woolf and S. S. Koteliansky*, ed. Stuart N. Clarke (London: Virginia Woolf Society of Great Britain, 2006), vii–xxiv.
[5] Marcus, "The European Dimensions of the Hogarth Press," 344.

concludes that in her study of Russian language and literature Woolf voyaged out and returned home: her rewriting of Chekhov in the short story "Uncle Vanya" shows how she "shaped the discourse of modernity by using the texts and genre sub-forms already existing in other languages and cultures."[6] My position, largely consistent with Reinhold's, is that Woolf used what she learned from translation to distance herself from realism. In addition she shared with Proust, whose work she began to read a decade later, an interest in the soul as a path to knowledge superior to that of the intellect, and written in a language that she could read.

When Woolf wrote of Tolstoy that "even in a translation we feel that we have been set on a mountain-top and had a telescope put into our hands," her image of translation as bringing the universe into view expresses the power of Russian fiction to enlarge the reader's sense of time and space. Her lifelong fascination with Tolstoy as "a man who sees what we see" led her to envision dialogue with a foreign culture as opening history to the sense of potentiality that is expressed at the end of *War and Peace* and in the drafts of *The Years* (*E*4: 188).[7] Although at first Woolf approached Tolstoy's work as a translator and reviewer of Russian fiction, her novels convert the questions she had asked as a reader into a sense that translation is the condition of historicity. The modernist innovations of plot in *Mrs. Dalloway*, and the turn to realism in *The Years* which has so puzzled Woolf's critics, are, I argue, her answer to questions about Tolstoy originally put by Matthew Arnold and Percy Lubbock that she had once considered. Unpublished sections of her review of *The Craft of Fiction* and her holograph notes on Tolstoy suggest that as a novelist she was stimulated to challenge the Victorians who first presented Tolstoy to British readers and then faulted him for not sounding more like Trollope or Henry James. As Woolf worked on *The Years* during the frightening events of the 1930s, her reading of Tolstoy provided a position from which to criticize the British nation as policing its borders in the name of the family, whereas she suggests that translation might transcend the barriers erected in the name of gender/class/nation.

Although Tolstoy's Russian spirituality and his attitude towards women complicated her response, Woolf turned to him again and again throughout her career.[8] She began reading Tolstoy about the time of his death in 1910.

---

[6] Natalya Reinhold, "Virginia Woolf's Russian Voyage Out," *Woolf Studies Annual* 9 (2003), 1–27.

[7] Gayla Diment, "Tolstoy and Bloomsbury," *Tolstoy Studies Journal* 5 (1992), 39–51.

[8] Woolf and S. S. Koteliansky translated A. B. Goldenveiser, *Talks with Tolstoi* (London: Hogarth Press, 1923), in which Tolstoy is recorded as saying, "I once said, but you must not talk about it, and I tell it you in secret: woman is generally so bad that the difference between a good and a bad woman scarcely exists," p. 24.

In a letter of 1928 she mentions reading *War and Peace*: "20 years ago, lying in bed one summer, I was enthralled and floated through week after week; and have lived in the recollection and called Tolstoi the greatest of novelists ever since" (*L*3: 570). Notes which Brenda Silver dates 1909–11 suggest the somewhat later date that appears in a letter of 1929, in which Woolf writes, "I've not read it for 15 years. *That* is the origin of all our discontent" (*L*4: 4). In "The Russian Point of View" (1925) Woolf refers to her reading of *Family Happiness*, *The Kreutzer Sonata*, and *The Cossacks*. Her library included as well *Plays* (1923), *Twenty-Three Tales* (1928), and *What Is Art?* (1930). In March 1926 she read and noted *Anna Karenina*, and in 1939 was planning to read the two major novels again (*L*6: 361).

In the aftermath of the Russian Revolution Tolstoy's reputation throughout the west rose to new heights, and by 1924 the sales of his books outstripped those of other Russian writers.[9] The Press published Countess Sophie Tolstoy's *Autobiography* (1922), A. B. Goldenveiser's *Talks with Tolstoi* (1923), *The Love Letters of Tolstoy* (1923), and Tolstoy's last work, his essay *On Socialism* (1936). Woolf's reviews helped to create the popularity of Russian writing. She reviewed Tolstoy's *The Cossacks*, two books by Dostoyevsky, and one by Aksakov in 1917, three on Russian topics in 1918, and one or two a year from 1919 to 1922. In "Notes on an Elizabethan Play" (1925) Tolstoy is compared favorably with Elizabethan dramatists, and he figures in "Character in Fiction" (1924) and "Phases of Fiction" (1929). He is discussed along with Dostoyevsky and Chekhov in "The Russian Point of View" (1925) as "the greatest of all novelists." Yet her ambivalence becomes apparent at the end of the essay: "of the three great Russian writers, it is Tolstoi who most enthralls us and most repels" (*E*4: 189).

Woolf's review of Percy Lubbock's *The Craft of Fiction* in the *Times Literary Supplement* (July 20, 1922) offered an occasion to situate Tolstoy in the context of European fiction. She took exception to Lubbock's concentration on "form," a term which he derived from painting ("Form, design, composition, are to be sought in a novel, as in any other work of Art"), because, she wrote, fiction differs from drama as well as from the visual arts.[10] The general structure of Lubbock's essay was to use Tolstoy's apparent disregard of form in order to praise the formal qualities of the novels of Flaubert and Henry James. The chapter on the structure of *War and Peace* initiated what Woolf called "a progression from Tolstoy" to the

[9] Alexander Fodor, *Tolstoy and the Russians: Reflections on a Relationship* (Ann Arbor, Mich.: Ardis, 1984), p. 123.

[10] Percy Lubbock, *The Craft of Fiction* (New York: Charles Scribner's Sons, 1921), p. 26.

work of Henry James. She countered Lubbock's argument by stressing the role of "emotion" in her reading of one of his texts, Flaubert's "Un coeur simple." The word "emotion" appears over and over in her notes, and is at the heart of her criticism of "form": "L dwells too much upon the form the emotions take . . . all rather problematic," and "He talks of 'form' as the work itself."[11]

Woolf's working notes for the essay include an unpublished section entitled "War and Peace," in which she defends the novel against Lubbock's criticism of what he called "a great and brilliant novel, a well-known novel . . . I wish to examine its form, I do not wish to argue its merit."[12] His criticism was that the double plot, which contains the narrative of the Napoleonic war and the stories of two families, forms in fact two distinct novels: "Neither is subordinate to the other, and there is nothing above them . . . to which they are both related."[13] In her notes Woolf argued for the primacy not of subject matter but of emotion. She first quotes his text, "that war is a big human motive / cut across by the irrelevant uproar. / the best form is that wh. makes the most / of its subject." Her comments follow: "there is no other definition of form / Surely you can't see form apart from the / emotion wh makes it," and she repeats "emotion" on nearly every page of her notes. Whereas Lubbock wrote of *War and Peace* that "its inadequate grasp of a great theme . . . is scarcely noticed – on a first reading of the book," Woolf countered, "to feel the thing – that is the first essential / that is the first reading."[14] These notes, which did not appear in the published version, make clear that by 1922, the year in which she began reading Proust as well as the Russians, she had become focused on the expression of feeling, although it went counter to some authoritative critical positions.

By the time she made her notes on *Anna Karenina* a few years later, Woolf had shifted to a new position. Although she appreciated Tolstoy's descriptive powers, of physical gesture for instance, she questioned his treatment of gender and his particular brand of realism. Her notes on *Anna Karenina* are pinned together with pages on Trollope, Peacock, and Balzac, and notes on Richardson's *Clarissa* dated June and July 1926.[15] The single sheet of Tolstoy notes, dated simply "23rd March," is presumably from the same year and thus postdates the publication of *Mrs. Dalloway*

---

[11] Berg Collection, Reel 13, XXVI, B 33.   [12] Lubbock, *The Craft of Fiction*, p. 26.
[13] *Ibid.*, p. 33.   [14] *Ibid.*, p. 41.
[15] My thanks to the curator of the Frances Hooper Collection of Virginia Woolf's Books and Manuscripts, in the Mortimer Rare Book Room, Smith College, for permission to quote.

(*D*3: 70). Woolf praised Tolstoy for his dialogue: "women's talk amazing," and for his sense of the visible: "His physical eye amazing." But like many of Tolstoy's early readers, she found his lack of exclusiveness, his giving the reader details which are not strictly subordinated to the plot, problematic: "What are the laws that govern realistic art? That one shd follow life exactly? Give all thrills & ups and down, even if they don't show character or philosophy, but only life?" The formal problems that she engaged in *The Years* had their origins in these questions.

Woolf's troubled observation of the apparently pointless quality of some Tolstoyan incident and detail locates her midway between Victorian and modernist readers. Matthew Arnold brought to his reading of Tolstoy certain expectations about the way plots should develop: "incidents are multiplied which we expect are to lead to something important, but which do not."[16] By the apparently simple gesture of turning Arnold's assumption into a question Woolf opened the possibilities of realism, for two years later in a letter to Vita Sackville-West (September 8, 1928) she praised her essay on Tolstoy: "The question you should have pushed home ... is precisely the one you raise, what made his realism which might have been photographic, not at all; but on the contrary moving and exciting and all the rest of it" (*L*3: 529).

Gary Morson argues that the extraneous incidents and characters in *War and Peace* signify Tolstoy's view of history. Russian critics who saw "a plague of small characters nibbling at the plot" failed to understand that Tolstoy deliberately violated the conventions of fiction. Morson cites among many possibilities the wolf hunt and the Christmas mummery as instances of "observations for observation's sake." He makes the point that the structure of the novel signifies the historical process as Tolstoy understood it. While some incidents lead to the reader's understanding, others manifest only that potential: "some potential is realized, some is not."[17] After some discussion of classical and romantic myths of composition, Morson ascribes to Tolstoy a creative process which he terms "creation by potential": "An author who follows this method ... does not know at the outset what the work will turn out to be when complete ... With no conclusion in mind, he deliberately cultivates the unexpected; structure is what it turns out to be, connections emerge without premeditation, and unity becomes only a unity of process."[18] To this end he quotes Tolstoy's draft of a proposed introduction to

---

[16] Matthew Arnold, "Count Leo Tolstoy," *Fortnightly Review* (December 1887), reprinted in *Essays in Criticism: Second Series* (London: Macmillan, 1888), p. 260.
[17] Gary Morson, *Hidden in Plain View: Narrative and Creative Potential in "War and Peace"* (Stanford: Stanford University Press, 1987), pp. 147–51.
[18] *Ibid.*, p. 182.

War and Peace: "In printing the beginning of my proposed work, I promise neither a continuation nor a conclusion for it. We Russians in general do not know how to write novels in the sense in which this genre is understood in Europe; and this proposed work ... can least of all be called a novel – with a plot that has constantly growing complexity, and a happy or unhappy denouement, with which interest in the narration ends."[19]

Whereas Lubbock, although critical of the characterization of Anna, did not fault the double plot of *Anna Karenina*, Woolf in her notes used the double plot to fuel her observations about gender: "What is so disturbing is the constant change from place to place one story to another the emotional continuity is broken up – unavoidable, but there seems to be a diversion of power," and a few lines later: "What seems to me is that the construction is a good deal hindered by the double story. It offends me that the book ends without any allusion to Anna. She's allowed to drop out never comes into Levin or Kitty's mind again. All the stress finally upon his religious feelings – as if they predominated momentarily as they wd in real life; but this is unsatisfactory in a work of art where the other feelings have been around for so long." Justin Weir explores the theme of language in *Anna Karenina* in a way that might answer Woolf's criticism. He observes that whereas Levin at certain moments has access to prayer, Anna becomes a modernist figure as she gradually loses her ability to communicate her emotions and retreats into a world of dreams.[20]

Yet in *Mrs. Dalloway* Woolf adapted the double plot of *War and Peace* and *Anna Karenina* to create a modernist narrative. As a reader she took one position, as a novelist its opposite. Her notes are those of a conservative reader whose views are beginning to diverge from those of Arnold and Lubbock. As a novelist Woolf made creative use of precisely those features that she had questioned, as though the creative act was motivated by reading, which set in motion a tension that stimulated the artist to dissent from the critic, whose views may be discerned as a kind of shadow text behind her own. This split subjectivity may also govern the narrative of Septimus Smith, which was like the narrative about Levin a relatively late addition. It defamiliarizes characterization, and draws the parallels between the lives of a London hostess and a soldier traumatized by war, by its treatment of narrative continuity and structure.[21]

[19] Quoted in Morson, *Hidden in Plain View*, p. 183.

[20] Justin Weir, "Anna Incommunicada: Language and Consciousness in *Anna Karenina*," *Tolstoy Studies Journal* 8 (1995–6), 99–111.

[21] Lydia Ginzburg, *On Psychological Prose*, trans. Judson Rosengrant (Princeton: Princeton University Press, 1991), p. 245.

In the five lines of notes that survive from Woolf's reading of *War and Peace* she refers in a tantalizing phrase to the well-known scene in which "Natasha at the window" is overheard by Prince Andrey standing at the window above.[22] The trope of the window and the possibility that it offers of a mode of communication beyond dialogue figures significantly in *Mrs. Dalloway*, where Clarissa at key moments in the narrative observes through her window an old woman preparing for bed. Septimus Smith, as though moving along the trajectory of Clarissa's gaze, jumps to his death through a window. In *To the Lighthouse* the first section, "The Window," points to the ideology of perspective that impedes Lily Briscoe's painting of Mrs. Ramsay. Yet these instances of the trope of the window, however intriguing, are to my mind less significant than Woolf's later attempt to create the essay-novel along Tolstoyan lines.

Tolstoy's technique, according to Robert Belknap never well understood, was to block the reading of the novel as "a simple morality text" and to "force the reader into active judgement ... What Western novelists achieved through the intimacies of narrators, Tolstoi often achieved through plotting that infects us with the moral malaise which Tolstoi considered the highest achievement of his civilization." When Woolf objected to the double narrative of *Anna Karenina*, while at the same time introducing the character of Septimus Smith into *Mrs. Dalloway*, she took up a particular modernist position. "From the end of the nineteenth century on, western novelists often use techniques from Russia ... as modernist departures from the nineteenth-century rules."[23] What might have been a novel about the domestic life of Clarissa Dalloway becomes by the addition of a second narrative a novel that problematizes the aftermath of World War I in the civilian population. The double plot averts moralizing by assigning the power of judgment not to the narrator but implicitly to the reader.

The historical context in which the language of fiction asserts its right to comment on the uses of narrative in history writing becomes more apparent when we take a comparative look at the composition of *War and Peace* (1869) and *The Years* (1938). What is at stake is not the problem of representing war but the way in which war comes to be represented as the history of a nation. As Karen Levenback observes of Woolf, "the place of war in dated history is insignificant when compared with experience of the

---

[22] The single page, numbered 19, is collected in notebook XIII, which Brenda Silver dates 1928–30. *Virginia Woolf's Reading Notebooks* (Princeton: Princeton University Press, 1983). Berg Reel 13. Woolf refers to the scene in "Phases of Fiction."

[23] Robert Belknap, "Novelist Technique," *The Cambridge Companion to the Classic Russian Novel*, ed. Malcolm V. Jones and Robin Feuer Miller (Cambridge: Cambridge University Press, 1998), 246.

war and how it is remembered."[24] The definition of the nation is a question that neither Tolstoy nor Woolf was content to leave in the hands of historians. Woolf wrote in an early version of *The Years*, "If you object that fiction is not history, I reply that though it would be far easier to write history . . . that method of telling the truth seems to me so elementary, and so clumsy, that I prefer, where truth is important, to write fiction."[25] In Russia the writing of history had not yet been professionalized and relegated to the university as was happening in the west. A number of well-known Russian novelists, having first earned a reputation in fiction, turned their hands to the writing of history. Pushkin wrote of the Pugachev uprising in *History of Pugachev* (1834), and again in his novel *The Captain's Daughter* (1836), two works that, begun at the same time, present the uprising first in terms of history and then fiction. Andrew Wachtel concludes that "Pushkin's choices were dictated primarily by considerations of genre; what was crucial for one genre was unnecessary for another and Pushkin wished, if anything, to emphasize the incompatibility of the historical perspectives that his various genres required in order to encourage intergeneric dialogue between them."[26] Tolstoy, like Pushkin and Gogol, believed that the languages of history and fiction were essentially different. Wachtel cites this passage from the notebooks for *War and Peace*: "When describing a historical epoch the artist and the historian have two entirely different objectives. Just as the historian would be wrong if he attempted to present a historical figure in all his entirety, in all his complicated connections to all aspects of life, so an artist would not be doing his duty if he presented that figure in all of his historical significance."[27] Wachtel goes on to distinguish three "narrative positions" in *War and Peace*, "the fictional, historical, and metahistorical voices."[28] The point is that the reader is forced into a position from which he must seek connections among these voices. But as we shall see, in England Woolf operated in an entirely different set of circumstances.

As Boris Eikhenbaum shows, in the steps by which Tolstoy moved during the period of composition (1863–9) from a study of individual lives lived during the Napoleonic era, to a novel about 1812, the process of

---

[24] Karen Levenback, *Virginia Woolf and the Great War* (Syracuse, N.Y.: Syracuse University Press, 1999), p. 120; and Melba Cuddy-Keane, "Virginia Woolf and the Varieties of Historicist Experience," *Virginia Woolf and the Essay*, ed. Beth Carole Rosenberg and Jeanne Dubino (New York: St. Martin's Press, 1997), 59–77.

[25] Virginia Woolf, *The Pargiters: The Novel-Essay Portion of "The Years,"* ed. Mitchell Leaska (New York: Harcourt Brace Jovanovich, 1977), p. 9.

[26] Andrew Wachtel, *An Obsession with History: Russian Writers Confront the Past* (Stanford: Stanford University Press, 1994), p. 82.

[27] *Ibid.*, p. 89.   [28] *Ibid.*, p. 90.

working in two genres created problems. The political dimension of the artistic process may be inferred from the resistance of readers and fellow artists, Turgenev and Flaubert among them, to the novel that is oriented towards both epic and essay. The hostility to Tolstoy's endeavor was exacerbated by the fact that as he worked on the novel at several periods, and published a book or two at a time, his conception changed. The titles themselves are suggestive: the first installment appeared in *The Russian Messenger* (1865) as *The Year 1805*, which although it contained no battle scenes immediately raised questions about the relationship of chronicle to fiction. As Eikhenbaum points out, Tolstoy chose "an era which was striking enough, and popular enough, so that its treatment from an unexpected angle would be . . . effective and convincing."[29] A version of 1863 was entitled "Three Eras." "All's Well that Ends Well" was to have been published in 1866, "with all possible marriages resolving all the family conflicts and unraveling all the knots of the plot."[30] Although the latter version preserved the emphasis on domestic life, "the military chapters were to introduce variety of tone and facilitate the transitions from one character to another."[31] To this end Tolstoy read widely in narratives about the Napoleonic period. But as this quotation from a draft makes clear, he retained an emphasis on family and private life: "Life, with its existing concern for health, sickness, wealth, poverty, love for one's brother, sister, son, father, wife, and lover, with its concern for work, leisure, hunting passions . . . all went on outside the decrees about ministries or boards, just as it always goes on outside all government control."[32]

Eikhenbaum characterizes the intellectual climate of the 1860s as marked by a general interest in questions of historical ethics, in particular one question "about how individual freedom and historical necessity are combined; and the second . . . about causality in history."[33] In this climate it is not difficult to appreciate that Tolstoy, self-educated and reading history in order to confirm his views, became discouraged: "The whole historical part is not sticking together and is going badly . . . I have fallen apart."[34] The turning point seems to have been his perception of the epic possibilities of narrative. Eikhenbaum stresses the importance to Tolstoy of the narrating voice in the *Iliad* as a way of introducing Homeric digressions. These historical digressions "based on relatively little historical material, and filled with family episodes which were entirely unrelated to the history or the

---

[29] Boris Eikhenbaum, *Tolstoy in the Sixties*, trans. Duffield White (Ann Arbor: Ardis, 1982), p. 135.
[30] *Ibid.*, p. 140.   [31] *Ibid.*, p. 148.   [32] Quoted in Eikhenbaum, *Tolstoy in the Sixties*, p. 150.
[33] *Ibid.*, pp. 195–6.   [34] Quoted in Eikhenbaum, *Tolstoy in the Sixties*, p. 159.

period of 1812 ... became ostensibly *historical* ... Genre and stylistic devices made up for the lack of historicity *per se*. The digressions played the role of a historical equivalent."[35]

Kathryn B. Feuer, writing a generation later, and with access to materials unavailable to Eikhenbaum, traces a pattern of development in which Tolstoy abandoned work on a political novel, since by 1856 the emancipation of the serfs was imminent, and the problem of landowner and serf was no longer primarily moral. Yet the change in Tolstoy's historical position did not mean that he argued on behalf of the political demands of the peasant. In a newly discovered chapter of *War and Peace* Tolstoy lists a number of reasons for drawing characters only from his own class, noting that he could not write of the inner lives of policemen, and concluding "Sixth, finally (and this, I know is the very best reason), because I belong to the highest class, to society, and I love it."[36] Although this passage never appeared in the printed version, Tolstoy worked during the preliminary stages of composition "to define the relationship he saw among Napoleon, Decembrism, and contemporary Russia in a manner that would provide a fictionally viable approach to the three epochs, working to find the one strand he must seize to untangle the temporal and conceptual skein."[37] Ultimately he identified the revolutionary aspects of all three, and Napoleon as "a symbol of the invasion of Russia by the ideas of the French Revolution."[38]

The hostility of early readers of *War and Peace* to the mix of fiction and history affected the establishment of the text. Turgenev, for instance, wrote that Tolstoy's arguments about free will simply revealed "the instability and immaturity of his thought, ... and the conceit of a half-educated person."[39] Tolstoy responded to his critics by reworking the novel for the 1873 edition: "not only was the French language eliminated, but the military-theoretical chapters were taken out of the basic text as well and put in a special appendix, 'Articles on the Campaign of 1812.'" Moreover, all of the philosophical-historical discourses, "which, as I have said, served as beginning-points of the various parts of the novel, were taken out altogether."[40] The effect on genre was to eliminate the Homeric digressions, and to move the novel closer to English models. Tolstoy did the work hastily and mechanically, so that the novel achieved "an even more

---

[35] *Ibid.*, p. 128.
[36] Quoted in Kathryn B. Feuer, *Tolstoy and the Genesis of War and Peace*, ed. Robin Feuer Miller and Donna Tussing Orwin (Ithaca, N.Y.: Cornell University Press, 1996), p. 146, and chapter seven.
[37] *Ibid.*, p. 194.   [38] *Ibid.*, p. 208.
[39] Quoted in Eikhenbaum, *Tolstoy in the Sixties*, p. 229.   [40] *Ibid.*, p. 239.

fragmentary 'montage' character." Posthumous editions were revised by Tolstoy's wife with respect to certain markets, so that the French passages were removed in cheap, but restored in expensive editions. As a result, "there is no obvious, definitive, 'canonical' text of *War and Peace* and it is not possible to establish it by any means."[41]

Western readers encountered a significantly less problematic *War and Peace*, that was more easily assimilated to other long nineteenth-century English and French novels. After all, in the early stages of writing, before the philosophical digressions appeared, Tolstoy had considered modeling his novel on Trollope's Barchester and Palliser series, which he admired. But the translators, who have "reduced the idiosyncrasies of his work . . . making it sound more 'classical' and less experimental," are also responsible for an anglicized novel.[42] French passages are seldom and German passages never retained, so that the use of language as an indication of class is suppressed: for instance on page 1 of the Constance Garnett translation we read that Prince Vassily "spoke in that elaborately choice French in which our forefathers not only spoke but thought." In 1909–11 Woolf would have read the Garnett translation (1900), which contains no table of contents, and is divided into fifteen "parts," followed by an "Epilogue in two parts." The Aylmer and Louise Maude translation (1922–3, revised 1933) changed Tolstoy's divisions of the novel into books and chapters in a way that corresponds to no Russian edition.[43] They divided the novel into fifteen "books," followed by a "First" and a "Second Epilogue." Even more significant was their decision to introduce each chapter with a synopsis that makes it easier to keep track of plot and characters. Their reader-friendly text has in fact compromised Tolstoy's sense of potentiality, and "committed the fallacy described in *War and Peace* as 'the law of retrospection.'"[44]

Woolf too started work with the plan of a family novel into which she gradually incorporated national events. The manuscript of *The Years* was written in eight holograph notebooks, dated at intervals from October 11, 1932 to September 30, 1934; a few sheets labeled "Revisions" are dated "Oct. 4."[45] Employing Tolstoy's hybrid term, she first described the work as "an Essay-Novel, called the Pargiters – & its to take in everything, sex, education, life &c: & come, with the most powerful & agile leaps, like a chamois across precipices from 1880 to here & now" (*D4*: 129). The list of tentative titles that appears in the seventh notebook emphasizes domestic

[41] *Ibid.*, pp. 241–2.   [42] Morson, *Hidden in Plain View*, p. 286, n. 3.
[43] *Ibid.*, pp. 78–9.   [44] *Ibid.*, p. 286, n. 3.   [45] Berg Reel 10.

themes: "The Pargiters, Here & Now, Brothers & Sisters, Dawn, Uncles & Aunts, Ordinary People, Sons & Daughters." None of these titles gestured towards large historical themes, and all sound a bit like Trollope. Nor does the holograph include the dates which in the printed version orient each chapter towards a place in a historical genealogy. Instead the manuscipt is divided into seven "Parts." As for the convention of chapters, the manuscript begins with the speech "Professions for Women," followed by "Chapter Fifty-six," which ironically introduces the narrative of the first section of the printed version.

During this period Woolf was questioning and exploring the limits of genre. In January 1933 she described the structure as "a curiously uneven time sequence – a series of great balloons, linked by straight narrow passages of narrative" (*D4*: 142). In April she described her broad vision: "to give the whole of the present society – nothing less: facts, as well as the vision. And to combine them both . . . It should include satire, comedy, poetry, narrative, & what form is to hold them all together? Should I bring in a play, letters, poems? . . . And there are to be millions of ideas but no preaching – history, politics, feminism, art, literature – in short a summing up of all I know, feel, laugh at, despise, like, admire hate & so on" (*D4*: 152 and see 162).

Work on *The Years* after the manuscript was completed in October 1934 suggests that Woolf gradually revised the novel to align the events of the family with the history of a nation. The holograph text mentioned a period thirty years after 1880, or an event that occurred ten years before 1927, and clearly the novel investigates the historical evolution of women's roles. Yet although in February 1933 she had contemplated "an appendix of dates" (*D4*: 146), the chapter-dates were added after the holograph draft had been completed. Tolstoy's dates refer to historical events that the Russian reader is expected to recognize; the dates in *The Years* are part of a more complex representation of time. Some chapters refer to well-known historical events: "1891" to the death of Charles Parnell, "1914" to World War I, and "1917" to the fighting at Ypres and Passchendaele as well as the Russian Revolution. After reading *The Life of Charles Stewart Parnell*, by R. Barry O'Brien in January 1933, Woolf returned to the "1880" chapter and added the scene of Abel Pargiter's visit to Mara, his mistress, which does not appear in the holograph. These implicit parallels between the Pargiter family and national events maintain, in the manner of Tolstoy, equivalent emphasis on family and history.[46]

---

[46] Laura Moss Gottlieb, "*The Years*: A Feminist Novel," *Virginia Woolf Centennial Essays*, ed. Elaine K. Ginsberg and Laura Moss Gottlieb (Troy, N.Y.: Whitsun Publishing Company, 1983), 215–29.

Once the holograph text was complete Woolf began a process of revision that drastically reduced the length of the novel, although the precise steps are not at all clear.[47] When the holograph was completed (September 30, 1934), it was "900 pages: L. says 200,000 words" (*D4*: 245). In November she began to revise so that by December "hardly a line of the original is left" (*D4*: 266). By July 1935 she had "finished my first wild retyping & find the book comes to 740 pages," minus apparently the final chapter and the "interludes . . . spaces of silence, & poetry & contrast" (*D4*: 332). In March 1936 she was at work on a typescript of 950 pages (*D5*: 17), and three months later she was correcting 600 pages of galley proofs. Grace Radin concludes from her study of the holograph, typescript, and galleys that revision compromised the coherence of the novel, and that "the holograph, which is many times the length of *The Years*, is replete with details that have been expunged from the final text."[48]

Woolf finished the novel in painful circumstances. She requested galley rather than page proofs, so that she might be free to revise. And the state of her mental health was, as Leonard describes it, worse than it had been since her major breakdown in 1913. The six months from April 9 to October 30, 1936 "were filled with an unending nightmare."[49] In these circumstances Leonard read the book for the first time in proof with the agreement "that she would accept my verdict of its merits and defects and whether it should or should not be published. It was for me a difficult and dangerous task." He was "greatly relieved" that it was not "in any way as bad as she thought it to be," although in light of her ill health he "praised the book more than I should have done if she had been well."[50] In these circumstances of collaboration during revision Woolf deleted hundreds of pages of text, including the "two enormous chunks" that she deleted in proof. Like the majority of Woolf's readers since, Leonard did not grasp the problem that the novel engages.

Two scholars who have studied the early versions of *The Years* see a novel that is more forceful, more grim, and more engaged with the representation of war than is apparent in the printed version. Karen Levenback observes, "When Woolf sent final corrections to the proofs . . . she had deleted what she called 'the first war scene,' made extensive cuts to what she called 'the raid scene,' and eliminated '1921' altogether."[51] Hitler was coming to power,

---

[47] Grace Radin, *Virginia Woolf's "The Years": The Evolution of a Novel* (Knoxville: Kentucky University Press, 1981), p. III.

[48] *Ibid.*, p. xxi.   [49] Leonard Woolf, *Downhill All the Way*, p. 153.   [50] *Ibid.*, p. 155.

[51] Levenback, *Virginia Woolf and the Great War*, p. 143.

and Leonard and Virginia were forced to consider the political climate. Woolf's diary notes war anxiety, and during their trip of May 1935 through Germany "every village had a painted sign 'Die Juden sind hier unwunscht'" (*D*4: 312). Leonard, Levenback argues, may have played a part in cautioning Virginia that the time was not right for anti-war sentiment. Grace Radin argues for the much greater historical specificity and the greater power of the earlier version. The deletion of expository passages has the effect of suppressing "radical and unorthodox ideas," so that they become in the printed version "absurd notions," affecting in particular the characterizations of Delia and Eleanor.[52] In one telling episode from the final chapter Eleanor in the earlier version "recalls the horrors of the last war [as] her instincts tell her the world is preparing for the next . . . Her remarks . . . create an atmosphere of grim foreboding in the MS that is lost in *The Years*."[53] Radin sees in the manuscript version "an unwritten novel" several times longer and a more compelling history of its time than the published text. Woolf's novel about the aftermath of the first World War had become a casualty of the second. And in fact faced with an audience unprepared to read an anti-war novel, Woolf reserved for *Three Guineas* her discussion of war and patriotism.

Nicholas, who appears in "1917" and in "Present Day," is the Tolstoyan character who contributes the sense that translation from a foreign culture is the condition of historicity. Of all the characters in *War and Peace* Nicholas Rostov is a singular choice, for Tolstoy characterizes him as having "that common sense of mediocrity which showed him what was his duty,"[54] and perhaps for that reason he has attracted less critical attention than Pierre Bezukhov or Prince Andrey Bolkonsky. Nicholas evolves from a wildly patriotic young man to a mature adult who becomes a good landowner and seeks spiritual companionship in marriage. As a sixteen-year-old Nicholas rushes onto a bridge that is under enemy fire in an attempt to impress the colonel, and has daydreams of being befriended by the Emperor Alexander. His experience of war and being wounded changes these sentiments. Visiting a friend who is recuperating from his wounds in a military hospital, Nicholas involuntarily makes a comparison between the stench and disease in the hospital and his glimpse of a ceremonial meeting between the Emperor and Bonaparte: "For what, then, had those legs and arms been torn off, those men been killed?" (468). Later when he encounters a French soldier who has been knocked off his horse and looks up in terror, Nicholas

---

[52] Radin, *Virginia Woolf's "The Years,"* p. 77.   [53] *Ibid.*, p. 93.
[54] Leo Tolstoy, *War and Peace*, trans. Constance Garnett (New York: Modern Library edition, 1994), p. 554. Subsequent page references appear in the text.

comes to a realization: "'So they are even more frightened than we are,' he thought. 'Why, is this all that's meant by heroism? And did I do it for the sake of my country? . . . Why should I kill him?'" (746). As Morson points out, Nicholas becomes more heroic than those characters who like Prince Andrey strive to be so: "It may well be Tolstoy's great achievement that his critics could not recognize Rostov as the only truly heroic figure in *War and Peace.*"[55]

Although Tolstoy's attitude towards patriotism was not constant, his work has had a special appeal to readers during wartime. The early stories that he wrote while serving in the military during the Crimean War and hoping for promotion show an erratic attitude, sometimes praising the patriotism of Russian soldiers, and sometimes revealing the needless suffering of the peasants.[56] Although in *War and Peace* the Russian forces and their commander Marshal Kutuzov are represented as superior to Napoleon's forces, Tolstoy's attitude vacillated. Donna Orwin writes that only in the late work, *The Kingdom of God Is Within You* (1890–3) did he "state outright that patriotism was impossible."[57] During World War II Russians enduring the siege of Leningrad found in *War and Peace* confirmation of their own feelings, and it is significant that only in the 1940s did the novel become a classic among western readers.[58]

Although in the printed version of *The Years* Nicholas is a Pole, on a corrected galley he is a Russian associated with the quality of "soul," which was as Woolf wrote "the chief character in Russian fiction" (Reel 12, M 128, and *E*4: 185). In the galley version Nicholas discusses with Eleanor "how to educate the soul . . . It wishes to rush; to expand; always adventuring; always forming new – he hesitated – combinations" (Reel 12, M 128, galley 202). Although in the dinner scene in "1917" he is discussing Napoleon with Renny, the latter's speech in the manuscript version makes a more explicitly historical connection: "That was how we came to Napoleon. What the Allies should have done at the end of the Napoleonic Wars."[59] Nicholas criticizes war as a mere interruption in the tendency of capitalist society to deprive women of rights and education. He says of Maggie and Sara, that they "are absolutely uneducated; they have received nothing from their

[55] Morson, *Hidden in Plain View*, p. 245.
[56] Alexander Fodor, "Ambiguities in Tolstoy's Views on Patriotism," *Lev Tolstoy and the Concept of Brotherhood*, ed. Andrew Donskov and John Woodsworth (New York: Legas, 1996), 181–93.
[57] Donna Orwin, "Tolstoy and Patriotism," *Lev Tolstoy and the Concept of Brotherhood*, ed. Andrew Donskov and John Woodsworth (New York: Legas, 1996), 70.
[58] Orwin, "Tolstoy and Patriotism," 51; but see Fodor, *Tolstoy*, p. 91.
[59] Cited in Radin, *Virginia Woolf's "The Years,"* p. 67.

country, from the institutions of their country; they cannot practice professions, they are kept purely as slaves for the breeding of children: & that
system it seems [has] abolished all feelings of patriotism."[60] It is as though
Woolf extrapolated from Tolstoy's criticism of patriotism the coupling with
patriarchy that is developed more explicitly in *Three Guineas*.

In the printed version the revolutionary theme is expressed during
Nicholas' conversation with Eleanor, in the trope of translation as "new
combinations." He begins a sentence, "if we do not know ourselves, how
then can we make religions, laws, that ... " that as he hesitates Eleanor
completes, "'That fit – that fit,' she said.'" (*Y*: 268). Her ability to complete
Nicholas' sentence has a liberating effect, for she begins to imagine "a new
world," where men will be liberated from living "like cripples in a cave" (*Y*:
282). Although several characters leave their sentences dangling, in this
exchange the words "made one intelligible sentence," which expresses
what each had been thinking (*Y*: 268). When the dinner and the air raid
are over, Eleanor emerges into the street, with the recognition that she has
been witness to "a happy marriage," between Maggie and Renny. In
"Family Happiness," Tolstoy's story of happy marriage, the unfinished
sentence occurs during the scenes of greatest bitterness between husband
and wife, when it appears that each assigns a different meaning to the same
word: "You call it love, but I call it torture." The happiness that the couple
achieves by the end depends to a great extent on the wife's intellectual and
semantic accommodation to the sentences begun by the husband. Woolf's
view of gender revises this discourse: Nicholas and Eleanor enjoy the special
intimacy between a gay man and an older woman who come from separate
cultures, in which the completion of the sentence translates new meaning
without pain.[61]

In Woolf's view war made translation more urgent. Eleanor sees a "fan of
light ... It seemed to take what she was feeling and to express it broadly and
simply, as if another voice were speaking in another language" (*Y*: 285). The
trope of voices heard speaking another language evokes the well-known
scene of Woolf's illness, when she heard the birds speaking Greek. More
significantly it evokes her lifelong interest in translation as mediating her
experience by opening a world "on the far side of language" that is necessary,
as she wrote in "On Not Knowing Greek," to express "the vast catastrophe
of the European war" (*E*4: 45 and 47–8). To complete the sentence begun

---

[60] Cited *ibid.*, p. 69.
[61] In a comparable scene in *Anna Karenina* Levin and Kitty reveal their love for each other in a series of
initial letters from which the other completes words and a sentence. Part IV, chapter thirteen.

by a foreigner would seem to be Woolf's twentieth-century trope of the cave: one is helped to emerge from darkness by means of a translation which Eleanor seems less to author than to witness in herself.

As Woolf worried over the last chapter of *The Years*, Tolstoy came to mind: "That is to say the last chapter is going to give me a deal of trouble . . . If the last chapter fails does the book fail? What is the last chapter of War & Peace? I forget" (*D*4: 249).[62] If we assume that Woolf's forgetting was temporary, we may look to the Epilogue to *War and Peace* for a sense of the problem she had characterized when writing of the Russian mind in "Modern Fiction": "the sense that there is no answer, that if honestly examined life presents question after question which must be left to sound on and on after the story is over in hopeless interrogation" (*E*4: 163). It would serve Woolf's purposes in both *The Years* and *Three Guineas* to read the second Epilogue as Tolstoy's study of the problematic of patriotism and the nation. Although in earlier times, he notes, the behavior of men was said to be motivated by divine intervention, modern historians retain the paradigm, merely substituting the notion of individual leadership. In a rhetorical technique that bears similarities to that of *Three Guineas* Tolstoy argues by repeating his central question, "What force moves nations?" (1347, 1348, 1360), while attacking the problem from the angle of a vocabulary that is also stressed by repetition. He considers the contradictory historical aims of "causality" and "description," the motivations of "power" both physical and moral, and "force" and "idea." The key idea is that history is not a transparent reporting of fact but a creation of language: "the subject of history is not the will of man, but our representation of its action."

Tolstoy's reflections on history and representation join the late nineteenth-century European debate on the meaning of "the nation." Eric Hobsbawm opens a chapter of *Nations and Nationalism since 1780* by asking a Tolstoyan question about the relationship between men and nations: "Why and how could a concept so remote from the real experience of most human beings as 'national patriotism' become such a powerful political force so quickly?"[63] After dismissing the possibility that the nation

---

[62] Pamela Caughie, one of the few critics to admire *The Years*, writes of the ending that it "cannot be contained, cannot be summed up, and, more important, cannot be appropriated by any one person, group, or reading. What is at issue in these narrative structures is a world that can be contained, controlled, and perfected versus a world that is constantly being rehearsed." *Virginia Woolf & Postmodernism: Literature in Quest & Question of Itself* (Urbana: University of Illinois Press, 1991), p. 106.

[63] Eric Hobsbawm, *Nations and Nationalism since 1780* (Cambridge: Cambridge University Press, 1990), p. 46.

is associated with common ethnicity, language, or culture, he concludes that the term is a "novelty," coined to represent a particular stage of historical and economic development. Rather the term depends on the construction of a national language by a system of higher education, for the purposes of communication, and the nation becomes a status to be claimed. Read in the context of Hobsbawm's argument, the function of Tolstoy's "Epilogue" would seem to be to argue that fictional representation keeps alive in the attentive reader a broad skepticism that maintains the potentiality of the complex and still unresolved questions of patriotism and the nation.

Woolf planned the final chapter around a speech by Nicholas that suggests the political urgency of translation. "I think I see that the last chapter should be formed round N.[icholas]'s speech" (*D4*: 332). She translates his name into a particularly Tolstoyan combination of the ordinary with the authoritative. Nicholas Pomjalovsky is known as a foreigner "called Brown" (*Y*: 296). Sara Pargiter, to whom he seems "a sunk part of her, coming to the surface" (*Y*: 349), sees him as an about-to-be-recognized ideological voice, a "Teacher . . . Master," who talks about "the soul" (*Y*: 306–7). Throughout the chapter the others identify him simply as "the foreigner." At the party Nicholas thumps the table with his fork, and Rose calls for silence as he prepares to speak, but the family continues to talk. Nicholas rises and begins, "'Ladies and gentlemen'" (*Y*: 397), but he is interrupted and sits down. "'What's the good?' he said. 'Nobody wants to listen'" (*Y*: 400). Near the end of the scene Nicholas says of his speech that "'It was to have been a miracle . . . a masterpiece,'" and after a series of half-finished sentences, "'I was going to drink to the human race . . . may it grow to maturity'" (*Y*: 404–5). He concludes, "'There is going to be no peroration . . . because there was no speech'" (*Y*: 410). Whereas the incomplete sentence extends to the attentive listener an invitation to co-author, in the context of the family such a listener does not exist. Eleanor, who had earlier been a creative listener, in the company of her family falls asleep. In the setting of the family party, as Nicholas summarizes what he would have said, translation becomes a merely potential mediation of two incommensurable languages. As a displaced person Nicholas' nationality has become a postulate, but when he wishes to "'drink to the human race,'" he has no listener.

Both the incomplete and the unheard sentence contrast with the closure-as-death that the Pargiter family experiences early in the novel as they wait for Rose, the mother, to die. Her husband, Abel, feels marooned in time as he sees his colleagues hurry off to appointments. At home Milly waits for the kettle to boil. Eleanor remarks to the impatient Delia: "'you've only to wait . . .' She meant but she could not say it, 'until Mama dies'" (*Y*: 19). The whole family lives in a state of imminence: "Morris had a book in his hand but he was not reading; Milly had some stuff in her hand but she was not sewing; Delia was lying back in her chair, doing nothing whatever" (*Y*: 42). When Rose eventually does die, Delia has the impression of "life mixing with death, of death becoming life" (*Y*: 84). If those scenes represent temporal process in the lives of the family, translation as incomplete sentence figures the power of language to suggest that history satisfies the need to defer closure.

Do we have then the ruins of a "War and Peace" by Virginia Woolf? Hermione Lee's sense that in *The Years* Woolf was aiming at "blotted history," and that "the novel seems to have had a 'failed' history" (xxv–xxvi) points to the historical and personal circumstances in which Woolf represented Tolstoy's sense of historical potentiality as a problem of translation. A comparison between two translators, Woolf and Edward Pargiter, the don who is engaged in translating *Antigone*, suggests the power of translation to create a future beyond imperialism. In a scene at the party Edward is approached by his nephew North, just back from Africa, and filled with a desire for "another life, a different life . . . There was the glass in his hand; in his mind a sentence. And he wanted to make other sentences" (*Y*: 389–90). Perhaps because North is drawn to the classics, and to Edward's earlier unfinished sentence (*Y*: 386), he asks for a translation of a line from *Antigone* that Edward has just quoted in Greek: "'Tis not my nature to join in hating but in loving." "'Translate it,'" says North, and Edward refuses, becoming once again "a guardian of beautiful words" (*Y*: 388). The exchange between the two men epitomizes Woolf's view that the university excludes the common reader, who approaches a foreign text with a mind that, ready to envision "a different life," seeks in translation the language that might answer his desire to "down barriers and simplify" (*Y*: 389).

The assignment of languages to nations is the philological component of the concept of the nation. It is significant that the challenge to Edward to translate comes from North, who has just sold his farm and terminated his involvement in British colonial Africa. He returns seeking "a different life. Not halls and reverberating megaphones; not marching in step after leaders, in herds, groups, societies . . . Not black shirts, green shirts, red shirts – always posing in the public eye" (*Y*: 389). Does North's distaste for the uniformity of the military pose, and specifically for the Black Shirts, which brought Mussolini to power in 1922, signal the wish to "brush up his classics" in order to investigate the mythical origins of British nationality? Like Rose he has taken an action that questions imperial Britain. Like Nicholas he has been cut loose from national identification and tries to approach by way of translation the possibility of a new perspective on history.

Translation creates the possibility of dialogue, which in Woolf's earlier novels often seems blocked. The conditions of "1917" favor the creation of a sentence capable of integrating the world views of different languages in a single syntax. M. M. Bakhtin points to the renovating aspect of translation:

A meaning only reveals its depths once it has encountered and come into contact with another, foreign meaning: they engage in a kind of dialogue, which surmounts the closedness and one-sidedness of these particular meanings, these cultures. We raise new questions for a foreign culture, ones that it did not raise itself; we seek answers to our own questions in it; and the foreign culture responds to us by revealing to us its new aspects and new semantic depths.[64]

The alternative, to remain within the language of one nation and family, is represented by Woolf as a failure to hear or answer questions that reduces language to the sounds of Milly and her husband: "tut-tut-tut and chew-chew-chew. It sounded like the half-inarticulate munchings of animals in a stall" (*Y:* 356).

I read Woolf in the context of the emerging discourse on the meaning of the nation. Although "nation" scarcely exists in her fiction, and in fact she more often used "civilization," we may discriminate her position from that of Nicholas/Tolstoy. "Qu'est-ce qu'une nation?" (1882), by Ernest Renan (five of whose books were in Woolf's library) expresses a sense of the contingency of the nation on translation that resembles the position of Nicholas. Putting aside the nation as an ethnographic or linguistic unit, Renan imagines the speaker of a national language who feels "cooped up in such and such a language ... Before French, German, or Italian culture there is human culture."[65] Healthy and warm-hearted men will in future create "the kind of moral conscience which we call a nation."[66] So Nicholas, celebrating "the men and women of goodwill" in a foreign language, drinks to "the human race." By the 1930s such an optimistic position was no longer tenable, and Woolf herself sought something more specific beyond the ideals of Nicholas' speech.[67]

---

[64] M. M. Bakhtin, "Response to a Question from the *Novy Mir* Editorial Staff," *Speech Genres and Other Later Essays*, trans. Vern W. McGee, ed. Caryl Emerson and Michael Holquist (Austin: University of Texas Press, 1986), 7.
[65] Ernest Renan, "What Is a Nation?," trans. Martin Thom, *Nation and Narration*, ed. Homi Bhabha (London: Routledge, 1990), 17.
[66] *Ibid.*, p. 20.
[67] Marion Eide uses the term "stigma of nation" to refer to women who are "located not fully outside of but neither fully included in a citizenship marked by military service." "'The Stigma of Nation': Feminist Just War, Privilege, and Responsibility," *Hypatia: A Journal of Feminist Philosophy* 23 (2008), 48–60.

Rather in terms like those of Ernest Gellner she makes clear that the institution of the family stands in the way of translation as a means of socialization. His definition of the nation as "an effect of industrial social organization," which stresses the need for a universal literacy in order to promote communication between strangers, permits us at least to see what is at stake in Woolf's trope of translation as incomplete sentence. "Exosocialization, the production and reproduction of men outside the local intimate unit, is now the norm, and must be so. The imperative of exosocialization is the main clue to why state and culture *must* now be linked, whereas in the past their connection was thin, fortuitous, varied, loose, and often minimal. Now it is unavoidable. That is what nationalism is about, and why we live in an age of nationalism."[68] *The Years* is clearest in its demonstration of the limits of the family as "the local intimate unit." At the level of class its failure to produce and reproduce men is literal: by the end of the novel the only children to appear are marked by alien speech: "Not a word was recognizable . . . the unintelligible words ran themselves together almost into a shriek" (*Y*: 408). A translator is needed to understand the speech of working-class children. Although at the end of the novel Maggie sees "the old brothers and sisters," standing in the window "as if they were carved in stone," the final lines of the novel, which celebrate the "beauty, simplicity and peace" of the rising sun, blunt Woolf's critique of the ossified family whose habits stand in the way of communication with strangers (*Y*: 413).

Writing of the relationship of modernism to nationalism and colonialism, Fredric Jameson observes that whereas "from 1884 to World War I, the relationship of domination between First and Third World was masked and displaced by . . . consciousness of imperialism as being essentially a relationship between First World powers," since that time "the axis of otherness" has shifted to the relationship between imperial subject and its others.[69] "Present Day" gives a snapshot of this phase of nationalism. The British nation is represented by a family that does not hear the request to be heard of a foreigner or a colonial settler, and cannot understand the voices of working-class children. Since the books in Latin and French taken from the shelves during the party by the family are not, and perhaps cannot be read, the family seems cut off as well from the history of European imperialism, so that it finds itself marooned in a time and space where class and nation mark the boundaries of its prison. Woolf's modernism in this realistic novel could

[68] Ernest Gellner, *Nations and Nationalism* (Ithaca, N.Y.: Cornell University Press, 1983), p. 38.
[69] Fredric Jameson, *Nationalism, Colonialism and Literature: Modernism and Imperialism* (Derry: Field Day Theatre Company, 1988), p. 9.

then be expressed as the silence between the speech that is heard and that unheard. Unlike Tolstoy, who never abandoned his belief in the family, she sees a future in which translation has become as necessary between classes as between national languages.

The *soul* is the elusive term that evolved in Woolf's writing to voice her concerns with spirituality, the body/mind relationship, and the limitations of the public language. She suggests to the reader hungry for spirituality, who is "sick of our own materialism," that he turn to Dostoyevsky and Chekhov: "If we want understanding of the soul and heart where else shall we find it of comparable profundity?" (*E4*: 163). Yet the soul was alien to English readers: "It has little sense of humour and no sense of comedy. It is formless. It has slight connection with the intellect. It is confused, diffuse, tumultuous, incapable, it seems, of submitting to the control of logic or the discipline of poetry" (*E4*: 186). Roberta Rubenstein cites Woolf's correction in the manuscript of her unpublished essay of 1925 "Tchekhov on Pope," in which she substituted *soul* for *heart*, that is "found to be more tumultuous than English literature has divined: under the Russian magnifying glass its boundaries are fluid: & the horizon is all a welter of wind and waves with all the booming & singing in our ears."[70] Illness brings the soul closer. In "On Being Ill" (1926), Woolf corrects the notion that "the body is a sheet of plain glass though which the soul looks straight and clear." Communication is an illusion of the healthy, "the army of the upright," whereas illness brings the knowledge that "We do not know our own souls, let alone the souls of others. Human beings do not go hand in hand the whole stretch of the way. There is a virgin forest in each; a snowfield where even the print of birds' feet is unknown" (*E5*: 198). The soul is associated with the body as a pristine site distant from the mundane demand that language communicate. In "The Novels of E. M. Forster" (1927) the soul formed the moral basis of her attack on realism: "It is the soul that matters; and the soul, as we have seen, is caged in a solid villa of red brick somewhere in the suburbs of London" (*E4*: 495). The confined soul appears as well in the short story "A Summing Up," as the "movement in her of some creature beating its way about her and trying to escape." It is tied to the cry of "a widow bird," who flies away in "wider and wider circles until it became (what she called her soul)" (*CSF*: 204–5).

In the 1920s the diary was temporarily conceived as a place to explore the soul: "How it would interest me if this diary were ever to become a real

---

[70] Roberta Rubenstein, *Virginia Woolf and the Russian Point of View* (New York: Palgrave Macmillan, 2009), p. 86.

diary: something in which I could see changes, trace moods developing; but then I should have to speak of the soul, & did I not banish the soul when I began?" (*D2*: 234). But always the soul is just out of reach in the present circumstances, for instance in a passage about "the violent moods of my soul: If I weren't so sleepy, I would write about the soul. I think its time to cancel that vow against soul description" (*D2*: 304). The soul is elusive, unknown, and infinitely precious, its recognition hampered by representation: "One always sees the soul through words" (*D2*: 184). In the final and poignant entry of her diary, written a few days before her death, Woolf recalled that "Nessa is at Brighton, & I am imagining how it wd be if we could infuse souls" (*D5*: 359). It was the final step in Woolf's search for a term larger than *mind* or *heart* that could express the furthest inward reaches of the questing spirit.

In *Night and Day*, the discovery of the soul is a moral and social goal. At the end of the scene in which Ralph Denham offers friendship to Katharine Hilbery, whom he believes to be engaged to marry William Rodney, Katharine, pondering her need for complete freedom of thought, maps the region of the soul: "Why, she reflected, should there be this perpetual disparity between the thought and the action, between the life of solitude and the life of society, this astonishing precipice on one side of which the soul was active and in broad daylight, on the other side of which it was contemplative and dark as night? Was it not possible to step from one to the other, erect, and without essential change?" (*ND*: 358). In contrast with the second pair of lovers, who are conventionally romantic, Woolf seems to say that whereas romantic love feeds on delusions inherited from the past, friendship offers Katharine, with her interest in mathematics and astronomy, a new kind of balance that respects the demands of the soul.[71] When at last Katharine and Ralph understand each other, they leave the realm of "the old believers" (itself a Russian expression) for a "region" that they create together, "where the unfinished, the unfulfilled, the unwritten, the unreturned, came together in their ghostly way and wore the semblance of the complete and the satisfactory" (*ND*: 488). That may be Woolf's translation of *soul*, into a language that can express it only in negative terms.

In "On Not Knowing Greek" the name of Dostoyevsky suggests the power of translation to release what has hitherto seemed inexpressible. Woolf cites a line from *Agamemnon* and the name of Dostoyevsky as

---

[71] Rubenstein notes the echoes in Katharine's character of Ippolit's speech in *The Idiot*, in particular "'It's life that matters, nothing but life – the process of discovering – the everlasting and perpetual process, not the discovery itself at all'" (*ND*: 130). *Virginia Woolf and the Russian Point of View*, p. 36.

representing "the meaning which in moments of astonishing excitement and stress we perceive in our minds without words; it is the meaning that Dostoyevsky (hampered as he was by prose and as we are by translation) leads us to by some astonishing run up the scale of emotions and points at but cannot indicate" (*E4*: 45). Dreams are a major feature of each of his novels, not only as an aspect of characterization, but as a heuristic device that puts the events of the rest of the novel in perspective. To compare the dream of Peter Walsh as he falls asleep on a bench in the park with that of Prince Myshkin in *The Idiot* (1868), who also falls asleep in the park, suggests the specific difficulties of translating Dostoyevsky's poetics into characterization in the English novel. The Prince dreams that a woman beckons him into a world of crime, remorse, and horror, and when he awakens his conscious thoughts remain colored by the dream. Prince Myshkin is an epileptic, whose dream revives a memory of the first year of his cure, when because he could not speak he felt outside the universe. In the dream he comes face to face with a familiar woman who beckons him to follow. At that moment he is awakened by Aglaia, with whom he discusses the attempted suicide of a friend. The liminal state of the dream entwines the history of the illness that had denied the Prince speech with his attraction to two women, under the shadow of a reported suicide. At several points Dostoyevsky interpolates a theory of dreams, the strangeness of their content, and the way that "the most fantastic dream seemed to have changed suddenly into the most vivid and sharply defined reality."[72] The narrator acknowledges the difficulty of telling a story that he does not fully understand: "yet we must, as far as possible, confine ourselves to the bare statement of facts and for a very simple reason: because we find it difficult in many instances to explain what occurred. Such a preliminary statement on our part must seem very strange and obscure to the reader, who may ask how we can describe that of which we have no clear idea, no personal opinion."[73]

The scene of Peter Walsh's dream reflects these themes in an English setting. After leaving Clarissa, Peter "pursued" a young woman to the doorway of her house, which has an air of "vague impropriety" (*MD*: 46–7). If indeed Peter stalks a woman whom he imagines is not quite "respectable," the scene is a much cooler, almost whimsical, version of Dostoyevsky's vision of such pursuits (as in *Crime and Punishment*, where

---

[72] Fyodor Dostoyevsky, *The Idiot*, trans. Constance Garnett (London: Heinemann, 1913, reprint 1969), p. 556.
[73] *Ibid.*, p. 562.

the girl being pursued is in real danger). Falling asleep on a bench in the park, he dreams of his wartime loss. Peter, who has spent the war years in India, dreams of the "spectral presences" of maternal loss, "the mother whose sons have been killed in the battles of the world," and "the solitary traveller." When he awakes, muttering "the death of the soul," the narrator suggests the power of the dream to articulate his history: "The words attached themselves to some scene, to some room, to some past he had been dreaming of" (*MD*: 51). By supplying a signifier where there had been none, the dream, like a translation, reinvents representation. In the manuscript draft of the dream scene the maternal presence is "the soul," but also "only a state of mind."[74] Woolf rewrote the passage, to say that Peter, although an atheist, "sees this giant figure displayed. It is the soul, he thinks."[75] (In the printed version he sees "the giant figure at the end of the ride," *MD*: 50.) When he awakens he recalls the moment of Clarissa's aversion, when she hears that a woman has given birth outside of marriage: "It is the death of the soul he had said to himself," a phrase that Woolf repeats in other drafts of the same passage.[76] Throughout the evolution of Peter's characterization *soul* defined the liminal state when the dreamer awakens and for an instant inhabits the two worlds that the narrator then relates to each other. But despite the importance of the dream as Peter's comment on Clarissa, his feelings of maternal loss are not comparable to the horror that Prince Myshkin experiences. Although a reader might be tempted to see that the two dreams engage parallel problems – the dreamer's love of two women and another character's drift towards suicide – in my view despite Woolf's narrator's pointed comment on the capacity of the dream to name Peter's experience, the dream cannot be said to exercise a heuristic force comparable with its function in *The Idiot*.

One of the troubles that beset translation, writes Venuti, is that it "never communicates in an untroubled fashion because the translator negotiates the linguistic and cultural differences of the foreign text by reducing them and supplying another set of differences, basically domestic, drawn from the receiving language and culture to enable the foreign to be received there. The foreign text, then, is not so much communicated as inscribed with domestic intelligibilities and interests."[77] That may describe what happens in a scene from *The Years* that expands the image of the soul in order to

---

[74] Virginia Woolf, *Virginia Woolf "The Hours": The British Museum Manuscript of Mrs. Dalloway*, ed. and transcribed by Helen M. Wussow (New York: Pace University Press, 1996), p. 25.

[75] *Ibid.*, p. 28.   [76] *Ibid.*, p. 31, repeated on p. 32, and in Appendix Two, p. 459.

[77] Lawrence Venuti, ed., *Translation Studies Reader* (New York and London: Routledge, 2000), p. 482.

make an ethical plea to decriminalize homosexuality. In "1917" Nicholas, the foreigner who echoes his namesake in *War and Peace*, explains to Eleanor that he seeks a world that offers an alternative to the "knot" that is his image of the crippling domestic arrangements of World War I Britain: "'The soul – the whole being,' he explained. He hollowed his hands as if to enclose a circle. 'It wishes to expand; to adventure; to form – new combinations'" (*Y*: 282). Sara, who overhears him as she awakens from sleep in front of the fire, thinks of the soul as a spark flying up the chimney. That Nicholas' spiritual authority is associated with his potential criminal status has a particularly Dostoyevskian flavor, since as a homosexual, Sara remarks ironically, "he ought to be in prison" (*Y*: 283). The scene confers a spiritual dimension on the sense of unlived possibilities that the novel associates with translation, implicit in Eleanor's sense that she might have married, or that she hears "another voice speaking in another language" (*Y*: 285).

By the time Woolf was accumulating notes for "Phases of Fiction" (1929) she was "negotiating" the cultural differences of Dostoyevsky's work by assimilating them to her reading of Proust. In her notes on *The Possessed* she frequently compared Dostoyevsky to Proust, for instance in her note on "the Ball Cf. Proust." A scene in which a man pours out his wounded feelings and weeps is "not so closely knit as P[roust]'s."[78] Another scene "violates the commonsense; more than Prousts."[79] In her study of the notes Rubenstein concludes that although they refer to "the crude scaffolding" of Dostoyevsky's narrative, the published version of the essay is more balanced: "There is a simplicity in violence which we find nowhere in Proust, but violence also lays bare regions deep down in the mind where contradiction prevails."[80]

Woolf's diminished interest in Dostoyevsky may be linked to her discovery in Proust, who was himself interested in Dostoevsky, of a capacity to represent soul, in a culture that she found less alienating. In *À la recherche du temps perdu* the narrator discusses with Albertine Dostoyevsky's creation of a "new kind of beauty ... just as, in Vermeer, there's the creation of a certain soul" (III: 384). After the death of Albertine the narrator feels himself "drawn into a vaster system in which souls move in time as bodies move in space" (III: 568).

This more intellectual version of *soul* figures in the draft version of "Time Passes," in the image of the sleeper who awakes to walk the beach seeking an

---

[78] Rubenstein transcribes Woolf's holograph notes in *Virginia Woolf and the Russian Point of View*, p. 166.
[79] *Ibid.*, p. 169.   [80] *Ibid.*, p. 52.

image of the world that would "reflect the compass of the soul" (*TL*: 122). Susan Dick, in an early study of the manuscript draft, focuses on the figure of the restless searcher, and transcribes two passages of meditation on the soul that do not appear in either the French translation or the printed version.[81] In them Woolf seems to defend an unspecified spirituality: "Then they say, after all, how there is no soul, & no immortality . . . they say the day is all; & what our duty is to the day."[82] The passage was rewritten after a few pages: "Yet if there is no soul, & the day is all, why should we, escaped from the house & pacing the beach, imagine robes flowing ~~down~~, & eyes with ~~the~~ lids compassionately lowered, as ~~if the presence regarded~~ as if to behold our ~~the~~ sufferings ~~on earth~~?"[83] In this figure *soul* recalls *Night and Day*, where Katharine Hilbery ponders her life, "on one side of which the soul was active and in broad daylight, on the other side of which it was contemplative and dark as night." "Time Passes" goes some distance towards resolving Katharine's dilemma by translating the diffuse foreign concept of spirit into the mind of an unnamed sleeper who walks the beach at night. In the sleeper's mind the word is fitted into the indictment of the "mindless warfare, the soulless bludgeoning" that links *soul* to the anti-war sentiment that is more in evidence in the draft version. Woolf accommodated the difficulties of an interlingual translation of the Dostoyevskian *soul* that seems to have alienated her from her native language, by detaching it from the conventional characterization that her readers would find "intelligible." In so doing she created the language that could, as she wrote of Dostoyevsky and Aeschylus in her essay on translation, "express the vast catastrophe of the European war" (*E4*: 45).

[81] Susan Dick, "The Restless Searcher: A Discussion of the Evolution of 'Time Passes' in *To the Lighthouse*," *English Studies in Canada* 5 (1979), 318–19.
[82] www.woolfonline.com/html/zoom/draft/151.php
[83] www.woolfonline.com/html/zoom/draft/153.php

CHAPTER 4

Proust and the fictions of the unconscious

> My great adventure is really Proust. Well – what remains to be written
> after that?
>
> (To Roger Fry, Oct. 3, 1922: *L2*: 565)

Woolf's work took a new direction after 1922, the year in which she began to
read *À la recherche du temps perdu*. Proust helped to shape the emphasis on
feeling that is so problematic in her early work into a prose whose aim was to
transform feeling into the language of spiritual apprehension. Her reading
notes, "The Hours" manuscript, and her diaries reveal that several of the
questions that she put to herself as she worked were in fact loose translations
of particular passages in the *Recherche* where Proust engaged questions of
memory and language. She responded, for instance, to Proust's idea that the
adjacent world of sleep focuses attention on the moment of awakening,
when the sleeper leaves the place of dreams for the language of the waking
world. Woolf read Proust largely in the translation of C. K. Scott Moncrieff,
who simplified Proust's extensive vocabulary of words for mental functions,
by reducing it to *conscious* and *unconscious*. Although his translation con-
veniently brought the novel into territory familiar to English readers of
Freud, his mistranslations resulted in Woolf's preference for the Proustian
image of the unconscious as the source, not of error and struggle as in Freud's
work, but of the artist's unique access to the underwater world of the mind.

Although Woolf's notes on the *Recherche* cover only the first two books,
Swann's Way and *Guermantes*, she and Vita Sackville-West read *Sodome et
Gomorrhe* together. At the point where Woolf's response to particular
passages is less demonstrable at the level of language, the presence of
Proust in her theory of writing may better be understood in terms of
translation as interpretation. Woolf shared with Proust a sense of the unseen
world that lies behind the seen, which is sometimes the world of the dead,
and sometimes the hidden world of sexual preferences and behaviors
that the narrator is forbidden to avow. The sign that represents a world so

divided creates a text designed to accommodate historical controversies and contradictions, and is necessarily contingent. Scenes of translation in *Orlando* seize the occasion when a term that is undergoing redefinition becomes untranslatable, as a means to undermine the sign. As in the *Recherche* the naked female body prompts a scene of awakening that questions the language of sexual identity, while the text relegates *gender* to the arcane vocabularies of law and grammar. The final pages of Woolf's novel rewrite the relationship of the translator to a dual readership in order to mediate the contradictions created by the untranslatable word.

Woolf's reading of Proust was part of the larger involvement of Bloomsbury with France. Virginia Woolf and her friends read Proust and other French writers avidly, and toured France on their holidays, but stopped short of integrating themselves in French intellectual life.[1] Although Woolf's relationship with French culture was limited by her difficulty with the language, her response to Proust was an intimate part of the language and subject position that she developed. Hermione Lee writes that Woolf's reading of Proust was "as important to her life-story as any of her relationships."[2] Eric Auerbach discusses *To the Lighthouse* in terms of the *Recherche*.[3] Jean Guiguet notes their temperamental similarity, as though Woolf saw in Proust her double, and sought in him confirmation of what she had long thought.[4] Harvena Richter explored in both the response to feeling, and theories of the unconscious.[5] Mary Ann Caws notes the Proustian sound of the gate opening in *Mrs. Dalloway*.[6] Pierre-Eric Villeneuve compares their theories of reading as "an alienating regime that they both want to break away from."[7] But although most recent studies of Woolf make passing reference to the importance of Proust, details of the relationship remain unexplored. I start with Woolf's reading notes to *Du côté de chez Swann* and to *Guermantes*, which are the key

[1] Mary Ann Caws and Sarah Bird Wright, "Introduction," *Bloomsbury and France: Art and Friends* (Oxford: Oxford University Press, 2000), 3–17.
[2] Hermione Lee, *Virginia Woolf* (London: Chatto & Windus, 1996), p. 403.
[3] Eric Auerbach, *Mimesis: The Representation of Reality in Western Literature*, trans. Willard Trask (Garden City, N.Y.: Doubleday, 1957), pp. 478–81.
[4] "Revenant au jugement de Virginia Woolf sur Proust, dont chaque terme est l'aveu parenté profonde, on se rend compte qu'il s'agit non d'une influence, mais d'une coïncidence complexe, faite d'une part de l'analogie de deux tempéraments." Jean Guiguet, *Virginia Woolf et son oeuvre: l'art et la quête du réel* (Paris: Didier, 1962), p. 247.
[5] Harvena Richter, *Virginia Woolf: The Inward Voyage* (Princeton: Princeton University Press, 1970), pp. 30–3 and 64.
[6] Mary Ann Caws, *Women and Bloomsbury: Virginia, Vanessa and Carrington* (New York and London: Routledge, 1990), p. 64.
[7] Pierre-Eric Villeneuve, "Communities of Desire: Woolf, Proust, and the Reading Process," *Virginia Woolf and Communities: Selected Papers from the Eighth Annual Conference on Virginia Woolf*, ed. Jeanette McVicker and Laura David (New York: Pace University Press, 1999), 27.

to work in which she developed a model of mind and language that like Proust's is derived from the tensions between an intellectual idea of truth and the authority of lived experience.

Woolf read *À la recherche du temps perdu* over a period of a dozen or so years, in the translation by C. K. Scott Moncrieff.[8] Although she had asked Roger Fry to bring her a volume of Proust in 1919 (*L2*: 396), she delayed reading, describing herself in January 1922 as "shivering on the brink, and waiting to be submerged with a horrid sort of notion that I shall go down and down and down and perhaps never come up again" (*L2*: 499). By October she was "only in the first volume . . . I am in a state of amazement; as if a miracle were being done before my eyes . . . One has to put the book down and gasp. The pleasure becomes physical – like sun and wine and grapes and perfect serenity and intense vitality combined" (*L2*: 566). She continued to read, recommending Proust to a friend in 1925, "Ten volumes however, difficult French; I've only read three" (*L3*: 166). Reading Proust for "that cursed book" ("Phases of Fiction," 1929), she copied some passages. In 1934 it was "impossible for me to finish Proust" (*D4*: 216). Her holograph notes cover *Swann's Way* and *Guermantes*, and in "Phases of Fiction" she alludes to the events of *Sodome et Gomorrhe*. J. Hillis Miller has noted the similarity between the final party scene in *Mrs. Dalloway* and *Le temps retrouvé*.[9] Although her library contained all seven volumes of the *Recherche* in French, including three copies of *Du côté de chez Swann*, the first page of her reading notes is labeled "Vol 1 (translation)," and the numbers in the left margin refer to the pages of the Moncrieff translation.[10]

Why would Woolf, whose language skills were impressive, have turned to a translation? In *Three Guineas* she cites the families who sent their sons to school and consoled their daughters with a few lessons in foreign languages, as though learning a foreign tongue were somehow both the key to and, in the eyes of their families, a substitute for university education. Among Woolf's peers the assumption was that everyone read French.[11] Mary Ann

[8] Cheryl Mares, "Woolf's Reading of Proust," reprinted in *Reading Proust*, ed. Mary Ann Caws and Eugène Nicole (New York and Paris: Peter Lang, 1990), 186.
[9] J. Hillis Miller, *Fiction and Repetition: Seven English Novels* (Cambridge, Mass.: Harvard University Press, 1982), p. 188.
[10] Marcel Proust's *À la recherche du temps perdu* appeared in several volumes in French (1913–27), and in English as *Remembrance of Things Past*, trans. C. K. Scott Moncrieff (New York: Random House, 1932–4). Subsequent references to Moncrieff appear in the text.
[11] Terry Hale writes that French was the second language of educated people everywhere in the nineteenth century, and that many could read it without the help of translation. "Readers and Publishers of Translations in Britain," *The Oxford History of Literary Translation in English*, vol. IV: *1790–1900*, ed. Peter France and Kenneth Hayes (Oxford: Oxford University Press, 2006), 34–47.

Caws writes: "The ten Strachey children, who had a French governess, seem to have been fluent in French from their childhood." Lytton's mother helped him to write French verse and read aloud from Racine every night. "Vita Sackville-West's mother was raised in France, and Vita was fluent in the language even as a toddler." E. M. Forster, Clive Bell, and Roger Fry all had a command of written and spoken French.[12] But Woolf did not grow up in a bilingual family, and save for her Greek lessons had no consistent formal training. In the company of her more fluent friends she felt herself at a disadvantage. In 1923 she wrote about "taking her fences gallantly ... save the French language, at which I failed ignominiously, & now must learn to speak French if I am in future to respect myself" (*D*2: 242). In the same year she asked her old friend Jacques Raverat, living in France, "How does one learn the language? I must & will. I want to know how the French think" (*L*3: 23). To that end she ordered a French grammar (*D*2: 259). Caws explains that Woolf was less at home in France than were Vanessa and Duncan Grant: "perhaps because she was far from fluent in French, she felt distanced from the country. She read French easily and even tried to become proficient at speaking it. At one time she wanted to keep a diary in French, and she later studied the language with Janie Bussy, the bilingual daughter of Simon and Dorothy Strachey Bussy."[13] Woolf's reading notes confirm that she read some French writers "easily": her notes on Montaigne and Stendhal were written in English; the notes on *Phèdre* cite the French text; the notes on George Sand were written in French. On occasion Woolf cites but does not translate lines of French, for instance the few lines by Rimbaud that appear untranslated in "On Being Ill."[14] But Proust was more important to her than other French writers, and his text more difficult.

To begin with, Woolf's reading of Proust corroborated her sense that illness forces attention to the body and challenges philosophical detachment. Her essay "On Being Ill" (1926) expands a diary entry of 1923 about the death of Katherine Mansfield: "In casting accounts, never forget to begin with the state of the body" (*D*2: 228). In the essay she turns to Proust: "there must be a volume or two about disease scattered through the pages of Proust – literature does its best to maintain that its concern is with the mind; that the body is a sheet of plain glass through which the soul looks straight and clear, and, save for one or two passions such as desire and greed,

---

[12] Caws and Wright, *Bloomsbury and France*, pp. 6–8.   [13] *Ibid.*, p. 49.
[14] The lines of French that appear in *Orlando* (*O*: 39) were apparently written in English, and at Woolf's request translated into French by Vita Sackville-West. *Letters of Vita Sackville-West to Virginia Woolf*, ed. Louise DeSalvo and Mitchell Leaska (New York: William Morrow, 1985), pp. 268–9.

is null, and negligible and non-existent. On the contrary, the very opposite
is true ... People write always of the doings of the mind; the thoughts
that come to it; its noble plans; how the mind has civilized the universe.
They show it ignoring the body in the philosopher's turret" (*E5*: 195–6).
Perhaps she had in mind a passage from *Guermantes*: "It is in sickness that
we are compelled to recognize that we do not live alone but are chained to a
being from a different realm, from whom we are worlds apart, who has no
knowledge of us and by whom it is impossible to make ourselves understood: our body" (II: 308).

In fact living with chronic illness gave both Proust and Woolf a special
opportunity to satirize physicians and criticize the medical profession.
Woolf's characterization of Drs. Holmes and Bradshaw in *Mrs. Dalloway*
is no less savage than Proust's satire of the doctors in the *Recherche* who treat
Marcel's grandmother after she suffers her first stroke while walking in the
Luxembourg Gardens. One is more ignorant and arrogant than the other;
what they know has been taught them by their patients. The first addresses
the dying woman: "'You will be cured, Madame, on the day, whenever it
comes – and it rests entirely on you whether it comes today – on which you
realize that there is nothing wrong with you and resume your ordinary life"
(II: 312). He is the double of Dr. Holmes, who brushes aside fears: "health is
largely a matter in our own control" (*MD*: 80). The second of Proust's
physicians is "a celebrated specialist in nervous diseases." He maintains a
hearty manner with his patients, "while quite ready to lend the strength of
his muscular arms to fastening them in strait-waistcoats later on" (II: 825).
The passage recalls the brutality of Sir William Bradshaw, who "shut people
up" as a means to deal with "these unsocial impulses, bred more than
anything by the lack of good blood," behavior "that endeared Sir William
so greatly to the relations of his victims" (*MD*: 90). Sir William's plan to
sequester Septimus, and Holmes' fatal, last-minute intervention measure
their distance from healing. Woolf's understanding of the medical profession as a repressive social apparatus goes further than Proust's, in her
suggestion that Sir William's insistence on "proportion" in fact upholds
the authority of the empire and the police, of whom Proust has little to say.

Woolf's concern about the role of the body as the arbiter of feeling was
part of her early history. One sees it for instance in the poignant letter she
wrote to Leonard in May 1912, explaining to him her fears that a conventional marriage would deaden feeling: "Of course I can't explain what I
feel," before she went on to describe her swings of mood from a desire for
intimacy to aloofness (*L1*: 496). When Woolf wrote of Proust in "Phases of
Fiction" (1929) "Everything that can be felt can be said. The mind of Proust

lies open with the sympathy of a poet and the detachment of a scientist to everything that it has the power to feel," she seized on the theme that had preoccupied her in the years before the *Recherche* was published, and would have disposed her to recognize that she and Proust were following parallel paths (*E5*: 67). It is the focus of characterization in "Melymbrosia," where both Rachel and the narrator focus on the difficulty of saying what one feels: "That was the result of wishing to share one's feelings; and the conclusions must be that to feel anything strongly is to create an abyss between oneself and others, who too, feel strongly, but differently. One had recourse to symbols" (*M*: 41). In the novel the male characters are remote from their feelings. Mr. Pepper, who deals in facts, "was never in a muddle about his feelings" (*M*: 20–1). During a discussion of love, Hirst remarks to Hewet, "'I feel practically nothing . . . except certain attractions and repulsions which have most of them an intellectual origin'" (*M*: 202).

The Proustian question about the capacity of "feeling" to undermine language as communication is more the concern of the female characters. When Rachel tells Helen that Richard has kissed her and she feels "'queer,'" she replies, "'But aren't you feeling what you think you ought to feel?'" (*M*: 97), and gives up trying to explain love "to people who've never felt it" (*M*: 98). Throughout her life Woolf, like Proust, found "love" a refractory term. Rachel understands feelings from the point of view of gender; owing to her father's forbidding her "'to walk down Bond Street alone . . . I shall never never have all [the] feelings I might have because of you'" (*M*: 222). Instead she turns to art: "'poems are full of things we feel – things we really feel, that people never say'" (*M*: 318). After Rachel's engagement to Hewet, Helen points out to Rachel that others have been in love, "'that we are all feeling what you feel'" (*M*: 278). "As they walked toward the boat it was Helen who felt the most of the four. At her age she understood better than the pair themselves the immense seriousness of what had happened" (*M*: 292). Only in the retrospective of memory it would seem does feeling become amenable to understanding and language.

What is at stake in Woolf's work is the manner in which feeling becomes a mode of thought capable of apprehending truth. In her notes on *Guermantes* she queried: "Prousts sympathy – is that not a philosophy?"[15] Her phrase identifies the central theme of the *Recherche*, the capacity of emotional affect to question intellect, although she did not yet engage the philosophical problem that Proust recognized: "We feel in one world, we think, we give

[15] Henry W. and Albert A. Berg Collection of English and American Literature, The New York Public Library, Reel 13.

names to things in another; between the two, we can establish a certain correspondence, but not bridge the gap" (II: 46). Woolf's interest in her own feelings is particularly marked in her diary during the period around 1923, when she was beginning to read Proust. He motivated her to examine her own ability to express feeling: "I am perhaps encouraged by Proust to search out and identify my feelings, but I have always felt this kind of thing in great profusion, only not tried to capture it, or perhaps lacked skill & confidence" (*D2*: 268). Two years earlier she had written of "my incessant search into what people are & feel" (*D2*: 119), or the dread of most readers of "being made to feel anything" (*D2*: 117). When Katherine Mansfield died in 1923, she devoted a long passage in her diary to tracing "the progress of one's feelings" (*D2*: 226), perhaps in response to her memory that Mansfield "said a good deal about feeling things deeply" (*D2*: 248). Apparently Woolf's love for Vita unleashed this capacity, for she wrote to her in 1926: "Always, always, always I try to say what I feel" (*L3*: 231). Several passages from her diary suggest that Proust and Mansfield also helped her to find a way out of the dilemma that she once shared with the female characters of "Melymbrosia." At the same time she was careful to distinguish her meaning from Vita's aristocratic notion of "no false reserves; anything can be said; but as usual, that fatal simplicity or rigidity of mind which makes it seem all a little unshaded, & empty" (*D2*: 307). In *Between the Acts* Woolf satirized the quality of unshaded emptiness, when Mrs. Manresa remarks to Isa, that "everything can be said in this house" (*BA*: 28).

Woolf's most important fiction after 1922 is sketched by the scene that engaged her in the first page of her notes, the "hours" scene of the *Recherche*, in which the narrator awakens from sleep and reads his position at the center of concentric worlds:

When a man is asleep, he has in a circle round him the chain of the hours, the sequence of the years, the order of the heavenly host. Instinctively, when he awakes, he looks to these, and in an instant reads off his own position on the earth's surface and the time that has elapsed during his slumbers; but this ordered procession is apt to grow confused, and to break its ranks. Suppose that, towards morning, after a night of insomnia, sleep descends upon him while he is reading, in quite a different position from that in which he normally goes to sleep, he has only to lift his arm to arrest the sun and turn it back in its course, and, at the moment of waking, he will have no idea of the time, but will conclude that he has just gone to bed. (I: 5)

Initially Woolf's notes on this passage expressed skepticism: "description of mind on waking – elaborate. My feeling that the relation between the [——] & the things described has to be right – is it? Otherwise curiosity

[——] things described Floating off from the person & the two becoming separate. A possible weakness."[16] Woolf's comment suggests that the moment of awakening is a kind of breaking point, when the description of things seen tests the referential aspect of language. She recognized the need to create a language that would represent solid objects as well as the narrator's experience of the dream world. That the "hours" passage lingered in her mind becomes apparent in a quick survey of those scenes in Woolf where the sleeping mind brings into play a larger world: the sense of concentric worlds and the creative power of the lifted arm in *The Waves*, access to other worlds during sleep in *Mrs. Dalloway* and *Orlando*, Lily Briscoe's awakening at the end of "Time Passes" in *To the Lighthouse*, and the early short story "A Haunted House." At the moment of awakening, the body is separated both from the world of sleep and the world of those already awake, in a place that is defined by the ability to read its position as a set of geographical and temporal coordinates.

Although "The Hours," Woolf's title of an early manuscript draft of *Mrs. Dalloway*, is broadly suggestive, its relationship to the *Recherche* was at first manifest in an aspect of character, until she introduced Septimus Smith and restructured the novel. She wrote in February 1923, "I wonder if this next lap will be influenced by Proust? I think his French language, tradition, &c, prevents that, yet his command of every resource is so extravagant that one can hardly fail to profit, & must not flinch, through cowardice" (*D*2: 234). The answer to her own question captures the complexity of a position composed equally of desire and fear, an attraction to something larger than narrative technique that is suggested by "resource," balanced by an admonition against cowardice and failure. The fact that the French language might be a barrier suggests her dependence on and also her mistrust of translation. The uncertainty did not hinder her ambitions: she wrote in the holograph of "The Hours": "the merit of this book so far lies in its design, wh. is original – very difficult."[17] In fact the complex relationship of the drafts of *Mrs. Dalloway* in the British Library, and another in the Berg Collection of the New York Public Library, is a daunting challenge, well beyond the scope of this chapter. I concentrate on the opening passage of the 1923 holograph in which the novel begins as Peter Walsh emerges from a scene of London church bells ringing.

---

[16] Berg Collection, Reel 13. The dashes in square brackets represent illegible words.
[17] British Library manuscript 51044: "NOTEBOOKS OF VIRGINIA WOOLF, vol. I (ff.ii + 150. '*The Hours?*' (f.2); June 1923 (f.2)–aft. 28 Jan 1924. *Drafts*, for *Mrs. Dalloway*." Holograph 421. www.bl.uk/catalogues/manuscripts/html.

The draft of "The Hours" dated "June 27, 1923"[18] begins: "In Westminster, where temples, meeting houses, conventicles, & steeples of all kinds are congregated together, there is, at all hours & halfhours, a sound of bells, ~~supplementing~~ correcting each other, asseverating that time has come a little earlier, or stayed a little later, here or here. Thus when Mr. Walsh walking with his head ~~a little~~ down & his coat flying loose came out by the Abbey the clock of St Margarets was saying two minutes later than Big Ben that it was half past eleven."[19] The paragraph was revised and rewritten a few pages further on. Although Woolf's brisk tone is her own as she deals with the waking world in which clocks inconsistently measure time, the passage suggests that in the presence of such temporal confusion the mind seeks and then creates. The bells give "something that lies below words . . . some grief from the past which holds it back, some impulse nevertheless to glide into the recesses of the heart . . . so that Mr. Walsh, as he walked past St. Margarets, & heard the bells toll the half hour felt . . . [Woolf's ellipsis]." Breaking off the sentence where she did suggests that Peter's feeling depends on his position in the space and time of London.

In her early notes for the novel, dated November 9, 1922, Woolf wrote, "There must be a reality which is not in human beings at all. What about death for instance? But what is death? Strange if that were the reality."[20] The sense of a reality that is hidden from view as the narrator strives to discover the truth of human behavior and the visible world is a major theme of the *Recherche* that reappears in Woolf's language. Her notes on "Vol 1" comment on the passage in which the narrator glimpses the steeples at Martinville from the various perspectives of a carriage moving through the landscape: "they appeared to be concealing, beneath what my eyes could see, something wh. they invited me to seize on – the steeples at Martinville." (Moncrieff has: "In noticing and registering the shape of their spires, their shifting lines, the sunny warmth of their surfaces, I felt that I was not penetrating to the core of my impression, that something more lay behind that mobility, that luminosity, something which they seemed at once to contain and to conceal," 1: 196.) Proust returned to the steeples of Martinville in *Le temps retrouvé*, to demonstrate that material impressions yield a truth superior to what the intellect can apprehend (III: 912). That the visible world of steeples has such power parallels Woolf's sense that the bells also contain and conceal "something that lies below words," presumably the reality of time and mortality.

---

[18] British Library manuscript 51044, vol. 1   [19] *Ibid.*, fol. 5.
[20] Berg Collection, Reel 6, M 19. A sentence in *Melymbrosia* suggests her early preoccupation with the theme: "Nothing is stranger than the position of the dead among the living" (*M*: 18).

The introduction of Septimus altered the design of the novel. In her notes of June 1922 Woolf wrote of his thematic significance: "not so much a character as an idea," that his character "becomes generalized – universalized . . . He must be topical enough to make the comparison between the two worlds."[21] He accuses himself of "the sin for which human nature had condemned him to death; that he did not feel" (*MD*: 80). But in the early drafts of the novel it is Peter Walsh, entwined with the image of the hours, who plays the larger part as a character at the center of a confusion of clock time that will open a narrative about the feeling that "lies below words." In the holograph that we are discussing the bells passage is followed by the scene in which Peter shadows a young woman on the London streets, suggesting a two-tier narrative, in which imaginary encounters stimulated by sexual desire run a course parallel to his meeting with Clarissa and his memory of their failed love. The 1923 holograph starts with a passage on the bells, whose sounds are heard by Peter Walsh, as he observes the boys in uniform. Following a break in the manuscript labeled "III" and a second revised bells passage, he remembers Clarissa, observes the boys, and begins the adventure of following a young woman whom he sees "coming down the steps of the National Gallery." Peter imagines her possessing an ease and gaiety that Clarissa, owing to her class position, lacks. "To embarrass her [the young woman] was the last thing he wished; but she still said, as she walked up the Haymarket yes, yes, & gave him changed him, into & made him feel that he would if she turned laugh like a boy & ask her in to have an ice & there would be no embarrassment, none whatever" (fol. 16). When she walks on, "he felt like a pursuer, who has been checked" (fol. 16). (In the printed version "He was a buccaneer" *MD*: 46.) Since "he had missed his opportunity," the moment "connected itself with every dream, every intensity, & fusing into one sudden diamond all the jewels of gems of all the hours; all those moments which at which shine out in the day" (fol. 17). (The printed version domesticates the moment: "it was half made up, as he knew very well . . . made up, as one makes up the better part of life, he thought," *MD*: 47.) Whereas the echoes in the passage of Molly Bloom's "yes" as well as Dostoyevsky's pursuers reinforce the Proustian emphasis on the imaginative power of missed opportunities, what is more distinctly Proustian is the structure of character as a point of intersection between purposeful movement and "moments which shine out." The dream that Peter creates has "confused" an orderly reading, so as to give equal priority to the world that he both seeks and invents. It is from this double perspective

---

[21] *Ibid.*

of a London world, peopled by pursuers and pursued, and by available women, that Peter judges Clarissa cold and timid.

At a later stage Woolf shifted the axis of the novel to Clarissa and Septimus, a task so difficult that she characterized it as "agony" (*D3*: 59) and "excruciating" (*D3*: 76). She transformed the much-revised beginning scene into the temporal scaffolding of the novel, and at the same time focused attention away from Peter. Paul Ricoeur reads the novel as concerning "the fissure opened up between the monumental time of the world and the mortal time of the soul."[22] He argues that Sir William Bradshaw and Septimus represent the poles between what Nietzsche called "monumental time" and the time of the soul, and that the novel explores "the variety of relations between the concrete temporal experience of the various characters and monumental time." Clarissa and Peter are oriented towards the poles, as they "experience . . . the mortal discordance between personal time and monumental time."[23] In the reordering of the structure of the novel the bells passage that is the image of monumental time was assimilated to characterization, and reduced to a few lines in the printed version: "Ah, said St. Margaret's, like a hostess who comes into her drawing-room on the very stroke of the hour and finds her guests there already. I am not late. No, it is precisely half-past eleven, she says. Yet, though she is perfectly right, her voice, being the voice of the hostess, is reluctant to inflict its individuality. Some grief for the past holds it back; some concern for the present" (*MD*: 42–3). The striking hour prompts Peter Walsh to remember Clarissa, in "an extraordinarily clear, yet puzzling, recollection of her, as if this bell had come into the room years ago, where they sat at some moment of great intimacy, and had gone from one to the other and had left, like a bee with honey, laden with the moment" (*MD*: 43). The bell "tolled for death that surprised in the midst of life" (*MD*: 43). At the same time the scene of Peter's imagined seduction, which by my count was about 1,900 words in the holograph, was reduced to about 700 in the printed version, and he makes his entry into the narrative after Clarissa's. Perhaps as Woolf developed the character of Septimus, her sense of "something that lies below words" was transformed by the themes of death and insanity that become increasingly in evidence in the *Recherche*.

Before going further with Woolf's image of mind it is important to note a stylistic trait of the Moncrieff translation, especially in light of Woolf's tantalizing note on *Guermantes*: "If one wants to see what style is, it is best to

---

[22] Paul Ricoeur, *Time and Narrative*, vol. II, trans. Kathleen McLaughlin and David Pellauer (Chicago: University of Chicago Press, 1985), p. 110.
[23] *Ibid.*, p. 108.

read a translation."[24] When Terence Kilmartin introduced a new edition of the *Recherche*, he acknowledged the general criticism of Moncrieff, "that his prose tends to the purple and the precious – or that is how he interpreted the tone of the original" (1: xi).[25] I note that Moncrieff drew on Freud's vocabulary to translate some common French phrases that have no colloquial English equivalent. In the "hours" passage Moncrieff translated Proust's "mon esprit" as "my consciousness," "au fond d'un animal" as "an animal's consciousness," and "mon moi" as "my ego."[26] Although on occasion Proust uses "conscience" in the sense of awareness, as in "la surface de ma claire conscience . . . soulever tout au fond de moi" (1: 46), he uses "l'inconscient" only seven times in the novel, four of them in the last two sections to be written.[27] Moncrieff by contrast relied heavily on *consciousness* and the *unconscious*. In the famous passage about the memory of drinking tea with the crumbs of a madeleine, he writes that the narrator tries "to follow it into my conscious mind" (1: 49), whereas Proust wrote that the image "tente de la suivre jusqu'à moi" (1: 47). In a passage from *Du côté de chez Swann* when the narrator considers from a philosophical perspective what kinds of books he might write, Moncrieff translates: "my consciousness would be faced with a blank" (1: 188), whereas Proust wrote: "mon esprit s'arrêtait de fonctionner" (1: 173). After Swann in a fit of jealousy raps on Odette's window, behind which he has seen a light, and surprises two old gentlemen, he remembers the incident: "But now and then his thoughts in their wandering course would come upon this memory where it lay unobserved, would startle it into life, thrust it forward into consciousness" (1: 300). The French text reads: "le souvenir qu'elle n'avait pas aperçu, le heurtait, l'enfonçait plus avant" (1: 275). In another passage, where Proust analyzes the difference in one's impression of a person before and after actually meeting him, Moncrieff translates: "I carried in my body the same consciousness. But on that consciousness . . ." (1: 716). In fact Proust used the word for "soul": "je portais en moi la même âme. Mais dans cette âme . . ." (1: 665). In a passage on what is incommunicable to his friends, Moncrieff has the narrator contemplate "my unconscious mind" (II: 358) whereas Proust wrote of "mon insu" (II: 642). The passage where Proust wrote of the dream: "La connaissance aurait-elle, réciproquement,

---

[24] In 1923, she wrote to Clive Bell, "Scott Moncrieff pesters for a few words – any words from *you*, Mrs Woolf – it don't matter if you haven't read – invent." She refused (*L*3: 11).
[25] Roger Shattuck notes that Moncrieff sometimes Bowdlerizes, and cites the occasional error. *Marcel Proust* (New York: Viking Press, 1974), p. 26.
[26] Lydia Davis, in her translation of *Du côté de chez Swann, The Way by Swann's* (London: Penguin Group, 2002), uses the vocabulary of "mind" and "self" to translate these phrases, p. 9.
[27] Robin Mackenzie, "Proust's 'Livre intérieur,'" *Modernism and the European Unconscious*, ed. Peter Collier and Judy Davies (New York: St. Martin's Press, 1990), 150.

l'irréalité du rêve?" (III: 375) appears translated as "might consciousness have the unreality of a dream?" (II: 1018). Where Proust's narrator writes of Charlus, "c'était sans s'en rendre compte à cause de ce vice" (III: 429), the translation reads, "Now it was, quite unconsciously, because of that vice" (II: 1075). Although I have not made a full comparison of the two texts, it should be apparent that the discrepancies raise a question about the meaning that emerges from a simplified vocabulary for mental function.

Translation itself signifies differently in English and in French. Whereas in English it means an equivalent text in another language, in French it "problematizes a shift of meaning – very close to the function of the metaphor."[28] Lawrence Venuti notes this cultural bias when he describes the Anglo-American preference for the immediate intelligibility of language. Such a readership "requires fluent translations that produce the illusory effect of transparency, and this means adhering to the current standard dialect while avoiding any dialect, register, or style that calls attention to words as words and therefore preempts the reader's identification."[29] The Moncrieff translation clearly satisfied such an audience when it simplified Proust's language by reducing his rich vocabulary to the pair *conscious/unconscious*.

It is my argument that the sense of consciousness in the Moncrieff translation, while it blurred significant distinctions, focused attention on an alternative to Freud's *unconscious*, linked as it is to theories of development and neurosis that speak to human weakness and illness. Proust dismissed "two-dimensional psychology" as lacking beauty (III: 1087). Elizabeth Abel points out that Woolf also deplored "the psychoanalytic simplification of character." The negative attitude to psychoanalysis that set her apart from Leonard and other members of the Bloomsbury community made her more hospitable to the mother-centered work of Melanie Klein.[30] Proust's sense of the unconscious, on the other hand, especially as it emerges from the Moncrieff translation, engaged Woolf's strengths, the power of imagination to provide a conscious perspective on the unconscious that for instance could turn illness into a demand for an enlarged literary vocabulary. Such a relationship to the unconscious, rather than representing a pathology, produced an empowered reader. Melba Cuddy-Keane, who also notes that Woolf differed from Freud in her emphasis on "the evocative possibilities

[28] Villeneuve, "Communities of Desire," 27.
[29] Lawrence Venuti, *The Scandals of Translation: Towards an Ethics of Difference* (London and New York: Routledge, 1998), p. 12.
[30] Elizabeth Abel, *Virginia Woolf and the Fictions of Psychoanalysis* (Chicago: University of Chicago Press, 1989), pp. 17–18.

of unconscious response," sums up the mental operations of Woolf's reader: "Unconscious response is first, followed by conscious articulation; the unconscious feels, while the conscious judges; the unconscious surrenders, while the conscious distances."[31]

The Proustian *unconscious* gave Woolf the authority to resist the critical consensus on realistic writing. As she composed *Mrs. Dalloway*, she explored the links between consciousness and creative discovery. In a much-cited passage of her diary where she describes the "tunnelling process, by which I tell the past by instalments, as I have need of it," she records her disagreement with Percy Lubbock, against whom she measured her judgment: "it proves, I think, how false Percy Lubbock's doctrine is – that you can do this sort of thing consciously. One feels about in a state of misery – indeed I made up my mind one night to abandon the book – & then one touches the hidden spring" (*D2*: 272).[32] Her phrasing recalls the narrator's realization in *Le temps retrouvé*: "But it is sometimes just at the moment when we think that everything is lost that the intimation arrives which may save us; one has knocked at all the doors which lead nowhere, and then one stumbles without knowing it on the only door through which one can enter – which one might have sought in vain for a hundred years – and it opens of its own accord" (III: 898).

What is at stake in Woolf's concept of consciousness is a theory of language and the unconscious that she derived in the context of translation. As she wrote in "On Not Knowing French" (1929), her review of *Climats* by M. [stet] Maurois:

One scarcely dare say it but it is true – nobody knows French but the French themselves. Every second Englishman reads French, and many speak it, and some write it, and there are a few who claim – and who shall deny them? – that it is the language of their dreams. But to know a language one must have forgotten it, and that is a stage that one cannot reach without having absorbed words unconsciously as a child. In reading a language that is not one's own, consciousness is awake, and keeps us aware of the surface glitter of words; but it never suffers them to sink into that region of the mind where old habits and instincts roll them round and shape them, a body rather different from their faces. (*E5*: 3)

---

[31] Cuddy-Keane, *Virginia Woolf, the Intellectual, and the Public Sphere*, pp. 122–4. Michel Dion concludes her study of Woolf and Proust: "Woolf tries to reconstitute the influence of the unconscious and the hidden history of events, behind our conceptions of life and time, so that without such a reconstituting process, we would lose access to a basic dimension of events we actually live." "Between the Dialectics of Time-Memory and the Dialectics of Duration-Moment: Marcel Proust and Virginia Woolf in Dialogue," *Analecta Husserliana* 86 (2007), 168.

[32] In 1927, in a letter to E. M. Forster, she said of Lubbock, "an able and painstaking pedant I should call him; who doesn't know what art is" (*L3*: 437).

Woolf's title echoes her earlier "On Not Knowing Greek," the essay for which she spent months reading and making notes, although in the format of the book review the irony of "not knowing" is less authoritative. Whereas in the Greek essay she had discussed the epic, dramatic, and lyric verse of an entire literature, and argued the position of the reader excluded from the university, the review unsettles assumptions about gender and education in order to sketch a theory of language. Those Englishmen who claim to read and speak French (among them most of her friends) serve merely to illustrate a theory that she derived from her study of translation, about childhood, body, and creativity. The essay introduces an image shared with Proust that reappears frequently in her work, of the mind as fertilized by the transforming power of childhood, body, and sleep. Her posture is as defensive as in her comments on Percy Lubbock, as once again the study of language led her to reconsider what it means to know something that men claim to know. Her argument is structured by a model of the mind that is divided between consciousness as wakefulness and an unconscious that is associated with childhood memories. If in fact reading a second language focuses the conscious aspect of a mind that faces outward, while subordinating the instinctive aspect of the mind that recognizes the body, reading a translation with enough knowledge of French to refer occasionally to the text of the *Recherche* would give the reader positioned between two languages a perspective on both body and language.

The narrator's authority is greatest when the moment of awakening provides an opportunity to realize consciousness. In the passage on Proust from "Phases of Fiction" Woolf chose his description of the narrator's being wakened by his mother to come to the bedside of his dying grandmother, as an instance of the difficulty of reading the *Recherche*: "Then, even in this crisis, he pauses to explain carefully and subtly why at the moment of waking we so often think for a second that we have not been to sleep. The pause, which is all the more marked because the reflection is not made by 'I' himself but is supplied impersonally by the narrator and therefore, from a different angle, lays a great strain upon the mind, stretched by the urgency of the situation to focus itself upon the dying woman in the next room" (*E5*: 66). As a result the reader struggles with what she calls "content obliquity," the difficulty of drawing together "thousands of small, irrelevant ideas," a project in which Proust gives the reader little help (*E5*: 67). Proust explains: "The great modification which the act of awakening effects in us is not so much that of ushering us into the clear life of consciousness, as that of making us lose all memory of the slightly more diffused light in which our mind had been resting as in the opaline depths of the sea" (II: 347).

Awakening splits the "I" from the narrator, whose consciousness becomes suffused by the watery depths of the unconscious: "It is from these depths that his characters arise, like waves forming, then break and sink again into the moving sea of thought and comment and analysis which gave them birth" (*E5*: 67).

Moncrieff's translation of Proust's vocabulary reflects a particular moment in the development of the concept of the unconscious in European history, when the term although in wide use was ambiguous. At the turn of the century it was marked by the sense of antagonism between the rational mind and the irrational forces of the unconscious, although the structure and mode of the unconscious mind remained obscure. Lancelot Law Whyte writes in *The Unconscious before Freud*, "the idea of unconscious mental processes was, in many of its aspects, conceivable around 1700, topical around 1800, and became effective around 1900, thanks to the imaginative efforts of a large number of individuals of varied interests in many lands."[33] But whereas the Germans and the English theorized the unconscious, the French "under the combined influence of Catholicism and of Descartes, played a relatively small role in the explicit development of the idea of the unconscious mind, compared with either the German or the English."[34] In 1909 a number of French scholars, members of the Société Française de Philosophie met to discuss the unconscious, but came to no agreement on its meaning.[35] Freud's work is also marked by the ambiguities of this era. On the one hand a reader of German and classical literature, and given to presenting the case history as a kind of literary narrative, he was at the same time silent on the connection of the unconscious with literary creation. Alasdair MacIntyre notes in his study of Freud's work on the unconscious the extreme ambiguity of the term, owing in part to his use of "unconscious (adj.)" as a descriptive term that accounts for behavior that cannot otherwise be accounted for in terms of conscious intentions. He reserves for "the unconscious (n.)" the status of an explanatory concept: "If I am right, then, Freud's indispensable terms are 'unconscious' and 'repression' used descriptively; except in so far as illuminating description may count as a kind of explanation, their place as

[33] Lancelot Law Whyte, *The Unconscious before Freud* (New York: Basic Books, 1960), pp. 63–75. Peter Gay traces the history of the unconscious in Austrian culture in *Freud: A Life for our Time* (New York and London: W. W. Norton and Company, 1988), pp. 129–30.
[34] Whyte, *The Unconscious before Freud*, p. 66.
[35] Jeremy Stubbs, "Between Medicine and Hermeticism: 'The' Unconscious in *Fin-de-siècle* France," *Symbolism, Decadence and the Fin-de-siècle: French and European Perspectives*, ed. Patrick McGuinness (Exeter: University of Exeter Press, 2000), 145.

explanatory terms is highly dubious." Nevertheless the "creative untidiness" of Freud's work invites discussion more than would "careful precision."[36]

Proust exploited this ambiguity of terms. He differed from Freud in attributing the creative act to the unconscious mind, as in this letter to Jacques Rivière: "Ahead of the intellect I place the unconscious, which the intellect will eventually clarify, but which itself provides the reality and the originality of a work."[37] But in his fiction he maintained what Malcolm Bowie sees as a tension in the *Recherche* between a narrator that "the tradition of the *moralistes* had made familiar, and a narrator who was the instrument of an alternative psychology, resembling psychoanalysis, that the Proustian text itself enacted in its discontinuities, contradictions and reversals."[38] Yet Proust maintained the tension between traditional and new theories of mind without a special scientific vocabulary: his use of *l'esprit, le moi, l'âme, l'insu,* and *la connaissance* is consistent with the anti-theoretical tendency of French culture in the developing history of the unconscious. In the historical context Moncrieff's translation blurs Proust's position. In a long passage on the effects of sleep on memory in *Guermantes* he translates: "What is it that guides us, when there has been a real interruption – whether it be that our unconsciousness has been complete or our dreams entirely different from ourselves?" (II: 86) Translating Proust's "le sommeil a été complet" (II: 88) as "our unconsciousness has been complete" (II: 86) effectively makes nonsense of the sentence and the term.

Proust and Woolf image the sleeping mind as a deep watery space into which the self plunges during sleep. While asleep, Proust wrote in *Le Côté de Guermantes*, "we turn our backs on the real" (II: 84). Sleep provides the moment when "the same story branches off and has a different ending," so that one dreams of dead relatives who after serious accidents recover from their injuries (II: 84). The narrator becomes "a dual creature whose different parts were not adapted to the same environment" (II: 87). As a result: "one cannot properly describe human life unless one bathes it in the sleep into

---

[36] Alasdair MacIntyre, *The Unconscious: A Conceptual Analysis*, revised edition (New York and London: Routledge, 2004), pp. 102–3. See Henri Ellenberger on the transformative effects of "creative illness" in Freud's life. *The Discovery of the Unconscious: The History and Evolution of Dynamic Psychiatry* (New York: Basic Books, 1970), pp. 449–50.

[37] Cited in Mackenzie, "Proust's 'Livre intérieur,'" 150. Proust also used *l'inconscient* in the sense of *unconscious* from time to time in his correspondence, as in this letter to Louis de Robert [1913]: "But since this sort of detail is never revealed to us through the intellect, since we have in some way to fish for it in the depths of the unconscious, it is, indeed, imperceptible because it is so remote, so difficult to grasp." *Letters of Marcel Proust*, trans. and ed. Mina Curtiss (New York: Helen Marx Books, 2006), pp. 294–5.

[38] Malcolm Bowie, *Freud, Proust and Lacan: Theory as Fiction* (Cambridge: Cambridge University Press, 1987), p. 97.

which it plunges night after night and which sweeps round it as a promontory is encircled by the sea" (II: 83). Peter Walsh, contemplating the government policy on India, assimilates the image to the soul: "For this is the truth about our soul, he thought, our self, who fish-like inhabits deep seas and plies among obscurities threading her way between the boles of giant weeds, over sun-flickered spaces and on and on into gloom, cold, deep, inscrutable; suddenly she shoots to the surface and sports on the wind-wrinkled waves" (*MD*: 161). The topographical motif of surface and depth, in which consciousness is the diver who plunges, may as Mackenzie remarks seem over-familiar.[39] But as he points out it differs from Freud's images of the unconscious in that it is not a source of error and struggle but rather "a store of internal signs which have to be deciphered in the production of a work of art."[40]

The image of the mind as a watery depth serves a feminist argument in the "Speech of January 21 1931," the holograph draft of "Professions for Women."[41] There Woolf's plea to let the unfettered imagination of the female novelist "sweep round every angle and rock and cranny of the world as it lies in the depths of her subconsciousness" became a few lines later an image of her mind: "She was not thinking; she was not reasoning; she was not constructing a plot; she was letting her imagination down into the depths of her consciousness while she sat above holding on by a thin <but quite necessary> thread of reason. She was letting her imagination feed unfettered upon every crumb of her experience; she was letting her imagination sweep unchecked round every rock and cranny of the world that lies submerged in our unconscious being."[42] The image fits easily into the European debate about the significance of the *unconscious*, while serving to justify what Woolf considered her own strength and weakness as a writer. It counters Lubbock's emphasis on the conscious aspect of writing, while giving free play to the imagination that controls but is not "fettered" by

---

[39] Woolf wrote in "More Dostoyevsky" (1917) of his ability "to suggest the dim and populous underworld of the mind's consciousness where desires and impulses are moving blindly beneath the sod" (*E*2: 85).

[40] Mackenzie, "Proust's 'Livre intérieur,'" pp. 154–5. Malcolm Bowie observes, "Where Proust's narrator, in *Le Temps retrouvé*, speaks of joy and ecstasy, Freud speaks of work. Intense moments of contact with the unconscious are, for Proust, a gratuitous grace – spontaneous, uncovenanted, ungoverned by rule; they are the culmination of an unplanned individual journey into the psychical underworld; they are the introspective's best reward, the last leap into apperceptive knowledge of a mind accustomed to solitary exertion." *Freud, Proust and Lacan: Theory as Fiction*, p. 96.

[41] Melba Cuddy-Keane emphasizes the motif of Narcissus and Woolf's openness to both conscious and unconscious processes in "The Fascination of the Pool" (1929), which she calls "Woolf's most detailed anatomy of the mind." *Virginia Woolf, the Intellectual, and the Public Sphere*, pp. 125–31.

[42] Woolf, *The Pargiters*, pp. xxxvii–xxxviii.

reason. The image of the novelist as a fisherwoman introduces a dialogue between imagination and reason concerning the conventions of writing about women's bodies. The passage, which Woolf did not publish, insists that the female writer free herself to explore the unconscious as the site of the female passions.[43]

The role of the unconscious as a source of truth is theorized by Proust in a passage from *Le temps retrouvé* in which he denied the priority of intellectual knowledge. In it he returned to the paradox that "the truths which the intellect apprehends directly in the world of full and unimpeded light have something less profound, less necessary than those which life communicates to us against our will in an impression which is material because it enters us through the senses but yet has a spiritual meaning which it is possible for us to extract" (III: 912). That he did not voluntarily choose these reminiscences "must be the mark of their authenticity" (III: 913). The passage is the occasion for one of his rare uses of *l'inconscient* as "the inner book of unknown symbols (symbols carved in relief they might have been, which my attention, as it explored my unconscious [l'inconscient], groped for and stumbled against and followed the contours of, like a diver exploring the ocean-bed [un plongeur qui sonde, IV: 458]), if I tried to read them no one could help me with any rules, for to read them was an act of creation in which no one can do our work for us or even collaborate with us" (III: 913).[44]

After *Guermantes* we no longer have Woolf's notes, if in fact she continued the practice. When her notes are abbreviated quotations from the *Recherche*, she seems to be assimilating Proust's images, in order to create for herself a language capable of linking narrative to feeling. In the absence of her notes, the congruities between their works become less demonstrable at the level of language and vocabulary, but more challenging. Woolf's reading became freer, more inventive, as it raised questions that reflect on the *Recherche* as well as on her own work. The two-way effect of this transformation is *abusive* in the special sense of the term that Philip E. Lewis has derived from Derrida's "une 'bonne' traduction doit toujours abuser," which he translates to mean "a 'good' translation must always commit abuses."[45] The theory is derived from the assumption that translation is a

---

[43] In a passage in her diary of September 15, 1926 Woolf's essay on "A State of Mind" explores the moment of painful awakening at 3 a.m., and in a second passage her "plunge into deep waters" that is at odds with the usual "curbing & controlling [of] this odd immeasurable soul" (*D3*: 110–12).

[44] Jeremy Stubbs notes that "'inconscient' as an adjective had long meant 'not awake', 'not aware', or even 'negligent' ... It has an accompanying noun, 'inconscience', evoking unconsciousness (not being awake), but also lack of prudence, heedlessness, moral irresponsibility." "Between Medicine and Hermeticism," 149.

[45] Lewis, "The Measure of Translation Effects," 39.

form of representation that involves interpretation. Whereas in expository
writing the translation "gives primacy of message, content, or concept over
language texture," and focuses on "the identification of substitute signifiers," an abusive translation "renews the energy and signifying behavior" of
the original.[46] In the process the translator no longer seeks to identify
his work with an original, but to recognize and compensate for the impossibility of the task. An *abusive* translation has the power to unsettle an
established reading; it becomes "an order of discovery," as it directs "a
critical thrust back toward the text that it translates and in relation to
which it becomes a kind of unsettling aftermath."[47] My argument is that
Woolf seized on a few of the famous moments in the *Recherche* to reflect on
that text as it might be inflected from the perspective of the female body.

Although we do not have Woolf's notes on "le plongeur" who explores
the ocean bed of the unconscious, the single phrase may illuminate the way
in which repetitions of language in *Mrs. Dalloway* reveal the Proustian
spiritual world.[48] On the opening page Clarissa's "What a plunge!" juxtaposes
to hers a world that is helpless against the spiritual meaning of impressions.
Her cry recalls Bourton, where "she had burst open the French windows and
plunged . . . into the open air," with a sense "that something awful was about
to happen," a passage that prefigures not only the war and her youth but
Septimus' suicidal plunge (*MD*: 1). Clarissa and Septimus are each isolated
within a different "book of unknown symbols" that, although it permits
another world to disturb their consciousness, fails of recognition. Their
common reference to a line from *Cymbeline* suggests that reading may integrate
their disparate experiences in a literary context. Like the figures from Proust's
Faubourg, Clarissa has been insulated by her class and her wealth from direct
knowledge of the war, although she lives in the shadow of fear. When Lady
Bradshaw communicates the news of Septimus' death at Clarissa's party, she
receives the news against her will as at the same time her body empathizes.
The fear of "something awful" that she had felt, once materialized becomes a
question: "But this young man who had killed himself – had he plunged
holding his treasure?" (*MD*: 163). Clarissa's lesser capacity to plunge is suggested as she looks through her window at an unnamed old woman preparing
for bed, a scene that assuages her fear: "She felt somehow very like him – the
young man who had killed himself. She felt glad that he had done it; thrown

[46] *Ibid.*, pp. 41–2.   [47] *Ibid.*
[48] Miller discusses "plunge" in *Fiction and Repetition*, p. 185. In the second paragraph of *Orlando*, where
the hero plays at slicing off the head of a Moor, it merely rhymes: "he would . . . go to his attic room
and there lunge and plunge and slice the air with his blade" (*O*: 3).

it away. The clock was striking" (*MD*: 165). In the absence of "truth," Septimus' death in the aftermath of war achieves its "spiritual meaning" when it enters unwilled "through the senses" of a character whose intellectual and emotional limitations are clearly on display. Proust's passage is heuristic in a double sense. The reader of *Mrs. Dalloway* surely feels adrift without rules. And like Proust's narrator, the reader faces the novel with a sense that although Septimus' "treasure" may be spiritual, its articulation is so imbedded in impression that it resists intellectual apprehension, and that precisely is his difficulty and its value.[49]

Whereas in the realm of the intellect feeling may remain inarticulate, the process of involuntary memory requires that language translate an experience of the body. A key passage of the *Recherche* is the narrator's contemplation of the image of the madeleine dipped in tea, the combination of an image with a taste that is chaotic and distant. So great is his confusion that I "cannot invite it, as the one possible interpreter, to translate for me the evidence of its contemporary, its inseparable paramour, the taste, cannot ask it to inform me what special circumstance is in question, from what period in my past life" (1: 49–50). Such a translation would use language to impose the order of time and place on images drawn from memory. Christie McDonald makes a compelling case for Proust's idea of a translation that lacks an original: "the question is how to bridge the passage between the language of memory and that of creation. As we have seen, conceptual thinking, as the realm of intellect, goes only so far: intelligence may cleverly formulate generalities, while individuation in feeling appears for a long time impoverished and inarticulate."[50] Language so charged does not link the mind with things, a problem that Woolf's note on the madeleine passage recognizes. Rather it links present and past.[51] McDonald aligns the *Recherche* with Benjamin's translation essay, to argue that the text must "recover the original book of the self unprompted and simultaneously translate it." The tension between the need to recover a past moment and the requirements of representation is "the truth of language."[52]

In *To the Lighthouse* the physical signs of Lily Briscoe's grief that free her to become a subject reflect and comment on the famous passage on

---

[49] In a letter to Ethel Smyth in 1930 Woolf wrote of her practice, that I "light a cigarette, take my writing board on my knee; and let myself down, like a diver, very cautiously into the last sentence I wrote yesterday. Then perhaps after 20 minutes, or it may be more, I shall see a light in the depths of the sea, and stealthily approach – for one's sentences are only an approximation, a net one flings over some sea pearl which may vanish" (*L*4: 223).

[50] Christie McDonald, *The Proustian Fabric: Associations of Memory* (Lincoln: University of Nebraska Press, 1991), p. 39.

[51] *Ibid.*, pp. 46–7. [52] *Ibid.*, p. 39.

involuntary memory in the *Recherche*. Proust's narrator, a year after the death of his grandmother, at a moment when he is suffering cardiac pain and leans over to unlace his boots, realizes for the first time the magnitude and nature of his loss (II: 783). At first he feels remorse for having so little missed the grandmother whose stroke he had witnessed, as he calls "ma grand-mère veritable," with whom the sick woman shares only a name (III: 153). "I now recaptured the living reality in a complete and involuntary recollec-tion. This reality does not exist for us so long as it has not been recreated by our thought ... and thus in my wild desire to fling myself into her arms, it was only at this moment – more than a year after her burial, because of the anachronism which so often prevents the calendar of facts from corresponding to the calendar of feelings – that I became conscious that she was dead" (II: 783). Thus, to take this complex passage step by step, the apparent stability of the sign as her name occludes its reference to two calendars and to more than one grandmother. Consciousness occurs at the moment when pain unites mind and body, thought and "wild desire" ("désir fou"), so that the narrator realizes what had formerly been merely potential. Just as the grandmother had restored him when years earlier "I had nothing left of myself," so her restorative function remains after her death. Involuntary memory preserves the trace of the uncon-scious that affirms the continued and salutary presence of the dead.

The passage is the source of the phrase, "the intermittencies of the heart," which Proust had at one time proposed as the title of his novel:

For with the perturbations of memory are linked the intermittencies of the heart. It is, no doubt, the existence of our body, which we may compare to a vase enclosing our spiritual nature, that induces us to suppose that all our inner wealth, our past joys, all our sorrows, are perpetually in our possession. Perhaps it is equally inexact to suppose that they escape or return. In any case if they remain within us, for most of the time it is in an unknown region where they are of no use to us ... But if the context of the sensations in which they are preserved is recaptured, they acquire in turn the same power of expelling everything that is incompatible with them, of installing alone in us the self that originally lived them. (II: 784)

The experience suggests a truth in death that the narrator barely grasps:

I did not know whether I should one day distil a grain of truth from this painful and for the moment incomprehensible impression, but I knew that if I ever did extract some truth from life, it could only be from such an impression and from none other, an impression at once so particular and so spontaneous, which had neither been traced by my intelligence nor attenuated by my pusillanimity, but which death itself, the sudden revelation of death, striking like a thunderbolt, had carved within me, along a supernatural and inhuman graph, in a double and mysterious furrow. (II: 787)

The living body is itself mortal and at the same time a kind of writing pad where the unintelligible is inscribed.

At the end of "Time Passes" Lily Briscoe awakens to ask herself the question about feeling that engages many of Woolf's characters: "What does it mean? . . . For really, what did she feel, come back after all these years and Mrs. Ramsay dead? Nothing, nothing – nothing that she could express at all" (*TL*: 139). She ponders the impossibility of "'knowing' people" (*TL*: 164) and the inadequacy of language to express "these emotions of the body . . . It was one's body feeling, not one's mind" (*TL*: 169). The intense pain that she feels as she cries the name "Mrs. Ramsay!" is the unmediated experience of the body that materializes the vision of Mrs. Ramsay as "some trick of the painter's eye" (*TL*: 172). In both novels involuntary memory opens the mind to the "truth in death" that is the condition of the contingency of the sign. Her violent eruption of grief and wild desire roots Lily's vision in an experience of the body. Whereas Proust separates the scene of grief from the narrator's realization of his calling by hundreds of pages that allow him to explore details of the phenomenon of memory, Lily seems by contrast almost instantly enabled to set up her easel and resume work on her painting. Perhaps Woolf anticipates her emphasis in "Professions for Women" on the female artist's relation to the body. For Lily's "getting hold of something that evaded her . . . that very jar on the nerves, the thing itself" (*TL*: 209) is Woolf's image of the subject that is briefly in control at the moment of awakening.

When certain terms are undergoing redefinition, translation may be impeded, at the same time as it opens new possibilities for narrative. The image of the underwater world when it appears again in *Orlando* has become part of Woolf's strategy to use the untranslatable word that originates in unconscious behavior as a means to shield lesbian experience from the law. *Orlando* was written during a period when the trial of *The Well of Loneliness*, which resulted in a verdict of obscene, served to remind the public that in Britain homosexual acts were a crime. Nicholas in *The Years* "ought to be in prison" (*Y*: 283). As for *Orlando*, the Home Office received and discussed a complaint about its obscenity that might have led to its being censored.[53] Among Woolf's friends the very term *homosexual*, in

---

[53] Celia Marshik, *British Modernism and Censorship* (Cambridge: Cambridge University Press, 2006), p. 118. Leslie Hankins discusses strategies that "reveal the text as both an accommodation to censorship and a profoundly witty and powerful critique of censorship." "*Orlando*: 'A Precipice Marked V': Between 'A Miracle of Discretion' and 'Lovemaking Unbelievable: Indiscretions Incredible,'" *Virginia Woolf: Lesbian Readings*, ed. Eileen Barrett and Patricia Cramer (New York and London: New York University Press, 1997), 183, and n. 7.

circulation since 1892, was problematic. E. M. Forster situated the action of *Maurice* in 1912, when male characters spoke of "sharing," or more painfully of a "criminal morbidity" in reference to "the word hitherto unmentioned."[54] Only the hypnotist doctor speaks of "homosexuality," and he is aware that in two European countries it has been decriminalized.[55] Lytton Strachey "issued his edict that certain Latin technical terms of sex were the correct words to use, that to avoid them was a grave error, and, even in mixed company a weakness, and the use of other synonyms a vulgarity."[56] Proust feared reprisal. Two letters from 1920 protest against a friend's calling him "feminine": "From feminine to effeminate is a mere step."[57]

Since, as Alison Finch has shown, Proust was "the first major novelist to deal at length with both homosexuality and homophobia, and . . . responsible for introducing the themes into the mainstream of modern literature," English readers looked to him for a language to describe their experiences.[58] So it is no surprise that when Proust died, and his English readers published a commemorative volume, *Marcel Proust: An English Tribute* (1923), his representation of homosexuality took center stage. The volume included essays by Clive Bell, Catherine Carswell, Arthur Symons, Violet Hunt, and Francis Birrell; Woolf had also been invited to contribute. Clive Bell set the tone of uneasiness with his statement that Proust writes of "certain relations of which they [British writers] may not treat freely."[59] His *Proust* (1929) went further: "I should have loathed Charlus," followed by a slighting reference to "English homosexuals" and to "rubbishy play in the Lesbian mode."[60] Arnold Bennett's essay was the most generous: "An unpromising subject, according to British notions! Proust evolves from it beauty, and a heartrending pathos. Nobody with any perception of tragedy can read these wonderful pages and afterwards regard the pervert as he had regarded the pervert before reading them. I reckon them as the high-water of Proust."[61] Since homosexual behavior was practiced and commonly acknowledged in the Bloomsbury group, the volume provided a good opportunity for public

---

[54] E. M. Forster, *Maurice* (New York: Norton, 1971), pp. 51 and 240.   [55] *Ibid.*, p. 196.

[56] Cited by John Maynard Keynes: "In 1903 those words [for homosexuality] were not even esoteric terms of common discourse." *Two Memoirs: Dr. Melchior: A Defeated Enemy and My Early Beliefs* (London: Rupert Hart-Davis, 1949), p. 84.

[57] Cited in the Pléiade edition, *À la recherche du temps perdu*, vol. III, ed. Jean-Yves Tadié, Antoine Compagnon, and Pierre-Edmond Robert (Paris: Gallimard, 1988), pp. 1254–5, and in Curtiss, ed., *Letters of Marcel Proust*, p. 427.

[58] Alison Finch, "Love, Sexuality and Friendship," *The Cambridge Companion to Proust*, ed. Richard Bales (Cambridge: Cambridge University Press, 2001), 174.

[59] C. K. Scott Moncrieff, ed., *Marcel Proust: An English Tribute* (London: Chatto & Windus, 1923), p. 88.

[60] Clive Bell, *Proust* (New York: Harcourt Brace & Company, 1929), pp. 79 and 95.

[61] Moncrieff, ed., *Marcel Proust*, p. 147.

denial. In 1934 Woolf wrote to Quentin Bell, that she was writing about sodomy: "In French, yes; but in Mr. Galsworthy's English, no" (*L5*: 273).

Woolf and Vita Sackville-West shared an interest in *Sodome et Gomorrhe* that became part of their private language. In February 1926 Vita, en route to Aden, wrote Virginia a letter full of longing, in which she mentions reading those volumes: "But why did he take 10 pages to say what could be said in 10 words?"[62] During their trip to Paris in September 1928 they started their lovers' holiday by visiting a bookshop, where Vita bought a copy of Gide's *L'Immoraliste*, and Virginia *J'adore*, by Jean Desbordes, a coming-out story that caused a scandal among the friends of Desbordes and Jean Cocteau, after which the two women went home to their hotel room and had "a heated argument about men and women."[63] Woolf scholars have focused on the personal aspects of the trip, to which I would add that both women seemed determined to use the opportunity to discover how homosexual life was portrayed in a culture where although homosexuals might fear exposure they were not in legal jeopardy.

The narrator of *Sodome* represents homosexual behavior in part as a problem of the history of nomenclature. Although the Napoleonic Code did not make homosexual behavior a crime in France, as it was in England, Proust was fearful of the consequences of the publication of *Sodome et Gomorrhe*. *Sodome* was published in May 1921, and *Gomorrhe* in April 1922, seven months before his death in November. Yves-Michel Ergal argues for an elaborate strategy of the forbidden (*l'interdit*) by which Proust distanced himself from the behavior of the *invert*, his preferred term.[64] *Sodome* opens with a long essay on "la race maudite" in which Proust argued for the existence of a homosexual society-within-a-society like that of the Jews. It is characterized by sexual behavior that he models on "the vegetable kingdom," where the pollination effected by the bumble-bee serves to invigorate the species and "brings back within the norm the flower that has exaggeratedly overstepped it" (II: 624–5). While denying "the slightest scientific claim to establish a relation between certain botanical laws and what is sometimes, most ineptly, termed homosexuality" (II: 629), the narrator uses botany to assimilate his narrative to nineteenth-century science, and so turn himself into a scientific observer.

---

[62] Louise DeSalvo and Mitchell A. Leaska, eds., *The Letters of Vita Sackville-West to Virginia Woolf* (New York: William Morrow, 1985), p. 97.
[63] Vita Sackville-West, "A Week in France with Virginia Woolf," *Virginia Woolf: Interviews and Recollections*, ed. J. H. Stape (London: Macmillan, 1995), 34–6.
[64] Yves-Michel Ergal, *"Sodome et Gomorrhe": l'écriture de l'innommable* (Paris: Éditions du Temps, 2000), p. 22.

The essay introduces the scene in which the narrator "could have opened the fanlight above and heard" Charlus and Jupien in the sexual act that is reported by its sounds: "For from what I heard at first in Jupien's quarters, which was only a series of inarticulate sounds, I imagine that few words had been exchanged. It is true that these sounds were so violent that, if they had not always been taken up an octave higher by a parallel plaint, I might have thought that one person was slitting another's throat within a few feet of me, and that subsequently the murderer and his resuscitated victim were taking a bath to wash away the traces of the crime" (II: 631). That the sexual act sounds like murder suggests the perception of an innocent child, so that the narrator, who in fact has seen nothing, appears doubly detached.

In the climate of nineteenth-century science the history of "invertism," Proust's term, serves to bridge history and Darwinian biology, since it forms a link "with the ancient East or the golden age of Greece, [that] might be traced back further still, to those experimental epochs in which there existed neither dioecious plants nor monosexual animals, to that initial hermaphroditism of which certain rudiments of male organs in the anatomy of women and of female organs in that of men seem still to preserve the trace" (II: 653). The narrator concludes by profiling his position as would-be observer against such a history: "I was distressed to find that, by my engrossment in the Jupien-Charlus conjunction I had missed perhaps an opportunity of witnessing the fertilization of the blossom by the bumble-bee" (II: 656).

Despite the narrator's strenuous attempts to maintain the rational tone of the historian of science, homosexuality in *Sodome et Gomorrhe* is a story of contradictions. Eve Kosofsky Sedgwick, after dismissing the chapter on "la race maudite" as "sentimental and reductive," focuses her argument on the range of contradictions around Proust's representation of Charlus and of homo/heterosexual definition. In the sex scene, for instance, Charlus is said to be a woman, although the narrative figures him as male and Jupien as female; in her reading the act is better represented as "a mirror-dance of two counterparts."[65] What she terms "the incoherent constructions of sexuality, gender, privacy, and minoritization" constitute "the viewpoint of the closet," that reflects "the turn-of-the-century crisis of homo/heterosexual definition."[66] In other words Proust's text was invaded by the incoherence that characterized the historical moment when a well-known forbidden practice could not yet be named in ordinary public discourse.

---

[65] Eve Kosofsky Sedgwick, *Epistemology of the Closet* (Berkeley: University of California Press, 1990), p. 219.
[66] *Ibid.*, p. 223.

It seems clear that *Orlando*, far from tolerating, exploits similar contradictions. Sedgwick shares the expectations of realism, that is that the themes of the novel ought to add up to resolution and closure. Woolf's reading of *Sodome et Gomorrhe* is better aligned with Lawrence Schehr's argument that the novel is virtually without plot, and that homosexuality, while unnamed, is at the center of a work about interpretation and reading. He reads the sentiments in the essay on "la race maudite" as problematic "not because they are banal, thematic, reductive . . . [but] because they complicate the way in which Proust articulates the structures and systems that are founded in and on a homosexual hermeneutic."[67] The most immediate question concerns the inconsistency between the essay and the naivety of the narrator of *Du côté de chez Swann*. As in the narrator's preoccupation with the Dreyfus Affair, the innocence of Dreyfus is "the nothing . . . the merest excuse, for the homosexual text." As a result the novel proposes "a theory of reading even when reading is not the theme, a theory of signs when there are no 'signs' to read, a theory of homosexuality even when it does not seem to be a question of homosexuality."[68] Woolf demands a reader who is similarly capable of reading *Orlando* as a narrative in which the visible signs of lesbianism are contingent and ambiguous.

Orlando, the most multilingual of Woolf's works, makes use of translation to exploit the contradictions of sexual identity. Since most of the references in the book create the history of an ethnocentric British culture, Orlando's experiences with foreigners require translation. He hears Sasha speaking Russian, a language that he does not understand. But he knows some Greek, speaks Turkish, and "perfect French" (*O*: 21), a language "which notoriously loses its flavour in translation" (*O*: 24). Immediately following the mirror scene in which Orlando becomes a woman, she encounters a culture as ethnocentric as her own that contemplates the violent behavior that an act of language might have avoided. Her sojourn with the gypsies comes to an end when a word that is apparently untranslatable points up the cultural differences that generate hostility on the part of the gypsies. They have no word for "beautiful," which they translate as "good to eat" (*O*: 90–1). The word focuses the difference between Orlando, who suffers from "the English disease, a love of nature," and a culture that is committed to crafts and hunting. The gypsies come to suspect that Orlando, who has the ability to see with her mind as well as her eyes, "is someone who sees . . . something else"

---

[67] Lawrence Schehr, *The Shock of Men: Homosexual Hermeneutics in French Writing* (Stanford: Stanford University Press, 1995), p. 58.
[68] *Ibid.*, p. 65.

(*O*: 92). They become suspicious and enraged; Orlando for her part "long[s] for pen and ink" (*O*: 92). Since the men are plotting to murder Orlando, the difference is not merely philosophical; a matter of aesthetics has become harshly ideological. The passage is heuristic: a culture that can make no room in its language for what is foreign to itself forces the writer to flee, in order to create another world in the written language. Whereas in *The Voyage Out* the contact of the British with a foreign culture is the prelude to and perhaps the source of the illness from which Rachel Vinrace dies, Orlando's "disease [is] a love of nature," and translation, in the literal sense of the departure of her person, affords a comic resolution.

As an untranslatable word "beauty" may be theorized as the *remainder* that resists translation into a signifying system. Drawing on a wide range of philosophical and literary works, Jean-Jacques Lecercle analyzes one of Edward Lear's nonsense texts to show that even in the absence of recognizable signs the reader comprehends in its rhythms the language of emotion. It is "the dark side [that] emerges in nonsensical and poetic texts . . . I have called it 'the remainder.'"[69] Arguing that language is in a constant process of change he defines "*The remainder* [as] *the return within language of the contradictions and struggles that make up the social; it is the persistence within language of past contradictions and struggles, and the anticipation of future ones.*"[70] Several of Woolf's works treat *beauty* as the site of contradictions and struggles, for instance in the constant reference in *To the Lighthouse* to the celebrated beauty of Mrs. Ramsay. Lily, recalling Mr. Bankes' phrase, that Mrs. Ramsay was "astonishingly beautiful," reflects as a painter: "But beauty was not everything. Beauty had this penalty – it came too readily, came too completely. It stilled life – froze it" (*TL*: 168). Woolf's sense in *Letter to a Young Poet* (1932) is that as a remainder *beauty* has not lost its power to anticipate struggle. Whereas the didactic function of *beauty* in *Orlando* is straightforward, in *Letter* it is linked to the reader's willingness to contemplate the undermining of sexual identity. Woolf notes that "for the first time in history there are readers . . . and they want to be told how to read and what to read" (*E5*: 308). In a rather elusive passage of the *Letter* Woolf engages "the malcontent" within who "bursts out, rather to my discomfort, 'Beauty.' Let me repeat, I take no responsibility for what my senses say when I read; I merely record the fact that there is a malcontent in me who complains . . . " but here she is interrupted. "For when it comes to saying that the poet should be bi-sexual, and that I think is what he was

[69] Jean-Jacques Lecercle, *The Violence of Language* (London and New York: Routledge, 1990), p. 6.
[70] *Ibid.*, p. 182.

about to say, even I, who have had no scientific training whatsoever, draw the line and tell that voice to be silent" (*E5*: 316–17). "Beauty" in this essay is the untranslatable remainder in the sense that it interrupts the argument in order to force attention to the fact that unresolved contradictions of sexual identity have been silenced in the name of Beauty.

Venuti takes the idea of the remainder one step further, arguing that it has the capacity "to shake the regime of English." Since in his view translation "is fundamentally ethnocentric," in the sense that it seeks to assimilate a foreign text, it exposes a power relationship between two languages. In these terms the gypsy tongue functions like a minor language, despite its claims to an antiquity of "two or three thousand years," in comparison with which the genealogy of the British aristocracy was "negligible" (*O*: 93). Perhaps because it is represented as a minor language it has the power, in Venuti's terms, to "expose the contradictory conditions of the standard dialect, the literary canon, the dominant culture, the major language."[71] He concludes that "good translation ... releases the remainder by cultivating a heterogeneous discourse, opening up the standard dialect and literary canons to what is foreign to themselves, to the substandard and the marginal."[72]

When at last Orlando is able to return to her writing, she has lost her illusions about the British past: "the bones of her ancestors ... had lost something of their sanctity since Rustum el Sadi had waved his hand that night in the Asian mountains" (*O*: 111). As a result her ethnocentric view of language has also changed. "Some black drop," perhaps Woolf's image of the remainder, prompts her reflections: "Slowly there had opened within her something intricate and many-chambered, which one must take a torch to explore, in prose not verse ... What the future might bring, Heaven only knew. Change was incessant, and change perhaps would never cease. High battlements of thought, habits that seemed durable as stone, went down like shadows at the touch of another mind and left a naked sky and fresh stars twinkling in it" (*O*: 112–13). As she starts work again on her poem, "The Oak Tree," her mind has been enriched by her experience of the difficulties and dangers of translation. The magnitude and significance of the transformation are suggested by the exchange of unlighted chambers for an image of the astronomical freedom of the skies.

In both *Orlando* and the *Recherche* a visual image of the naked female body poses the question, how sexuality is to be determined. Judith Butler asks, "what will be taken as the true determinant of meaning: the phantasy

---

[71] Venuti, *Scandals of Translation*, p. 10.   [72] *Ibid.*, p. 11.

structure, the act, the orifice, the gender, the anatomy?"[73] Proust's narrator delights in watching his beloved Albertine sleep, when she seemed "an unconscious and unresisting object of dumb nature" (III: 67), "the image precisely of what was mine and not of the unknown" (III: 70). As the narrator's captive she "obeys" the command to disrobe: "Her two little uplifted breasts were so round that they seemed not so much to be an integral part of her body as to have ripened there like fruit; and her belly (concealing the place where a man is disfigured as though by an iron clamp left sticking in a statue that has been taken down from its niche) was closed, at the junction of her thighs, by two valves with a curve as languid, as reposeful, as cloistral as that of the horizon after the sun has set" (III: 74). The similes figure the female body as assimilated to those vegetal rhythms where the penis is literally disfigured as a "place." Rather than provoking male desire, the image of "cloistral" closed thighs visualizes the horizon made briefly visible after sunset. Edward J. Hughes analyzes the vegetal terms in which the narrator assimilates Albertine to himself: "the independence and complexity of her being is subverted by the Narrator, the effect being to allay the incessant doubting generated by his jealousy."[74] Butler argues that in such circumstances the sign becomes provisional: "How to use the sign and avow its temporal contingency at once?"[75]

  The remainder as visual image serves to sustain those historical contradictions that forestall the sign. The image of a sexual identity made unstable by the viewer occurred in Proust's work and in Woolf's during a period when *gender* more commonly referred to grammar. In order to discriminate between social and sexual practice, Proust represented the contingency of social identity as a problem of visibility. After the scene where the narrator overhears Charlus and Jupien having sex, he sees differently: "Until that moment, in the presence of M. de Charlus I had been in the position of an unobservant man who, standing before a pregnant woman whose distended outline he has failed to remark ... suddenly catches sight of her stomach and ceases to see anything else" (II: 636). Reflecting on his earlier impression of Charlus, "I had managed to arrive at the conclusion that M. de Charlus looked like a woman: he was one! He belonged to that race of beings, less paradoxical than they appear, whose ideal is manly precisely because their temperament is feminine, and who in ordinary life resemble other men in

---

[73] Judith Butler, "Imitation and Gender Subordination," *Inside/Out: Lesbian Theories, Gay Theories*, ed. Diana Fuss (New York and London: Routledge, 1991), 17.
[74] Edward J. Hughes, *Marcel Proust: A Study in the Quality of Awareness* (Cambridge: Cambridge University Press, 1983), p. 153.
[75] Butler, "Imitation and Gender Subordination," 19.

appearance only" (II: 637). Charlus' sexuality depends less on his social identity than on the narrator's new perception of him as a "centaur," an abstraction that once "materialized, the creature at last discerned had lost its power of remaining invisible" (II: 637). As a result the narrator seems to have developed a kind of sight that enables him to see double. Under these conditions *gender* functions in the domain of language as a reminder of constraint: homosexual men are obliged "to change the gender of many of the adjectives in their vocabulary, a social constraint that is slight in comparison with the inward constraint imposed upon them by their vice, or what is improperly so called" (II: 640).

Orlando transforms into comedy the very principle of awakening to the realities of gender determination that in the *Recherche* is the cause of the narrator's prolonged suffering, "the fatal and inevitably painful road of Knowledge" (II: 1152). Whereas Proust's narrator observes the body of the sleeping Albertine, the moment when Woolf's narrator perceives the naked body as the occasion to consider the language of gender occurs when Orlando awakens. Here we recall an earlier passage that meditates on Orlando's week-long trance: "But if sleep it was, of what nature, we can scarcely refrain from asking, are such sleeps as these? . . . what strange powers are these that penetrate our most secret ways and change our most treasured possessions without our willing it?" (O: 39–40). The paragraph invites comparison with one of Proust's long digressions on sleep, in chapter three of *Sodome*. There sleep is "a second dwelling" with its own servants and visitors: "The race that inhabits it, like that of our first human ancestors, is androgynous. A man in it appears a moment later in the form of a woman. Things in it show a tendency to turn into men, men into friends and enemies" (II: 1013). Woolf, in a more playful mood, challenges the theories of identity and reference that determine gender.[76] "The change of sex, though it altered their future, did nothing whatever to alter their identity" (O: 87). In fact in the holograph "Orlando stood for a moment in all his/her beauty [?] stark naked."[77] The changes instead

[76] Pamela Caughie argues that "this play side of Woolf's writing be accounted for in terms of different conceptions of self, language, and reality – in terms of a dramatic self not an appropriate one, in terms of a performative view of language not a cognitive one, in terms of a rhetorical reality not a referential one," in "Virginia Woolf's Double Discourse," *Discontented Discourses: Feminism/Textual Intervention/Psychoanalysis*, ed. Marleen S. Barr and Richard Feldstein (Urbana: University of Illinois Press, 1989), 49.
[77] Virginia Woolf, *Orlando: The Original Holograph Draft*, ed. Stuart Nelson Clarke (London: S. N. Clarke, 1993), p. 109.

concern grammar: "in future we must, for convention's sake, say 'her' for 'his', and 'she' for 'he'" (*O*: 87).[78]

The novel connects that language to the law, which for the purposes of inheritance requires stable signs of gender identification. When Orlando receives notice that her lawsuits have been resolved, she learns that in order to settle a matter of inheritance, *male* must be a stable sign: "The estates which are now desequestrated in perpetuity descend and are tailed and entailed upon the heirs male of my body" (*O*: 166). James McDaniel puts this scene into the context of British legal history: inheritance law associated real property with males, personal property such as writing with females, and a loss of property is linked to a loss of identity. *Orlando* moves "from associating identity with real property to associating identity with personal property."[79] I would add that the laws linking inheritance to identity come into play after a death, when the living body no longer poses a challenge to the stable sign.

In this context clothing becomes a protest against the identity imposed by fifteenth-century legal jargon. In the *Recherche* "By dint of thinking tenderly of men one becomes a woman, and an imaginary skirt hampers one's movements" (ii: 939). As for Orlando, "when Captain Bartolus saw Orlando's skirt, he had an awning stretched for her immediately, pressed her to take another slice of beef, and invited her to go ashore with him in the long-boat. These compliments would certainly not have been paid her had her skirts, instead of flowing, been cut tight to her legs in the fashion of breeches" (*O*: 120). As her sex vacillates with her clothing, she "enjoyed the love of both sexes equally." She spends the morning "in a China robe of ambiguous gender," before changing to knee-breeches and later a taffeta gown (*O*: 142). Woolf goes further than Proust in suggesting the performative nature of costume. In *Orlando* clothes demonstrate the inscrutability of the visible: "clothes are but a symbol of something hid deep beneath . . . In every human being a vacillation from one sex to the other takes place, and often it is only the clothes that keep the male or female likeness, while underneath the sex is the very opposite of what it is above" (*O*: 121).

As translation helped Orlando to discover during her visit to the gypsies the ethnocentric limits of language, so following her meeting with Shelmerdine, her understanding changes again: "'You're a woman, Shel!' she cried. 'You're

---

[78] Charles Mauron in his translation of *Orlando* into French "was able to maintain an ambiguity of gender in key passages that would be impossible in English." Caws and Wright, *Bloomsbury and France*, pp. 353–4.

[79] Private communication from James McDaniel, graduate student at Case Western Reserve University, Cleveland, Ohio.

a man, Orlando!' he cried" (*O*: 164).[80] But more than sexual identity has been shattered. What emerges from the narrative that follows is a theory of the effects of death and desire on the referential aspects of language. Woolf's first move is destructive: since "it has come about, by the wise economy of nature, that our modern spirit can almost dispense with language; the commonest expressions do, since no expressions do; hence the most ordinary conversation is often the most poetic, and the most poetic is precisely that which cannot be written down. For which reasons we leave a great blank here, which must be taken to indicate that the space is filled to repletion" (*O*: 165). In a world reduced to a blank, Woolf seems to say, naming becomes a fundamental model of sign making: the name *Bonthrop* "should signify to the reader that she [Orlando] was in a solitary mood . . . was desirous only of meeting death by herself . . . for him too the same word signified, mystically, separation and isolation" (*O*: 169). The special signifying system that Orlando and Shelmerdine create between them is an echo to be sure of the coded nature of the novel as a love letter to Vita.[81] In addition their communication is based on an acknowledgement of death: "saying 'Bonthrop', she said in effect, 'I'm dead'" (*O*: 169). As in *The Waves* Woolf struggled with a demand that language in theory accommodate the unspeakable and hence untranslatable effects of death and mourning. That Orlando experiences her solitude while absent from the narrative (she returns a few lines later) suggests that the vitality of language entails a movement of departure and return.

After Shelmerdine departs, Orlando develops a theory of the self that affords an intimacy achieved in solitude, theorized by Proust's sense that "in order that we may discover that we are in love, perhaps indeed in order that we may fall in love, the day of separation must first have come" (III: 516). The gaiety of Woolf's narrator in the face of absence strongly contrasts with the somber tone of Proust's, who believes in "the valuable agony" of unhappiness (III: 945). During the absence of the beloved he realizes more fully his earlier perception, that his mistresses "have never coincided with my love for them," so that he is scarcely aware of their appearance, since it is "within us that the beloved creature was" (II: 1164–5). To realize that he has internalized the beloved Albertine puts identity of self in question, as the

---

[80] Jeffrey Mehlman interprets the chiasmus of this moment by a reference to Laplanche's idea, "that every Oedipus complex is both positive and negative, and that, paradoxically, it is the positive Oedipal position which results in a homosexual identification and the negative one which issues in a normal or heterosexual one . . . One will end up loving precisely as one *did not love* (predominantly) during the Oedipal moment. The question of Oedipal identification is opened to the freedom and rhetorical complexity of dream-work." *Revolution and Repetition: Marx/Hugo/Balzac* (Berkeley: University of California Press, 1977), pp. 102–3.

[81] Hankins, "*Orlando*: 'A Precipice Marked V,'" 180–202.

narrator is led to the recognition of "those innumerable and humble 'selves' that compose our personality," some of whom he had not encountered for some time (III: 437). As Orlando motors out of London, she too experiences a process that so "resembles the chopping up small of identity which precedes unconsciousness and perhaps death itself that it is an open question in what sense Orlando can be said to have existed at the present moment" (*O*: 201). Despite the association with death, Woolf converts what Proust's narrator experiences as suffering into a game of numbers. At the point when Orlando might have been "entirely disassembled," she comes to Proust's realization of numerous selves: "For if there are (at a venture) seventy-six different times all ticking in the mind at once, how many different people are there not – Heaven help us – all having lodgment at one time or another in the human spirit? Some say two thousand and fifty-two. So that it is the most usual thing in the world for a person to call, directly they are alone, Orlando? . . . still the Orlando she needs may not come" (*O*: 201). The passage directs a "critical thrust" back towards the *Recherche*, where by contrast such prolonged absence has melancholy consequences: "We construct our lives for one person, and when at length it is ready to receive her that person does not come; presently she is dead to us, and we live on, prisoners within the walls which were intended only for her" (I: 682). Whereas Proust's narrator finds himself imprisoned within a relationship as well as a room, Woolf's image suggests that the public setting, where clocks keep different times and so put identity in question, frees Orlando to experience her several selves.

Uncertainty about the stability of the self affects the reader's position as well. In *Sexuality and the Reading Encounter*, Emma Wilson argues for the centrality of Albertine's lesbianism to Proust's conception of the reader. Since, she argues, heterosexual desiring relations depend on the narrator's obsessive attention to lesbian activity, Proust challenged the normative social function of heterosexuality by destabilizing reading positions. That is, there is a kind of continuum between heterosexual and homosexual: "Proust's achievement here is in the very destabilizing of desiring reading positions. It is thus that his text makes its challenge to the regulatory matrix of heterosexuality, exploding as it does any normative function it might hold."[82] We can see something similar going on in *Orlando*. Heterosexual desiring relations are characterized by Orlando's pursuit of the Russian Princess Romanovitch. When like Albertine she silently abandons the

[82] Emma Wilson, *Sexuality and the Reading Encounter: Identity and Desire in Proust, Duras, Tournier, and Cixous* (Oxford: Clarendon Press, 1996), p. 91.

narrator, he then seeks to engage the mystery of female identity. Glimpsing Sasha seated on a sailor's knee, Orlando seems to perceive in her "something rank . . . something coarse flavoured" (*O*: 29). The rankness of heterosexual desiring prompts Orlando after Sasha's departure to put to himself a list of questions like those asked by Proust's narrator after the departure of Albertine: "In her heart of hearts what was she? What were her thoughts? What were her loves? Did she lie to me?" (III: 527). Orlando's questions address the problems of identity that arise from kinship: "Where was she; and why had she left him? Was the Ambassador her uncle or her lover? Had they plotted? Was she forced? Was she married? Was she dead?" (*O*: 47). Although the conventional novel whose plot reveals family relationships would answer such questions, in *Orlando* they serve to trouble the narrative by making identity untenable. Yet heterosexual identities remain available as roles, so that when Orlando encounters the Archduke, "they acted the parts of man and woman for ten minutes with great vigour and then fell into natural discourse" (*O*: 115). In these circumstances love becomes "highly ridiculous" (*O*: 115), and the traditional romantic union impossible.

If the *abusive* translation is a kind of "controlled disruption" that results in an exchange of energy between two conceptual systems, what is the impact of such an exchange on the image of the reader? In the *Recherche* Charlus recites lines from love poems written to women as though they were addressed to men: "How should he suppose that he is not like every-body else when he recognizes the substance of what he feels in reading Mme de La Fayette, Racine, Baudelaire." The example is a poem addressed to Chloe: "I love but Chloe in the world, / For Chloe is divine; / Her golden hair is sweetly curled, / For her my heart doth pine" (II: 646–7). The name of Chloe appears in the draft version of *A Room of One's Own*, in a passage on what a female novelist may and may not write: "Chloe liked Olivia; they shared a –." As the pages that the narrator is reading stick together, "there flashed into my mind the inevitable policeman; the summons; the order to attend the court; the dreary waiting; the Magistrate coming in." Like the novelist who fears court proceedings Woolf censored herself: "But the thread by which we hold to a book is so stretched, so attenuated, is so intense a process, that one jar like this breaks it, & away the mind flew, thankful for a rest, or some other theme."[83] The elaboration of the image suggests that the legal threat imposes on the reader a kind of self-censorship

---

[83] Virginia Woolf, *Women and Fiction: The Manuscript Versions of "A Room Of One's Own,"* ed. S. P. Rosenbaum (Oxford and Cambridge, Mass.: Blackwell, 1992), p. 114. In *Jacob's Room* Edwin Mallett addresses a poem about "Chloe" to Clara Durant (*JR*: 84–5).

that manifests itself as distraction. Not only is the mind prompted to flee, but Woolf did not include the passage in the published version. Whereas in the *Recherche* Charlus as reader suffers personally, in Britain the "normative function" of the reader's text acknowledges the possible legal proceedings against the representation of same-sex relationships.

Proust hoped that the *Recherche* might furnish his readers "with the means of reading what lay inside themselves," although, he cautioned, it "could also be that the reader had eyes for which my book was not a suitable instrument" (III: 1089). The sense of two audiences obtained as well in Britain, where historical circumstances gave a particular urgency to the collaborative process by which Woolf invited readers to read the contingent sign. In October 1928, the date inscribed in the final lines of *Orlando*, and one month before *The Well of Loneliness* went on trial, some of Woolf's readers could reasonably be asked to recognize a theory of sex and gender even when, or especially because, key terms were so disavowed that they had not yet entered the lexicon. In such circumstances the sign behaves queerly: a feather may tip the scale in favor of its performative aspects. Whereas in "Time Passes," "One feather, and the house, sinking, falling, would have turned and pitched downwards to the depths of darkness" (*TL*: 132), in *Orlando* the name of Shelmerdine that falls out of the sky like a feather produces his reappearance. The feather signals the afterlife of a history that haunts the structures of a culture: the phantom castle is readied "as for the coming of a dead queen" (*O*: 115). The lesson of translation would seem to be that the sign has more than a cognitive function, so that the reader's primary task is to orient himself in a new conception of time and space. Perhaps this aspect of translation in *Orlando* is imaged by Proust's final sentence, in which he described his aim "to describe men first and foremost as occupying a place, a very considerable place compared with the restricted one which is allotted to them in space, a place on the contrary prolonged past measure, for ... they touch epochs that are immensely far apart, separated by the slow accretion of many, many days – in the dimension of Time" (III: 1107). It is the place made accessible by translation.

CHAPTER 5

Translation and iterability

A text lives only if it lives on [*sur-vit*], and it lives *on* only if it is *at once* translatable *and* untranslatable.

> Jacques Derrida, "Living On: Border Lines," *Deconstruction and Criticism* (1979), 102

It would be misleading to conclude that the impact of translation on Woolf's language was of interest only to readers in the English-language community. The overall argument of this book would not be complete without some study of foreign writers who share her sense that translation in postcolonial culture resists what Bakhtin has called the centralizing tendency of European languages, in order to create a space that is defined by crossing borders. In the process translators abandon a commitment to accuracy in order to accommodate the historical contingency of the sign. Scenes from several of Woolf's novels play out the social consequences of Derrida's "iterability," that is the sign read in the absence of either the sender or the receiver. In such circumstances the translation becomes heuristic, in the sense that it sends the reader back to interpret the relationship between or among texts.

The distinguishing features of Woolf's vision of translation emerge most distinctly in the perspective of European writers whose experience of nations and nationality was diasporic.[1] In her work we see that moving a text into a different language and culture asks new questions and creates a new reader. In my reading, a sentence or two hitherto unexamined in one of her paragraphs makes theoretical sense when read in the context of European discourses of translation. The striking difference is that whereas Walter Benjamin and Jacques Derrida assumed the institutional position of

---

[1] I have adapted the term "diasporic imagination" used by Gabriel Josipovici to refer to modernist artists like Beckett, Kafka, and Woolf, whose feelings of rootlessness although they disable them personally orient their work in an era of postrevolutionary upheaval. "Fail again. Fail better," *Times Literary Supplement* 5461 (November 30, 2007), 14–16.

translator-as-heir, as a British female Woolf occupied a different position. Although her family legacy and her position as a co-founder of the Hogarth Press are the marks of social authority, one has only to recall the role of entail in the fortunes of Vita Sackville-West to realize how contingent was the agency of a female in matters of inheritance. In such a split position Woolf emphasized instead the changing role of the reader, and translation as a linguistic activity with specific results for language and culture. In effect she shifted the discourse from an ethnographic emphasis on translation and filiation, to her observations of the way that translation alienates one's own language, and in so doing she raised an entirely different set of questions.

In chapter three of *The Waves* Louis, who sees himself as "the companion of Plato, or Virgil," reads at lunch from a book of poetry that he has "propped against the bottle of Worcester sauce. It contains some forged rings, some perfect statements, a few words, but poetry. You, all of you, ignore it. What the dead poet said, you have forgotten. And I cannot translate it to you so that its binding power ropes you in, and makes it clear to you that you are aimless; and the rhythm is cheap and worthless; and so remove that degradation which, if you are unaware of your aimlessness, pervades you, making you senile, even while you are young. To translate that poem so that it is easily read is to be my endeavour" (*W*: 61). The problem that Louis faces as translator is to move an ancient text into a contemporary historical setting where the demands of new readers may alter its significance. He starts from the assumptions of his class and gender, when he speaks of the "dead poet" writing in a language that has been forgotten. Yet his task is considerably more complex than merely to restore what was once known, for his potential readers, "prehensile like monkeys," are characterized by the aimlessness and degradation of a senile person who ignores the poet because his mental capacities have failed so totally that he does not recognize his loss (*W*: 60). Such a reader represents a culture in which males, Jacob Flanders for instance, have received an education that makes it possible to forget classical languages. Had Louis considered female readers like those in *The Voyage Out* who hunger for translations, he might have imagined a more receptive audience. Convinced of the "binding power" of the poems he has in mind, he is committed to a translation that "is easily read." Yet Louis' reiteration of the hortatory "you" lends the passage a less than confident air. The project is riven by the tension between the reader whose taste is utterly degraded and Louis' paralyzing sense that he both can and cannot translate the poem for such a reader. The text that is both translatable and untranslatable reflects a fractured readership: as a colonial Louis inhabits both the position of translator and reader-as-consumer.

As a colonial subject Louis draws attention to the older and less familiar sense of translation as movement from one location to another.[2] His training in the British educational system has only exacerbated Louis's sense that he speaks as a foreigner: "If I speak, imitating their accent, they prick their ears, waiting for me to speak again, in order that they may place me – if I come from Canada or Australia" (*W*: 94).[3] His view of translation ignores the unnamed text in order to focus on the gulf between himself and the reader. Woolf shows him in an isolated position, unaware both of Arnold's criterion of translation, that it satisfy the university scholars, and equally of her plea on behalf of the common reader. By the end of the novel he has become in Bernard's self-serving narrative a truly marginal figure: "How then, I asked, would Louis roof us all in? How would he confine us, make us one, with his red ink, with his very fine nib?" (*W*: 189).

Louis has received relatively little attention in discussions of *The Waves*.[4] If, however, we focus on the politics by which culture is transmitted as another aspect of colonialism, his role as a translator becomes central. Jane Marcus was the first to claim that *The Waves*, like *The Years* and *Three Guineas*, "investigates the origin of cultural power in the generation or group formed by the British public school and its values."[5] Bernard is the figure who illustrates an ideology of conquest in language, often misquoted, from Wordsworth and other Romantic poets, in the service of "patriotism and nationalist claims for English genius."[6] Gabrielle McIntire builds on Marcus' essay when she analyzes Bernard's "summing up" in terms of Bakhtin's monologism and heteroglossia, in order to argue that Woolf "constructs a text that is enthralled with its heteroglossic experiment, yet curiously resistant to its own polyphony. We might say that *The Waves* places heteroglossic and monologic modes side by side throughout, and then in Bernard's section, performatively enacts heteroglossia's failure ... [when] she asks us to consider what it means to speak of and for others by reducing

---

[2] Woolf notes the effect of such translation in "Ode Written Partly in Prose on Seeing the Name of Cutbush Above a Butcher's Shop in Pentonville." Among the crowds passing in the street: "These are semblances of human faces seen in passing / translated from a foreign language. / And the language always makes up new words" (*CSF*: 234).
[3] In Draft I Louis says "I never speak without trying to alter my Australian accent" (*Hol W*: 218).
[4] Gillian Beer notes his similarity to T. S. Eliot in *Virginia Woolf: The Common Ground* (Ann Arbor: University of Michigan Press, 1996), pp. 87–8. Makiko Minow-Pinkney calls him "a proto-fascist," *Virginia Woolf and the Problem of the Subject* (New Brunswick, N.J.: Rutgers University Press, 1987), p. 159.
[5] Jane Marcus, "Britannia Rules *The Waves*," *Decolonizing Tradition: New Views of Twentieth-Century "British" Literary Canons*, ed. Karen R. Lawrence (Urbana: University of Illinois Press, 1992), 142.
[6] *Ibid.*, p. 145.

plural lives to a suddenly decipherable and tellable 'order.'"[7] Her argument, in which Louis scarcely figures, is compelling. But Bakhtin's sense that "discourse lives, as it were, on the boundary between its own context and another, alien, context" would seem to suggest that translation, which he does not mention, is one way to represent the "alien context."[8] In particular "the novel senses itself on the border between the completed, dominant literary language and the extraliterary languages that know heteroglossia; the novel either serves to further the centralizing tendencies of a new literary language in the process of taking shape . . . or, on the contrary – the novel fights for the renovation of an antiquated literary language."[9] *The Waves* is structured by the tension between Bernard's summing up within the dominant language, albeit deformed by misquotation, and Woolf's ear for extraliterary language and extralingual cries and birdsong. The two seem yoked, for when the authority of monologism is compromised by misquotation, heteroglossia also fails.

The scene at lunch when read in Bakhtin's broad geographical and historical context is but one example of the "centralizing and unifying" of European languages that involves "the incorporation of barbarians and lower social strata into a unitary language of culture and truth, the canonization of ideological systems, [and] philology with its methods of studying and teaching dead languages."[10] Louis' open disdain for men of a lower social stratum, whom he sees as "prehensile like monkeys, greased to this particular moment" (*W*: 61), marks his complicity in producing "dead languages." His anxiety stems in my view from a fear that he resembles these men in his confinement to "this particular moment." For Louis history is focused on the present: "The weight of the world is on our shoulders; . . . if we blink or look aside, or turn back to finger what Plato said or remember Napoleon and his conquests, we inflict on the world the injury of some obliquity. This is life" (*W*: 169). "Obliquity" would seem rather to characterize a history that fails to consider the example of Napoleon. By the end of the novel Louis has so altered his sense of history

[7] Gabrielle McIntire, "Heteroglossia, Monologism, and Fascism: Bernard reads *The Waves*," *Narrative* 13 (2005), 33.

[8] M. M. Bakhtin, "Discourse in the Novel," *The Dialogic Imagination: Four Essays by M. M. Bakhtin*, trans. Caryl Emerson and Michael Holquist, ed. Michael Holquist (Austin: University of Texas Press, 1981), p. 284.

[9] M. M. Bakhtin, "From the Prehistory of Novelistic Discourse," *The Dialogic Imagination: Four Essays by M. M. Bakhtin*, trans. Caryl Emerson and Michael Holquist, ed. Michael Holquist (Austin: University of Texas Press, 1981), p. 67.

[10] Bakhtin, "Discourse in the Novel," p. 271.

that he has come to realize that the dead require a language: "How shall we put it together, the confused and composite message that they send back to us, and not they only, but many dead, boys and girls, grown men and women, who have wandered here, under one king or another?" (*W*: 153). The monologism learned in the British school system, and hence largely confined to the male characters, is connected to the sense that a language becomes "dead" when it is made unavailable to readers outside the system. Neville writes poetry, Bernard tells stories, Louis is a would-be translator. Acting as individuals none is equal to the task of vivifying the native language. Woolf's emphasis is rather on the translation of a classical text as the site of disputed colonial theories of history, class, and gender.

No aspect of translation is more important than its ability to renew the life of texts from another era or a different culture as a way to preserve the lives of the dead. Woolf understood the element of "boredom" that readers experienced when they read Greek drama: "The ordinary reader resents the bareness of their literature. There is nothing in the way of anecdote to browse upon, nothing handy and personal to help oneself up by; nothing is left but the literature itself, cut off from us by time and language, unvulgarised by association, pure from contamination, but steep and isolated" (*M*: 169). Although she shared Louis' worry that readers might not recognize the need for translation, she also understood that unless the text can be made to signify anew, its language is dead. Her concern spread to her native tongue, for what she knew and practiced of translation focused attention on the inertia of the semiotic and social aspects of the dominant discourse in English.

If we now turn to Walter Benjamin, and go back and forth between "The Task of the Translator" and Woolf's position at a comparable moment of postwar European history, we can observe significant similarities in their attitudes to language, as well as the substantial differences that become apparent in their interpretation of canonical texts.[11] As a European Jew, Benjamin was drawn to Genesis and the Kabbalah. In the context of nineteenth-century educational opportunities for girls, Woolf turned, as we saw in chapter two, to *Antigone*. As a result Benjamin periodizes history before and after the Fall, Woolf since the Greeks. He envisions a Biblical, she a Darwinian prehistory. Despite such fundamental differences, both produced reflections that defied the contemporary conventions of translation in order to envision another realm of linguistic possibility. A comparison with Benjamin puts in perspective major questions in

---

[11] I paid some attention to this question in *Virginia Woolf and the Visible World*, pp. 38–9 and 183.

Woolf's work: the importance of translation to the theory of reading and language, resistance to "bourgeois" ideas of language, and the sense of foreignness in one's native tongue.[12]

Benjamin's discussion of translation assumes a sacred text that records the word of god. For instance his argument that "a real translation is transparent; it does not cover the original, does not block its light, but allows the pure language ... to shine upon the original all the more fully" uses the language of Genesis 1, god's "Let there be light" to suggest that closeness to the divine rather than fidelity to the original text is the standard of translation.[13] Although he concludes the essay with praise for "the interlinear version of the Scriptures [as] the prototype or ideal of all translation," in fact the more usual model of translation is the story of the Tower of Babel from Genesis 11.[14] It begins with an image of simplified language: "Now the whole earth had one language and few words." Men built the Tower out of a desire to identify themselves: "let us make a name for ourselves, lest we be scattered abroad upon the face of the whole earth." When the Lord saw the Tower he said: "Behold, they are one people, and they have all one language; and this is only the beginning of what they will do; and nothing that they propose to do will now be impossible for them. Come, let us go down, and there confuse their language, that they may not understand one another's speech" (11:6–7). The narrative is framed by the genealogy of the sons of Noah, Shem, Ham, and Japheth that were born after the Flood, and the subsequent award of Canaan to the descendants of Abram. It is important to note that in Genesis translation is entwined with a narrative about the privileges of inheritance.

"The Task of the Translator" although it does not mention Babel is oriented towards the Bible as a sacred text. Benjamin begins by setting aside the notion that a translation recreates the original text for a reader who cannot read its language, and the accompanying notions of fidelity and freedom. As Carol Jacobs argues, "translation does not transform an original foreign language into one we may call our own, but rather, renders radically

[12] Makiko Minow-Pinkney considers the relationship of "The Task of the Translator" to Woolf's modernism in "'The Meaning on the Far Side of Language': Walter Benjamin's Translation Theory and Virginia Woolf's Modernism," *Virginia Woolf Across Cultures*, ed. Natalya Reinhold (New York: Pace University Press, 2004), 79–84. Angeliki Spiropoulou links Woolf's historiographical views with Benjamin's philosophy of history and theory of modernity, in *Virginia Woolf, Modernity and History: Constellations with Walter Benjamin* (London: Palgrave Macmillan, 2010).
[13] Walter Benjamin, *Selected Writings*, vol. 1: *1913–1926*, ed. Marcus Bullock and Michael W. Jennings (Cambridge, Mass.: Belknap Press of Harvard University Press, 1996), p. 79.
[14] *Ibid.*, p. 82.

foreign that language we believe to be ours."[15] She rejects Benjamin's language of the "natural" connection of the translation to its original that is manifest in his vocabulary of growth and development, germination and seeds: "Nowhere in the essay does translation develop into the future promised by the germ, the kernel, the seed."[16] Rather a concept of "pure language," that derives from the Biblical word of god, is at the center of the essay. In a translation it is that untranslatable residue of the original that signals a connection to the sacred word. Jacobs makes her point by a new "germanized" translation of Benjamin: "All suprahistorical kinship of languages rests in the fact that in every one of them as a whole . . . one and the same is meant, which, however, is not reachable by any one of them, but only by the totality of their mutually supplementing intentions – pure language."[17] It follows that the most important task of the translator is "to release in his own language that pure language which is under the spell of another, to liberate the language imprisoned in a work in his re-creation of that work. For the sake of pure language he breaks through decayed barriers of his own language."[18] To illustrate, Benjamin concludes his essay with praise for the interlinear translation of the Bible: "to some degree all great texts contain their potential translation between the lines, this is true to the highest degree of sacred writings. The interlinear version of the Scriptures is the prototype or ideal of all translation." His is the view of translation as capable of receiving and conveying divine revelation.

Benjamin's earlier essay "On Language as Such and on the Language of Man" (1916), his most fundamental essay on language, shows even more clearly the importance of the Bible to his theory of translation. Taking the Creation story in Genesis as his model, Benjamin questioned ideas of language as communication that also disturbed Woolf: "the bourgeois conception of language . . . holds that the means of communication is the word, its object factual, and its addressee a human being. The other conception of language, in contrast, knows no means, no object, and no addressee of communication."[19] "Bourgeois" language, in other words, assumes a language that conveys information among the living members of a community, on the assumption that they speak the same language. It defines the field of the novel narrowly, by ignoring figurative language and the words spoken to the dead, for instance Bernard's lament after the death

---

[15] Carol Jacobs, *In the Language of Walter Benjamin* (Baltimore, Md.: Johns Hopkins University Press, 1999), p. 76.
[16] *Ibid.*, p. 77.   [17] *Ibid.*, p. 81.   [18] *Ibid.*, p. 80.
[19] Benjamin, *Selected Writings*, vol. 1, p. 65.

of Percival, when he asks "if I shall never see you again and fix my eyes on that solidity, what form will our communication take?" (*W*: 101). Woolf's mistrust of "bourgeois" language as the language of communication is expressed elsewhere as distaste for "representation" and "common sense," the characteristics of the realistic novel written by Wells, Bennett, and Galsworthy.[20] To follow their example would have meant, she wrote: "Describe cancer. Describe calico. Describe – But I cried, 'Stop! Stop!' . . . for I knew that if I began describing the cancer and the calico . . . that vision to which I cling though I know no way of imparting it to you, would have been dulled and tarnished and vanished for ever" (*E3*: 432).

One chapter of *Jacob's Room* conflates two myths from Genesis, god's creation of light and the Tower of Babel, as the background of Jacob's fatal inheritance. In the novel the inability to translate ancient texts is paradoxically wedded to an ideology that uses them to signify male inheritance. Jacob, although he "knew no more Greek than served him to stumble through a play," imagines himself the heir of Socrates, who would if they met greet him as a friend. Chapter three, concerning Jacob's time at Cambridge, is structured by the narrator's play on god's command, "Let there be light," and the lights of Cambridge. The narrator comments on the educational system: "Such is the fabric through which the light must shine, if shine it can – the light of all these languages, Chinese and Russian, Persian and Arabic, of symbols and figures, of history of things that are known and things that are about to be known" (*JR*: 36). Narrative transitions among paragraphs that associate "the light" with the lights of Cambridge lead to the central question of the novel: "Was it to receive this gift from the past that the young man came to the window and stood there, looking out across the court? It was Jacob . . . he looked satisfied; indeed masterly; which expression changed slightly as he stood there, the sound of the clock conveying to him (it may be) a sense of old buildings and time; and himself the inheritor" (*JR*: 39). The masterly satisfaction of an heir limits Jacob's understanding: it lies with the narrator to ask what it means to inherit as a gift not only old buildings but a sense of history that is based on the knowledge of ancient languages.

The image of "the veiled lady" in the Courts of Trinity suggests another view of genealogy, as a form of history that in the interests of the elite represses the disparity of origins. It is, writes Lawrence Venuti, a definition of genealogy that in Europe challenged "the complicity with

---

[20] For instance, "The peculiar combination of suavity, gravity, malignity & common sense always repels me" (*D2*: 128).

the continuance of past domination and exclusion into the present."[21] In *Jacob's Room* the name of a ghost in the Courts of Trinity suggests that translation in other hands might have challenged this complicity with domination. The scene is haunted by Julian the Apostate, the last pagan Roman emperor, whose name was associated with the Cambridge Apostles. Among his works Julian's "Oration upon the Mother of the Gods" is a lengthy tribute to the Great Mother, whom he associates with Ceres. Much of the "Oration" concerns her relationship with Attis, "who at first is called *insane* and then *sane*, in consequence of his castration." Of her wider powers Julian wrote, "Who then is the Mother of the Gods? She is the Source of the Intelligible and Creative Powers, which direct the visible ones; she that gave birth to and copulated with the mighty Jupiter ... generating without passion; ... herself a virgin, without mother, sharing the throne of Jupiter, the mother in very truth of all the gods."[22] In *Jacob's Room* she is figured as the "veiled lady," whose presence "washed over everything, mollifying, kindling, and coating the mind with the lustre of pearl, so that if you talk of a light of Cambridge burning, it's not languages only. It's Julian the Apostate" (*JR*: 40). In other words, the transmission of "the light" is to be found in the university, in the hands of ordinary mortals, who as males conflate economic with spiritual privilege, in order to regard themselves as "inheritors." Whereas their education has prepared them for lives in imperial Britain, another narrative of the Roman past that included the Mother of the Gods would have authorized a different history. The master narrative of inheritance obscures a narrative about insanity harnessed by the virgin mother whose unrecognized spirit permeates the university.

Without translation skills those narratives of ancient history that happen not to be among the canonized texts of Jacob's formal education are reduced to ghostly presences that can be summoned by calling a name. In *Between the Acts* Woolf imagines a world where this has already happened. At a point during the pageant the villagers sing a song about seasonal work: "*All passes, but we, all changes ... but we remain forever the same ... Digging and delving we break with the share of the plough the clod ... Where Clytemnestra watched for her Lord ... saw the beacons blaze on the hill ... we see only the clod ... Digging and delving we pass ... and the Queen and the Watch Tower fall ... for*

---

[21] Lawrence Venuti, *The Translator's Invisibility: A History of Translation* (London and New York: Routledge, 1995), p. 39.
[22] The full text, translated into English: www.tertullian.org/fathers/julian_apostate_2_mother.htm.

Agamemnon has ridden away . . . Clytemnestra is nothing but . . ." (*BA*: 86–7).
In this passage history has become prehistory, when the signal of the beacon
that is seen and read by the watchman and Clytemnestra must be interpol-
ated from a clod of soil. Excavation as an accident of the farmer's ploughing
suggests the contributions of archeology to the knowledge of classical
culture. But artifacts alone reduce texts to names: "Only a few great
names – Babylon, Nineveh, Clytemnestra, Agamamnon, Troy – floated
across the open space. Then the wind rose, and in the rustle of the leaves
even the great words became inaudible; and the audience sat staring at
the villagers, whose mouths opened, but no sound came" (*BA*: 87). As a
means to teach history the pageant is limited by the need to appeal to
an audience that reads the newspaper or, in the case of Mrs. Swithin, a
fabulous prehistory of "the iguanodon, the mammoth, and the mastodon;
from whom presumably, she thought, jerking the window open, we
descend" (*BA*: 4). The frightening image of words lost in the wind and
open silent mouths suggests that in a new era when classical texts are finally
lost communication will also fail.

Derrida's "Des Tours de Babel" (1985) moves the question of translation
into the domain of colonial politics, where he maps its significance in the
world of nations and institutions. His essay in effect rewrites Benjamin's
translation essay so as to draw parallels with colonial policy. Whereas
Benjamin assumes all the difficulties of translating a sacred text, Derrida's
phrase, "since the sacred would be nothing without translation, and translation would not take place without the sacred; the one and the other are
inseparable," in effect exploits the contingency of translation in order to
shift the emphasis to filiation.[23] Derrida reads the Tower of Babel as the
myth of a colonial encounter, of "the inadequation of one tongue to
another." He builds on the French translation of the Bible by Louis
Segond, that from the sons of Shem emerged "the nations which spread
over the earth."[24] On that assumption Derrida deconstructs translation as
an institution within the university and the nation, from the position of
someone whose own lifelong association with the university was marked by
a particular colonial/Algerian ambivalence. On several occasions he related
the story of himself as the Algerian Jew who was expelled from a French
school, leaving Algeria for France at age nineteen, so that subsequently "my
language, the only one I hear myself speak and agree to speak, is the

---

[23] Jacques Derrida, "Des Tours de Babel," *Difference in Translation*, ed. Joseph F. Graham (Ithaca,
    N.Y.: Cornell University Press, 1985), 204.
[24] *Ibid.*, p. 168.

language of the other."²⁵ Paradoxically in this situation he read himself into the role of translator-as-heir, at the center of the Biblical myth of kinship: "For this entire history deploys filiations, generations and genealogies: all Semitic. Before the deconstruction of Babel, the great Semitic family was establishing its empire, which it wanted universal, and its tongue, which it also attempts to impose on the universe. The moment of this project immediately precedes the deconstruction of the tower."²⁶ Thus in the hands of the translator the text becomes an imperial legacy. In this reading he sees Benjamin as "an indebted subject, obligated by a duty, already in the position of heir, entered as survivor in a genealogy, as survivor or agent of sur-vival."²⁷ Perhaps Derrida's personal experience of diaspora gave him a double perspective on colonial institutions, and on the translator as legatee.

The title of Benjamin's essay, in particular the responsibility of undertaking a task, is an "injunction" that multiplies genealogical motifs. Derrida reads Benjamin's emphasis on the kinship among languages not from the perspective of "pure language," but as "the marriage between the author of the 'original' and his own language," that implies a contract.²⁸ In effect he directs attention away from the translator's language to his relationship to the text. The contract, that is necessary to any transfer, is in this instance a trace rather than a written document, but "subsequently will authorize every sort of contract in the originary sense."²⁹ Such a contract binds the translator to the translation as well as the author to his native tongue. In fact the whole essay is framed by a vocabulary of the contract. The word "task" requires "duty, debt, tax, levy, toll, inheritance and estate tax, nobiliary obligation . . . as if the presumed creator of the original were not – he too – indebted, taxed, obligated by another text, and a priori translating."³⁰ That Louis' authority in *The Waves* derives from his skill in international negotiations that require his signature many times over suggests some limits to the trace of the imperial contract as a model of the translator's obligation.

To speak of translation as a marriage contract emphasizes filiation and inheritance. Derrida writes of Benjamin's task as "what I have called the translation contract: hymen or marriage contract with the promise to produce a child whose seed will give rise to history and growth."³¹ The translation resembles a child "with the power to speak on its own which makes of a child something other than a product subjected to the law of

---

²⁵ Jacques Derrida, *Monolingualism of the Other; or, The Prosthesis of Origin*, trans. Patrick Mensah (Stanford, Calif.: Stanford University Press, 1998), p. 25. On p. 52 Derrida identifies himself as "an indigenous Jew."
²⁶ Derrida, "Des Tours de Babel," *Difference in Translation*, 167.
²⁷ *Ibid.*, p. 179.   ²⁸ *Ibid.*, p. 176.   ²⁹ *Ibid.*, p. 185.   ³⁰ *Ibid.*, p. 199.   ³¹ *Ibid.*, p. 191.

reproduction. This promise signals a kingdom which is at once 'promised and forbidden where the languages will be reconciled and fulfilled.' This is the most Babelian note in an analysis of sacred writing as the model and the limit of all writing."[32] Elsewhere Derrida has expressed a more nuanced sense of himself as legatee within a colonial structure: "I have always recognized myself in the figure of the heir ... I came to think that, far from the secure comfort that we rather too quickly associate with this word, the heir must always respond to a sort of double injunction, a contradictory assignation."[33] That is, he embraces a tradition, which in this interview consists of the thinkers who have preceded him, Heidegger but also Lacan and Levi-Strauss for instance, in an attempt "to appropriate a past even though we know that it remains fundamentally inappropriable, whether it is a question of philosophical memory or the precedence of a language, a culture, and a filiation in general."[34] In order to keep the past alive, the heir has the responsibility to choose.

By refusing to translate Louis has refused to become the heir of Plato and Napoleon, which is tantamount to refusing responsibility for a history that he is nevertheless helping to write. Woolf associated male inheritance with education when, for instance, she wrote in "The Leaning Tower" (1940) of educated men living before World War I as "the unconscious inheritors of a great tradition. Put a page of their writing under the magnifying glass and you will see, far away in the distance, the Greeks, the Romans" (*M*: 139). Although Woolf's knowledge of Greek language and literature is beyond dispute, her attitude was not that of the legatee. In a well-known passage of *A Room of One's Own* she writes of the moment "when [a woman] from being the natural inheritor of that civilization, ... becomes, on the contrary, outside of it, alien and critical," inclined to "think back through our mothers" (*RO*: 88). Apparently inheritance is a matter neither of genetics nor of free choice. Whereas Derrida defined the role of heir from within an institution and a tradition in a manner that allowed him to think of himself as legatee, as a British woman Woolf's gender complicated the question. Perhaps the phrase to "think back through our mothers" figures the female alternative to the heir. In the passage where the narrator encounters the ghost of "J – H – " (Jane Harrison), the "natural inheritor" is the mere ghost of a memory, whereas in the present she experienced the split that brings

---

[32] *Ibid.*, p. 191.
[33] Jacques Derrida and Elizabeth Roudinesco, *For What Tomorrow ... A Dialogue*, trans. Jeff Fort (Stanford, Calif.: Stanford University Press, 2004), p. 3.
[34] *Ibid.*

into being the feminine subject that although lacking a signifier occupies a historical position.[35]

Paul de Man's essay on Benjamin raises the question of the capacity of the translation to create a sense of alienation towards one's native tongue. He elaborates the implication that translation is less like poetry than like history or the theory of literature. Far from merely imitating the original, translation questions its authority. The very fact of translation suggests that the original text was not canonical, and transfers that quality to itself.[36] The propensities of translation to become literary theory or history "disarticulate, they undo the original, they reveal that the original was always already disarticulated."[37] As a result translation defamiliarizes one's native language: "What translation reveals is that this alienation is at its strongest in our relation to our own original language, that the original language within which we are engaged is disarticulated in a way which imposes upon us a particular alienation, a particular suffering."[38]

The narrative structure of *Jacob's Room*, for instance, is a form of disarticulation that is attributed to the postwar disruption of patterns of kinship and gender. Since to establish a bond of kinship in this novel would require the exchange of vows, the silence that Jacob and Clara Durrant impose on their mutual desire for each other effectively cancels the possibility of marriage. Florinda is pregnant, although she cannot name the father, who might be Jacob. Bonamy and Jacob separate when Bonamy walks away angry at Jacob's talk of Sandra Williams, who is herself an unsatisfied and childless wife. The narrator attributes closure to untimely death most simply in her comment on a pair of minor characters who fail to marry: "And now Jimmy feeds crows in Flanders and Helen visits hospitals" (*JR*: 97). The disruption of patterns of kinship "disarticulates" as well a diachronic narrative sequence that is based on "clock time." Instead paragraphs are synchronically paired by the repetition of key words, *light* or *window* for instance. The final lines, in which Jacob's remains are represented as a pair of shoes and the contents of his desk, mimic closure: Bonamy holds a bill that "seems to be paid" (*JR*: 173). Although Jacob and other male characters are committed to a narrative of material inheritance that is reinforced by their education, the narrator takes a kind of

---

[35] Woolf asked in "Reading at Random," "The writer – [*the f*] what is his mark? That he enjoys dispassionately: has a split in his consciousness?" *The Gender of Modernism*, ed. Bonnie Kime Scott (Bloomington: Indiana University Press, 1990), p. 678.
[36] Paul de Man, "Conclusions: Walter Benjamin's 'The Task of the Translator,'" *The Resistance to Theory* (Minneapolis: University of Minnesota Press, 1986), pp. 82–3.
[37] *Ibid.*, p. 84. [38] *Ibid.*

perverse pleasure in representing the Tower of Babel from the perspective of the god of Genesis 11, who said, "Come, let us go down, and there confuse their language, that they may not understand one another's speech."

In the same essay de Man asks a central question: "Why, in this text, to begin with, is the translator the exemplary figure? Why is the translator held up in relation to the very general questions about the nature of poetic language which the text asks? The text is a poetics, a theory of poetic language, so why does Benjamin not go to the poets? Or to the reader, possibly; or the pair poet-reader, as in the model of reception?" After reviewing other possibilities de Man prefers to think that the translator acknowledges defeat in his "task of refinding what was there in the original."[39] The translation questions the original text in a manner that decanonizes it; it "disarticulates" the original in a manner that alienates us from our mother tongue.

Let me try to suggest what is involved by Woolf's taking one of de Man's alternate routes. Although in her work Woolf usually translated passages of Greek, she left the occasional citation untranslated, as though to signal her authority as a reader of Greek. By refusing to translate, and thus presenting the text as both translatable and untranslatable, she was able to shift attention away from the idea of the text as a finished product and focus attention instead on the reader as her "exemplary figure." Woolf's "common reader" reads foreign texts from a position outside the institutions that teach language in a setting that links translation to filiation. Studies of the development of Woolf's common reader put in play many forces in Bourdieu's "field of cultural production" that include improvements in secondary education, use of the free library, and the introduction of the professional study of English literature. Perhaps owing to her teaching at Morley College and her observations of the university Woolf developed an alternative method of instruction and reading that stressed dialogue.[40] The "common reader" emerged as well from Woolf's explorations of the female reader's position in her novels, although as Susan Friedman notes, the "common reader" sustains greater critical distance and flexibility.[41] In these various settings translation comes to mark the position of the outsider

[39] *Ibid.*, p. 80.
[40] Melba Cuddy-Keane, chapter two: "Woolf, English Studies, and the Making of the (New) Common Reader," *Virginia Woolf, the Intellectual, and the Public Sphere* (Cambridge and New York: Cambridge University Press, 2003), 59–114.
[41] Susan Friedman, "Virginia Woolf's Pedagogical Scenes of Reading: *The Voyage Out, The Common Reader,* and her 'Common Readers,'" *Modern Fiction Studies* 38 (1992), 101–24. See also Kate Flint, "Reading Uncommonly: Virginia Woolf and the Practice of Reading," *YES* (1996), 187–98.

who, excluded from the traditions of university teaching, reads a foreign text without institutional support. At this historical moment, when women and Louis' clerks were not admitted to matriculation, the reader of a translation who like Woolf understood its provisional nature in effect challenged university pedagogy, the canon, and the boundaries of fields of study, as well as the dominant discourse.

In "On Being Ill" (1926) Woolf makes the sickbed into a kind of counterculture where the reader may approach language like a foreigner: "In health meaning has encroached upon sound. Our intelligence domineers over our senses. But in illness, with the police off duty, we creep beneath some obscure poem by Mallarmé or Donne, some phrase in Latin or Greek, and the words give out their scent, and ripple like leaves, and chequer us with light and shadow, and then, if at last we grasp the meaning, it is all the richer for having travelled slowly up with all the bloom upon its wings. Foreigners, to whom the tongue is strange, have us at a disadvantage" (*E*4: 324–5). In his study of the phonotext as the continual play between the aural and the graphic, Garrett Stewart reads Woolf's essay as a manifesto of reading that puts "aural before logical sense."[42] That is it proffers an alternative to stylistics, in which recurrence is read as inflecting structure and syntax: "Stylistics is concerned at most with phonological patterns, while phonemic reading takes up their morphological implications, the junctural overlaps and detachments that make and undo words ... In stylistics the lexical code usually stays in place and only the message is submitted to examination. In phonemic reading, the lexical code remains perpetually in play."[43] Perhaps because translation deconstructs the sign, it effectively loosens the bond that keeps the lexical code in place.

Translating the myth of the Tower of Babel into the sickroom, Woolf has her way with the sacred word of god. The Woolf who wrote in *Three Guineas* of a "'God,' who is now very generally held to be a conception, of patriarchal origin, valid only for certain races, at certain stages and times," is not likely to have held the Genesis myth in much esteem (*TG*: 166). In "On Being Ill" she turns healthy reading on its ear and substitutes for a foundational text the primal scene of reading in bed. Like Sara Pargiter in *The Years* she discovers that the translated text defamiliarizes her native language and her behavior as a reader. In the essay the Tower of Babel becomes part of

---

[42] Garrett Stewart, *Reading Voices: Literature and the Phonotext* (Berkeley: University of California Press, 1990), pp. 22–3. Gillian Beer notes Woolf's "ear that heard the auditory likeness between the most improbable concepts, as in *The Waves* the word 'tea-urn' generates 'eternity' a few lines down." *Virginia Woolf: The Common Ground* (Ann Arbor: University of Michigan Press, 1996), p. 133.
[43] *Ibid.*, p. 27.

Woolf's plea for a language that can represent not the word of god, but the suffering body. The sick person who tries to describe his pain to a doctor "is forced to coin words himself, and taking his pain in one hand, and a lump of pure sound in the other (as perhaps the people of Babel did in the beginning), so as to crush them together that a brand new word in the end drops out. Probably it will be something laughable. For who of English birth can take liberties with the language? To us it is a sacred thing and therefore doomed to die" (*E4*: 318–19). The story of Babel in the absence of god or a sacred text "puts in play the lexical code" by reducing language to sound. The notion of the sacred, which is at the heart of Benjamin's essay, in Woolf's view guarantees a dead language, and "pure" modifies not "language" but "sound." In this scene language has become a laughable extrusion that escapes the body, like a fart.[44] The value of illness is that it apprehends the body and its functions, at the moment before they are named, a position of original naming that Benjamin reserves for god. The Rabelaisian Woolf, so rarely in evidence, emerges in her plea for "a new language that we need, subtle, primitive, sensual, obscene" (*E4*: 319).[45]

Like Derrida Woolf recognized that any change in the national language can be perceived as a threat. In her "Speech of January 21, 1931" she writes of women waiting "in a state of fury" for the moment when it will be possible to write "about womens bodies for instance – their passions," the moment "when a woman speaks the truth about her body" (*TP*: xl). Can we say that in these essays the female body has replaced the sacred text as the site of an original that, in Derrida's phrase, "requires translation even if no translator is there, fit to respond to this injunction"?[46] There is little to suggest that within her lifetime Woolf saw a future when translation in the sense suggested in these essays might bring about what Derrida calls "this linguistic supplementarity by which one language gives to another what it lacks, and gives it harmoniously [in order to] assure the growth of languages."[47] After her death, as I show in chapter six, the system of colonial education circulated her work among other languages, in a manner that without her intervention brought this ideal closer.

---

[44] See her letter about a poem deemed obscene, Penis in the Mount of Venus (*L5*: 27–8). Jeanne Dubino explores the Rabelaisian metaphors of carnival and illness in the essay, and ties them to a new language of the soul. "A Dialogue with Imperialist Discourse," *Virginia Woolf: Emerging Perspectives: Selected Papers from the Third Annual Conference on Virginia Woolf*, ed. Mark Hussey and Vara Neverow (New York: Pace University Press, 1994), 38–43.

[45] Kate Flint argues for Woolf's "sexualization of the activity of reading" as a radical contribution to the debates of her time. "Reading Uncommonly," 193.

[46] Derrida, "Des Tours de Babel," 182.   [47] *Ibid.*, 202.

What happens when translation moves a text into new territory, where under the conditions of narrative it asks new questions?[48] In "Signature Event Context" (1972) Derrida, in the context of his criticism of Austin's *How to Do Things with Words*, formulated a critique of speech acts that explored the conditions under which a sign becomes iterable. The written sign is distinguished from the spoken by the fact that it may be read in the absence of either the sender or the receiver: "In order for my 'written communication' to retain its function as writing, i.e., its readability, it must remain readable despite the absolute disappearance of any receiver, determined in general. My communication must be repeatable – iterable – in the absolute absence of the receiver or of any empirically determinable collectivity of receivers."[49] Yet such iterability is never exact: "at the same time, a written sign carries with it a force that breaks with its context, that is, with the collectivity of presences organizing the moment of its inscription. This breaking force (*force de rupture*) is not an accidental predicate but the very structure of the written text."[50] I ask whether the scenes of translation in Woolf's fiction exhibit the characteristics of iterability that would allow the Greek text to pose new questions, under the conditions outlined by Derrida: "if one admits that writing (and the mark in general) *must be able* to function in the absence of the sender, the receiver, the context of production, etc., that implies this power, this *being able*, this *possibility* is *always* inscribed, hence *necessarily* inscribed *as possibility* in the functioning or the functional structure of the mark."[51] Derrida's assertion, which I have drawn from a long essay, is in fact investigated as a proposition by Woolf. That is, she asks whether and under what circumstances a work in Greek for instance can be inscribed in a contemporary setting, and with what consequences for its significance and survival. Whereas the Greek lines that she quotes in her essays remain citations, in that they refer to Greek history and tragedy, in her fiction the title or citation creates a new context in which she investigates the historical forces that occasion the break with context, the "*force de rupture*," in order to pose new questions.

Translation in *The Voyage Out* is less about acquiring new knowledge than about failed attempts to unlearn subjection to the discourse of the

---

[48] Benjamin approached the question as a cultural phenomenon: "The medium through which works of art continue to influence later ages is always different from the one in which they affect their own age. Moreover, in those later times its impact on older works constantly changes, too." "The Medium through Which Works of Art Continue to Influence Later Ages," *Selected Writings*, vol. I, p. 235.

[49] Jacques Derrida, *Limited Inc*, trans. Samuel Weber and Jeffrey Mehlman (Evanston, Ill.: Northwestern University Press, 1988), p. 7.

[50] *Ibid.*, p. 9.   [51] *Ibid.*, p. 48.

university and the church. The main characters are defined by reading tastes that unite and divide them across lines of class and gender. Reading Greek effectively divides men from women and university graduates from all others. Mr. Ambrose, who is at work on an edition of Pindar, declares to Rachel, who has come looking for a book, "what's the use of reading if you don't read Greek? After all, if you read Greek, you need never read anything else, pure waste of time" (*VO*: 171). Living in scholarly seclusion he is able to deny the need of translation. Mrs. Flushing on the other hand, uncertain whether the *Symposium* were written in Latin or Greek, craves a translation. Hirst reads the poems of Sappho in Swinburne's translation during a church service, as though seeking the protection of a sacred space for his undercover exploration of love and gender. Hewet asks "Why go to church . . . merely in order to read Sappho?" (*VO*: 237). By contrast Rachel's reading awakens her desire to enter the masculine world of learning. She responds to a passage from Gibbon about the conquest of barbarians with an appreciation of names as visual objects, rather than as signs: "Never had any words been so vivid and so beautiful – Arabia Felix – Aethiopia," and of Hirst and Hewet, who have given her the books, she thinks: "Any clear analysis of them was impossible owing to the haze of wonder in which they were enveloped . . . and her mind dwelt on them with a kind of physical pleasure such as is caused by the contemplation of bright things hanging in the sun" (*VO*: 175). As a result she wonders about love, while at the same time she returns home with her books "much as a soldier prepared for battle" (*VO*: 176). No wonder that love is a confused emotion in her mind, when her reading under male direction has fused the roles of divine lover and colonial conqueror.

Derrida's deconstruction of the teaching practices of the pedagogical institution is played out in two scenes of translation in *The Years*. Translation practice, he argues, is determined by the fact that languages and literatures are taught. The teaching of languages imposes certain limits on translation that are then "governed by the classical model of trans-portable univocality or of formalizable polysemia . . . What this institution cannot bear, is for anyone to tamper with . . . language, meaning *both* the *national* language *and*, paradoxically, an idea of translatability that neutral-izes this national language."[52] In other words university pedagogy by a narrow attention to the text denies that iterability can be a problem. The

[52] Derrida, "Living On: Border Lines," trans. Hulbert, *Deconstruction and Criticism*, by Bloom, de Man, et al., 93–5.

Greek text becomes a reified document, its language a border to be defended.

Two scenes in *The Years* show how translation has become part of the linguistic hegemony maintained by the university. During the family reunion in the final chapter Edward Pargiter, aware that the study of Greek has become unfashionable among a younger generation, recites in Greek the line that Antigone addresses to Creon after she has sprinkled dust on the corpse of her brother and been apprehended. Creon responds, "Pass, then, to the world of the dead, and if thou must needs love, love them. While I live, no woman shall rule me." When Edward's nephew North, who has just returned from farming in Africa, and has attempted to translate, asks him to translate the line, Edward refuses: "'It's the language,' he said." To what does Edward's "it" refer? Perhaps to the sound of Greek. In "On Not Knowing Greek" Woolf cites several lines in Greek, leaving untranslated Cassandra's cry as she foresees Clytemnestra's bloody murder. In the rest of the essay Woolf refers to sentences that "explode on striking the ear." Since Antigone's line remains untranslated in the novel, Woolf may have shared Edward's pleasure in the phonotext that handily defends against tampering with either Greek or the national language. But "it" shrouds Edward's motive in obscurity, as beyond his recognition or intention. As though to mimic his action, Woolf left the line of Greek that he recites untranslated. For the reader of *The Years* who knows no Greek the line remains a series of marks on the page that the narrative tells us represents Edward's oral delivery: "οὖτοι συνέχθειν, αλλα ουμφιλείν έφυν" (*Y*: 393). The sense of a text that is "at once translatable and untranslatable" means that the common reader is quarantined for the moment in a univocal language, with the advantage that unlike North he can turn to the notes to satisfy his curiosity.

A second scene of translation shows how *Antigone* has shed its Greek context in order to serve as part of the critique of the university as a colonial institution. The scene in which Edward is seen translating *Antigone* shows how the text participates in a chain of events that in effect shifts its meaning. In the chapter "1880" Edward prepares a translation that he hopes will qualify him for entrance into the university and thus assure him a place in the lineage of his father and grandfather, who had both studied there. Stimulated by a glass of port, he imagines his cousin Kitty who "lived, laughed and breathed" as Antigone (*Y*: 43). Translation transacts "the difference between signified and signifier" in Edward's mind in a way that recreates the dead Antigone as a living phantom. His translation is read in the chapter "1907," not by the woman he imagines, but by his cousin Sara, as she lies in her sickbed dreaming of love. In her reading the subtext is visual rather than phonological. She visualizes the violence that in the play occurs offstage. As she listens to dance music coming from the neighborhood she imagines the blackened foot of the corpse, and the mason who taps the last brick into Antigone's tomb. Finally she arranges her body so as to mimic the bodily position of the dead Antigone, literally reenacting Edward's image of the phantom woman. In her reading she picks a few words at random, so that the play becomes largely a dumb show enacted against a background of popular music. In both scenes Edward has successfully defended the border between university men on the one hand, and women and colonials on the other, in effect using translation to create a colonized subject.[53] He has created a reader for whom music, sound, and personal fantasy so condition the reading process that the text of the play all but disappears.

Derrida's "Living On: Border Lines" (1979) juxtaposes "The Triumph of Life," the poem that Shelley was writing at the time of his death, with the versions of a *récit* by Maurice Blanchot about a disappearing shoreline, as translating each other.[54] To erase the borders of a text, as though each text endlessly iterated others, leads him to redefine narrative less as an achievement than as a demand for narrative.[55] The third strand of his argument, and the one which concerns me, is the discussion of the "translation-effect" that is carried on in a band at the bottom of the page. There Derrida follows "the massive movement of . . . this *cortège*, over the border of another language, into the language of the other."[56] He begins by attacking "the limits of the prevalent concept of translation," as it has been shaped by a university pedagogy that defends the national language against "tampering." As translation "suspends, and sets in motion" Derrida's own language, he finds that some portions of Shelley's poem remain unreadable, an indication to him that the text remains alive. In this context "a text lives only if it lives on, and it lives on only if it is at once translatable and untranslatable at the same time. Totally translatable, it disappears as a text, as writing, as a body of language. Totally untranslatable, even within what is believed to be one language, it dies immediately . . . The same thing will be said of what I call writing, mark, trace, and so on. It neither lives nor dies; it lives on."[57] How does *The Waves* balance the behaviors and the circumstances under which a text that is both translatable and untranslatable might "live on"?

---

[53] A longer analysis of the scene appears in my *Virginia Woolf and the Visible World*, pp. 96–100.
[54] Derrida, "Living On: Border Lines," 92.
[55] *Ibid.*, p. 103.   [56] *Ibid.*, p. 77.   [57] *Ibid.*, pp. 102–3.

Following the death of Percival, Bernard self-consciously lives on, "shedding one of my life-skins" by spending a few days in Rome (*W*: 124). His memory while there of a scene of translation from the *Prelude* underscores the difficulty of moving the cortège of mourning over the border "into the language of the other." His is a Romantic sensibility that combines the language of Byron with *Prelude* V: "'Look where she comes against a waste of waters.' A meaningless observation, but to me, solemn, slate-colored, with a fatal sound of ruining worlds and waters falling to destruction" (*W*: 125). Bernard reads himself into the well-known passage in which Wordsworth's narrator, while dozing over *Don Quixote*, dreams of an Arab who bears the shell and the stone. It is a scene of language creation as translation: "He seemed an Arab of the Bedouin tribes: / A lance he bore, and underneath one arm / A stone, and in the opposite hand, a shell / Of a surpassing brightness. At the sight / Much I rejoiced, not doubting but a guide / Was present, one who with unerring skill / Would through the desert lead me" (1850 version, lines 77–83). Bernard echoes the language of the Arab's departure, as he "Went hurrying o'er the illimitable waste, / With the fleet waters of a drowning world / In chase of him" (lines 135–7). The dream vision is historically unavailable to Bernard. His reading of *Prelude* V is selective, in that he neither notes Wordsworth's tribute to madness that is paired with reason, nor recognizes that he fits right in with those whom the narrator dismisses: "Enow there are on earth to take in charge / Their wives, their children, and their virgin loves, / Or whatsoever else the heart holds dear" (lines 153–5). "Summing up," the title that Woolf gave to the final chapter of *The Waves*, is what we may expect from a Bernard unaware that colonial ideology has nullified Arab culture to the degree that it is no longer available even to the reader-as-dreamer.[58]

At first glance Louis' position as an agent of colonial commerce seems less blinkered. He has a wide knowledge of languages: in the draft version "he knew all languages: Greek was merely another."[59] His is the largest view of time and space: "we are gone; our civilization; the Nile; and all life . . . we are extinct, lost in the abysses of time, in the darkness" (*W*: 150). He sees human suffering everywhere as the condition of colonialism. Even as the group gathers for the reunion dinner, "This moment of reconciliation, when we meet together united, this evening moment, with its wine and shaking

---

[58] Jane de Gay studies echoes of the *Prelude* in *The Waves*, but does not include Book V. *Virginia Woolf's Novels and the Literary Past* (Edinburgh: Edinburgh University Press, 2006), pp. 165–72.

[59] Virginia Woolf, *The Waves: The Two Holograph Drafts*, ed. J. W. Graham (London: Hogarth Press, 1976), p. 367. Louis' school report notes his gift for translation, p. 53.

leaves, and youth coming up from the river in white flannels, carrying cushions, is to me black with the shadows of dungeons and the tortures and infamies practiced by man upon man. So imperfect are my senses that they never blot out with one purple the serious charge that my reason adds and adds against us, even as we sit here. What is the solution, I ask myself, and the bridge?" (*W*: 145).

But as a colonial legatee Louis is blinded to the participation of the translator in the culture of inheritance.[60] Bernard's biographer might note that he inherited a small sum from an uncle, but Bernard sees himself as the inheritor of the tradition of Byron and Shelley, and at table with his wife, as one of "those who have inherited the spoils of all the ages" as preparation "to assume command of the British Empire" (*W*: 174). The prospect that Louis might work to inherit an armchair is the basis of his hatred of Bernard and Neville, who see their material and cultural inheritance in an unconflicted manner, with no sense of Derrida's "obligation." Yet Louis sees the peak of his career as the moment when he will have "inherited a desk of solid mahogany in a room hung with maps" (*W*: 146). His sense of history is archeological: "I have lived a thousand lives already. Every day I unbury – I dig up. I find relics of myself in the sand that women made thousands of years ago, when I heard songs by the Nile and the chained beast stamping. What you see beside you, this man, this Louis, is only the cinders and refuse of something once splendid. I was an Arab prince" (*W*: 83). As though his refusal to translate has come back to haunt him, Louis' cultural inheritance is comprised of the songs and the sounds that remain when "Arab" is merely a name and the text has been lost. He is no more able than Bernard to create a narrative in which the translated/untranslated text lives on.

In keeping with Louis' tendency throughout the novel to open its questions to wider scope, he also queries the conventions of elegy as encouraging imperialist ideology. Following Woolf's suggestion that "elegy" might supplant "novel" as a name for her work, many critics see elegy as dominating *The Waves*.[61] Louis' cool remark, "Percival whom I most admire," strikes a different note (*W*: 133). Whereas the "Death"

[60] Susanna Rich, in an article on the echoes of Lucretius in *The Waves*, deconstructs Lucretius' name as a combination of "Louis" and "creti," which suggests *cretio*, "a declaration by an heir accepting an inheritance." "*De Undarum Natura*: Lucretius and Woolf in *The Waves*," *Journal of Modern Literature* 23 (1999–2000), 256.

[61] Jane Marcus reads the novel against its critical history as a canonical text: Woolf "exposes the cult of the hero and the complicity of the poet in the making of culture as he exudes cultural glue (in the form of an elegy for the dead hero) as a source of social cohesion, the grounding for nationalism, war, and, eventually, fascism." *Hearts of Darkness: White Women Write Race* (New Brunswick, N.J.: Rutgers University Press, 2004), p. 64.

chapter is dominated by the mourning of Neville and Bernard, and Louis is silent, his voice opens the "Life" chapter with a meditation on his position at the pinnacle of his commercial career. Is the reader invited to balance Bernard's mourning voice with Louis' note of personal triumph? Unlike Bernard, who went to Rome but no further, Louis seizes the occasion of death and mourning to deny national borders: "Percival has died (he died in Egypt; he died in Greece; all deaths are one death)" (*W*: 112). Yet in the passage that meditates on his love of Rhoda and the lines "O western wind, when wilt thou blow," he becomes a poet who mourns Percival in an image of spring aborted: "Percival was flowering with green leaves and was laid in the earth with all his branches still sighing in the summer wind" (*W*: 135). His is an elegy in prose that refrains from dramatizing self or nation.

The difficulty of living on, in a world where a text is both translatable and untranslatable, seems to be Woolf's sense of imperial history, in which she figures herself as well as her characters. Translation that is no longer oriented towards a sacred text assumes the task of preserving a history that is instead comprised of the lives of the dead. When in her work translation is refused, the emphasis often shifts to archeological excavation, which in these circumstances no longer supplements ancient texts. When Woolf imagines it otherwise as replacing them, names only remain, and tongues fall silent. At the reunion dinner Louis images the nightingale, but not in the language of Woolf's Greek essay as "the nightingale whose song echoes through English literature" (*E*4: 42). Rather he makes her tongue an image of diaspora: "'Listen,' I say, 'to the nightingale, who sings among the trampling feet; the conquests and migrations. Believe –' and then am twitched asunder. Over broken tiles and splinters of glass I pick my way" (*W*: 145). "Believe" makes the slightest gesture towards the sacred as a fragment, nevertheless imperative, without which Louis becomes the inhabitant of dangerous ruins.

CHAPTER 6

Assia Djebar and the poetics of lamentation

Haunting belongs to the structure of every hegemony.
Jacques Derrida, *Specters of Marx* (London and New York:
Routledge, 1994), p. 46

The *abusive* translation, which in Philip E. Lewis' essay forces a reinterpretation of the original work, finds its home in postcolonial literature when the translator's primary concern is no longer to translate a text from one into another dominant language. While it is true that Assia Djebar cites a Woolf short story in a text she wrote in French, the more significant role of translation is to be found in their reading of lamentation in *Antigone* as a means to question the policies of the twentieth-century state, and in scenes where narrative strategy begins with the act of translating the mourning cry. In the aftermath of war the scene of female mourning provides the occasion to "renew the energy and signifying behavior that a translation is likely to diffuse."[1] In the work of Woolf and Djebar the narrator participates in the female rites of mourning, while charging herself with their translation into a dominant language that has hitherto been deaf to their cries of grief. The female narrator who resists assimilating the mourning cry to the conventions of narrative that demand closure establishes an ethical position that is derived from translation.

The premise of Lewis' argument is that the translator cannot overcome the difference between the two texts. He acknowledges the cultural difference between the word *abusive* in English, and in French where it means false, deceptive, misleading (and in my *Hachette* dictionary excessive and unfair as well), as he considers the willingness of an English-speaking audience to tolerate a typically French elliptical use of language. The translator's predicament is that since the referential structures of

---

[1] Philip Lewis, "The Measure of Translation Effects," *Difference in Translation*, ed. Joseph F. Graham (Ithaca, N.Y.: Cornell University Press, 1985), 42.

English and French are not identical, an adequate translation is unlikely. The problem for the translator is to move away from the logic of identity, and rather to compensate for losses and justify differences.[2] Lewis queries how much freedom to grant the translator's interpretation, and whether the *abusive* translation can become a model. "The translator's aim is to rearticulate analogically the abuse that occurs in the original text, thus to take on the force, the resistance, the densification that this abuse occasions in its own habitat, yet, at the same time, also to displace, remobilize, and extend this abuse in another milieu where, once again, it will have a dual function – on the one hand, that of forcing the linguistic and conceptual system of which it is a dependent, and on the other hand, of directing a critical thrust back toward the text that it translates and in relation to which it becomes a kind of unsettling aftermath."[3] Yet in these difficult and unpromising conditions, it seems to me that Woolf's and Djebar's translation of *Antigone*, and Djebar's interpretation of Woolf's challenges to the language of colonialism, demonstrate that despite, or perhaps because of, these cultural differences the translation of Woolf's work exerts an unsettling and energizing force both on the work of a postcolonial novelist and in retrospect on her own.

Woolf's readers are not accustomed to linking her name with that of writers from the Maghreb.[4] Yet perhaps owing to the fact that Woolf and Djebar both knew some Greek and read *Antigone* as part of their education, each developed a feminine subject that emerges during wartime in response to the dominant language, and manifests itself at the intersection of translation and mourning. Djebar was born in Cherchel, and earned a degree in history in French institutions. When Algeria gained its independence in 1962, she returned to teach North African history and theatre science. There she offered a course at the University of Algiers in the work of three European writers: Elsa Morante, Ingeborg Bachmann, and Virginia Woolf, all novelists whose account of war, she wrote, had deepened their writing, and brought them as women to an understanding of tragedy. In the company of these women she queried: "is it not there that I situate myself in the return or not of the migrations of languages and narrative?" ("leur condition feminine, leur témoignage de la guerre creusent leur écriture et entraînent aux rives d'une vérité de tragédie leurs corps vulnérables, est-ce

---

[2] *Ibid.*, p. 42.   [3] *Ibid.*, p. 43.
[4] Anne Fernald discusses "Woolf in Africa," the work of Lessing, El Saadwi, and Aidoo, in chapter four of *Virginia Woolf: Feminism and the Reader* (New York: Palgrave Macmillan, 2006).

que je ne me situe pas là dans les retours, ou le non-retour, des migrations des langues et du récit?").[5]

Djebar's "there," as she explained in an interview, signals her decision to ignore the French writers who in her mind were too closely associated with colonialism, and nevertheless to take her place with other women who wrote in hegemonic languages.[6] The elements of that complex decision are played out in her definition of the novel as a space to think. In *L'amour, la fantasia* (1985) Sophocles' *Antigone* structures a novel that rethinks the history of the Algerian war and the French occupation from the perspective of an Algerian woman, in terms that recall Woolf's in *Three Guineas*. A later novel, *Vaste est la prison* (1995), is prefaced by lines from a Woolf story in which the ghost of colonial hegemony awakens the sleepers and sets the stage for the emergence of the subject. The novel opens and closes with an image of the writer's hand, that like Woolf's hand as she wrote the last pages of *The Waves* is driven by uncontrollable force. But whereas Woolf imaged the writer at that moment as helpless and mad, in *Vaste est la prison* the driven subject seizes language from the hand of the father. Translation under such conditions may account for the fact that in many passages Djebar seems more at home than Woolf in positions that a half-century after her death the Algerian writer might occupy as her own.

One may ask, what is the common ground between Woolf, a modernist writer living in a colonial society, and Djebar, an Algerian writer now residing in the postcolonial society of Paris and New York. The geography of Woolf's fiction is essentially the territory of the British Empire mapped onto the Roman, and expanded to include India, Ceylon, and South Africa. Although Woolf wrote in "The Leaning Tower" (1940) that literature "is not cut up into nations; there are no wars there," her works reference the boundaries of nation and empire, and save for the Dreadnought Hoax, a youthful escapade, Africa was scarcely in the picture (*M*: 154).[7] Until the Spanish Civil War she appeared largely insensitive to massacres and forced migrations, and as Kathy Phillips notes, she did not represent colonized people.[8] But the Hogarth Press was a significant focus of postcolonial

[5] Assia Djebar, *Ces voix qui m'assiègent . . . en marge de ma francophonie* (Paris: Albin Michel, 1999), p. 191. Paraphrase and translation mine. Subsequent references appear in the text, with the abbreviation *CV*.
[6] In answer to a question put to her at the African Visions Conference in Cheltenham in 2003.
[7] But see Heidi Stalla, "William Bankes: Echoes of Egypt in Virginia Woolf's *To the Lighthouse*," *Woolf Studies Annual* 14 (2008), 21–34.
[8] On May 12, 1919 she wrote of the massacre of the Armenians by the Turks: "I laughed to myself over the quantities of Armenians. How can one mind whether they number 4,000 or 4,000,000?" (*D1*: 271). But see Trudi Tate, who argues that *Mrs. Dalloway* is "judgmental of [Clarissa] and of her entire class, particularly on the question of the war and its consequences (including distant events, such as the

culture in London. In the 1920s and 1930s it published a number of books on Africa. Anna Snaith has studied the relationship of the Press with two writers from Trinidad and India. One of them, Mulk Raj Amand, wrote after meeting Woolf of her "desire to see beyond her own cultural boundaries and create points of transcultural understanding."[9] In my argument her view of language as opening the minds of others and paying a debt to the dead was an invitation.[10] In *Le blanc de l'Algérie* (1995) Djebar asked a question that might with a change of time and place have been Woolf's as well: "why on Algerian land, and in the year '95 specifically, am I so obsessed by the coupling of death ... and writing?"[11] In their work the mourning subject translates the voices of the dead in order to admonish official history with an authority that cannot be challenged.

Because translation disrupts the sign and hence its referential structures, its construction plays a part in colonial hegemony. Rodolphe Gasché argues that the point is implicit in Walter Benjamin's translation essay: "Translatability is the means by which the work of art rises above itself, above its own linguistic enmeshments." That is, a translation unless it is merely literal "destroys the original's structures of reference and sense communication."[12] Djebar wrote of her experience of this phenomenon in the autobiographical passages of *Fantasia*, when as a girl she studied French and noticed the references to flowers and birds she had never seen, or to strange social practices like men and women walking together in the street: "I write and speak French outside: the words I use convey no flesh-and-blood reality ... So, the world of the school is expunged from the daily life of my native city, as it is from the life of my family. The latter is refused any referential role."[13] ("J'écris et je parle français au-dehors: mes mots ne se chargent pas de réalité charnelle ... Ainsi, le monde de l'école est expurgé

sufferings of the Armenians)," "*Mrs. Dalloway* and the Armenian Question," *Textual Practice* 8/3 (1994), 467–86. Kathy J. Phillips, *Virginia Woolf Against Empire* (Knoxville: University of Tennessee Press, 1994), p. xxxiv.

[9] Anna Snaith, "Conversations in Bloomsbury: Colonial Writers and the Hogarth Press," *Virginia Woolf's Bloomsbury*, vol. II: *International Influence and Politics*, ed. Lisa Shahriari and Gina Potts (Basingstoke and New York: Palgrave Macmillan, 2010), 148–9.

[10] For instance in "Street Haunting," a walk in the London streets cultivates "the illusion that one is not tethered to a single mind, but can put on briefly for a few minutes the bodies and minds of others" (*DM*: 28).

[11] Assia Djebar, *Algerian White: A Narrative*, trans. David Kelley and Marjolijn de Jager (New York and London: Seven Stories Press, 2000), p. 219.

[12] Rodolphe Gasché, "Saturnine Vision and the Question of Difference: Reflections on Walter Benjamin's Theory of Language," *Studies in Twentieth Century Literature* (1986), 76–7.

[13] Assia Djebar, *Fantasia: An Algerian Cavalcade*, trans. Dorothy S. Blair (Portsmouth: Heinemann, 1993), p. 185. Subsequent references to this translation are given in the text, with the abbreviation *FE*. Quotations from the original edition, *L'amour, la fantasia* (Paris: Albin Michel, 1985), will also be referenced subsequently in the text, with the abbreviation *F*.

du quotidien de ma ville natale tout comme celui de ma famille. A ce dernier est dénié tout rôle réferential," *F*: 261.)

As part of western notions of representation and reality, translation also plays a role in colonial hegemony. Tejaswini Niranjana begins a study that is focused on translation theory as it is manifested in Indian texts with a powerful argument about the lack of awareness of the historical nature of theories of translation: "Is there something in the very nature of the problems posed – and the kinds of solutions adopted – in translation studies and ethnography that lends itself, borrows from, authorizes the discourse of colonization that underwrites the project of imperialism?"[14] The book argues that translation as a function of imperialist ideology interpellates the colonized subject as an object without a history. Simultaneously translation studies fail to note the inequality of languages in the colonial encounter, or to press questions about its history. As a result the colonial subject is created by an act of what Pierre Bourdieu, who has studied Berber culture, called "symbolic domination." It combines "recognition and misrecognition (*reconnaissance* and *méconnaissance*) – recognition that the dominant language is legitimate ... and 'a misrecognition of the fact that this language ... is imposed as dominant.'"[15]

As a result of French colonial policy Djebar found herself situated among three languages: Berber, the mother tongue which she understands imperfectly; Arabic, both the language of the Koran and spoken on the street; and French, the language of her education and of the colonial occupier. A good portion of *Ces voix qui m'assiègent* (1999), a book of essays about her emergence as a writer, concerns the difficulties and conflicts of her writing position. One cannot speak of Djebar as having chosen to write in French without considering the complexities of a diasporic position. During the ten years of what she terms her "mutism" as a novelist, she listened to the non-French voices that besieged her: those of her characters, who spoke "un arabe dialectal," or a Berber "que je comprends mal," while she sought an "equivalence" that neither deforms nor hastily translates these languages (*CV*: 29). During a period of Algerian history when Arabic monolingualism was enforced, she sought a passage among languages (*CV*: 32–3). Situated between the language of maternal tenderness, and French, which she called

---

[14] Tejaswini Niranjana, *Siting Translation: History, Post-Structuralism, and the Colonial Context* (Berkeley: University of California Press, 1992), p. 48.

[15] *Ibid.*, p. 32. The socially constituted subject of symbolic domination in language is explored in Pierre Bourdieu, "The Production and Reproduction of Legitimate Language," *Language and Symbolic Power*, trans. Gino Raymond and Matthew Adamson, ed. John B. Thompson (Cambridge, Mass.: Harvard University Press, 1991), 43–65.

the "stepmother language of adversity," she envisioned Berber as a third language, the source of myths and proverbs, that had been separated from its alphabet and thus lost to the world of books.[16]

In *Loin de Médine* (1991), written in response to street riots in Algeria, Djebar recognized in French "the language of laicity" that gave her "the freedom to depict anyone and anything." The novel treats the role of women in the life of the Prophet Mohammed in the aftermath of his death. The process of mourning is marked by quarrels between his daughter Fatima and her male relatives about her right to inherit, a problem that was resolved only by her untimely death. In writing about the divisive subject of women, property, and mourning, Djebar, like Woolf, found that translation widened her field of reference. French served as "essentially a lay medium . . . It put to rest the question of the relationship between France and Algeria. The consequence for me . . . was that I considerably enlarged my field of vision and my field of scription. The experience was, for me, crucial: it gave me my freedom."[17]

Djebar's decision to choose French bears on a complex argument about colonized language. Christopher L. Miller asks in *Nationalists and Nomads: Essays on Francophone African Literature and Culture*, "To whom do the languages of the former colonizers belong? Must we interpret the use of European languages as a sign of unending dependence and alienation? Is it possible for Africans to *appropriate* these languages, lend them an African inflection in literature, and thereby escape the cycle of dependence?"[18] In fact Anne Donadey argues that Djebar "arabicizes French."[19] As for the Berber voices that play such a critical role in Djebar's fiction, Stuart Hall notes that the moment when the colonized discover that they have a history and a language other than that of the colonizer, "It is an enormous moment. The world begins to be decolonized at that moment."[20] Djebar seized that moment, when in an interview she said of her response to the nineteenth-

---

[16] Her situation was not unique. Adapting a line from Kafka, Pascale Casanova writes that Kateb Yacine was also torn among "the impossibility of not writing, the impossibility of writing in French, the impossibility of writing in Arabic, and the impossibility of writing otherwise." *The World Republic of Letters*, trans. M. B. DeBevoise (Cambridge, Mass.: Harvard University Press, 2004), p. 272.

[17] Clarisse Zimra, "'When the Past Answers our Present': Assia Djebar Talks About *Loin de Médine*," *Callaloo* 16 (1993), 128–9.

[18] Christopher L. Miller, *Nationalists and Nomads: Essays on Francophone African Literature and Culture* (Chicago: University of Chicago Press, 1998), p. 165.

[19] Anne Donadey, "The Multilingual Strategies of Postcolonial Literature: Assia Djebar's Algerian Palimpsest," *World Literature Today* 74 (2000), 27.

[20] Stuart Hall, "The Local and the Global: Globalization and Ethnicity," *Dangerous Liaisons*, ed. Anne McClintock, Aamir Mufti, and Ella Shohat (Minneapolis: University of Minnesota Press, 1997), 173–85.

century history of Algeria: "Hence, in the language known as the language of the other I found myself possessed by the need to reminisce about an elsewhere, about a dead Arabo-Berber past, my own. As if the heredity of blood was to be transmuted into a welcoming language, and in fact this is the true welcome, rather than merely stepping over the threshold of the other's home."[21]

In this context translation no longer concerns making a foreign text available to a European reader. Each section of *Vaste est la prison* is prefaced by citations from a group of writers for whom translation has a special meaning. They include besides Woolf: Malek Alloula, an Algerian poet and photographer; Charles Dobzynski, a Jewish poet writing in Yiddish; Hermann Broch, the Austrian modernist novelist; Jeanne Hyvrard, whose early novels deal with the language of madness; Hölderlin, the German lyric poet and translator of *Antigone*; and the fourteenth-century Persian poet Hafiz. They are not Woolf's usual company, nor do I claim for her an exclusive relationship to Djebar's work. Rather Woolf joins a collection of European, Maghrebian, and Middle Eastern artists writing in a variety of languages. Theirs is a literature in which translation serves to keep alive and available the several languages required for the purposes of rewriting their and by implication European history. Translation is no longer oriented along the lines articulated by Matthew Arnold, but rather seeks to create a history that includes the languages of the defeated as well as those of the victors. It serves to define the diasporic writer as one who discovers her subject position by means of translation or the refusal on ethical grounds to translate. These circumstances reorient translation, in Dobzynski's words from Djebar's citation, towards "an alphabet that I did not use to think or write, but to cross borders."[22] Thinking back to Woolf's position in *Three Guineas* as a mediator among languages, we can see that she anticipates the diasporic writer who crosses borders in order to write the history of the dead.

The discovery of the stele that records the Berber language, as Djebar recounts its history in *Vaste est la prison*, is the story of a spoken language that has been reclaimed for the domain of script. At first a matter of

---

[21] Assia Djebar, "Writing in the Language of the Other," *Lives in Translation: Bilingual Writers on Identity and Creativity*, ed. Isabelle de Courtivron (Basingstoke and New York: Palgrave Macmillan, 2003), 25.

[22] Assia Djebar, *So Vast the Prison*, trans. Betsy Wing (New York: Seven Stories Press, 1999), p. 121. Subsequent references to this translation are given in the text, with the abbreviation *VPE*. Quotations from the original edition, *Vaste est la prison* (Paris: Albin Michel, 1995), will also be referenced subsequently in the text, with the abbreviation *VP*.

negotiation among Europeans, it is ultimately a story of the interaction between two systems of writing that brings to the fore "the question of the locus of enunciation from which the understanding subject perceives colonial situations."[23] As an object the stele has a long history. It was discovered in 1631 by Thomas-Osmann, a native of La Ciotat in Provençe, after he was captured by pirates during a sea voyage and taken to Tunisia. Near Dougga he discovered a mausoleum, and later transcribed an inscription that he found there on two parallel steles, which he understood as a bilingual text written in Punic and another language. When Thomas-Osmann converted to Islam and made his home in Tunis he became a man "between two shores, between two beliefs" (*VPE*: 130). Although his discovery led to nothing, the steles were repeatedly rediscovered and the parallel texts transcribed, by Camille Borgia of Naples in 1832, by a British lord, Sir Granville Temple, and finally by Thomas Reade, the consul general of England in Tunis, who sold the stele with its seven lines of text to the British Museum. Eventually the language of the second stele was identified as Libyan, the language of the first translated, and a Berber dictionary compiled. The narrator comments on the circuit of intellectual and economic interests: "This lost writing was resurrected in various stages over the course of several decades and once more with an Anglo-French rivalry as their basis" (*VPE*: 148). ("Étapes de cette résurrection de l'écriture perdue: elles se déroulent sur quelques décennies, là encore, sur fond de rivalité anglo-française," *VP*: 146.) After three centuries of intervention by European amateurs, the oral language that had been preserved in memory recovered its alphabet.

The narrative of the stele suggests what is at stake for Djebar in the recuperation of a language that she does not fully understand. Of all the languages current in Algeria: Koranic Arabic, Standard Arabic, and French, which are all written; and the three Berber languages and Farabé, a French-Creole-Arabic language, which are spoken at home and in the street, Berber is the most ancient. It dates from 4000 BC, and is the mother tongue of 20 percent of the population of Algeria. As part of a vast chamito-semitic group that includes ancient Egyptian and semitic languages, its use predates the invasion by the Arabs in the seventh century, and by the French in 1830. In the second century BC Berber was already marginal, since the official language of the Berber kings was Punic, and the use of Berber was limited to rural and tribal matters. Until the arrival of the Turks at the beginning of the sixteenth century, Berber was virtually eliminated. Nor did the language find a place during the debate about Algeria as a nation-state.[24] Giuliva Milò, who has written about Djebar as a historian of "la longue durée," points out that the transformation of the status of Berber from a dialect to a language inscribed on a monument reveals a civilization at least as old as the Egyptian.[25]

Yet during Djebar's education in French schools, Berber, her maternal language, was inscribed as a silence. Djebar felt herself "sur les frontières," which she found alarming as well as inspiring. Several of her essays describe the effects of an experience in which she chose French, and conceptualized the position of the Berber language as a ghost. The rumbling ("le gronde-ment") that may be heard, as of an animal or a storm, becomes in her account the sign of a living language that is associated with the ghosts of the dead ("des fantômes des morts," *CV*: 31). Between two languages, Arabic and French, lies a third whose absence or loss persists as a brush with the other, or a sign suspended. The hegemonic languages face up to their coupling, on the basis of their response to Berber, "langue de la mémoire berbère immémoriale, langue non civilisée, non maîtrisée, redevenue cavale sauvage" (*CV*: 34). Berber brings to the union its oral treasure of legends, stories, myths, and proverbs. Djebar represents these turbulent voices in the rhythm and style of a writing that is inflected for Arab or Berber ears (*CV*: 29).

The narrator of *Vaste est la prison* takes as the model of a writer who accommodates such ghosts Polybe of Megalopolis, who witnessed the destruction of his native Carthage and of Corinth by the Romans. Deported in his youth to Corinth and returning later to a Carthage that had been despoiled, his writing "is nourished by all this simultaneous destruction." Writing of death and bloodshed puts him "at the very center of a strange triangle, in a neutral zone that he discovers, though he did not expect it or seek it out." His writing, largely erased, exists "only in scattered scraps." As a deported writer who has lost his country, "all that he has is a language whose beauty warms him and that he uses to enlighten the enemies of yesterday who are now his allies." Rather than seeking to mount resistance, Djebar's narrator models herself on Polybe, who is "neither a loyalist nor a collaborator," but mediates among languages in order to write revisionist history (*VPE*: 161–2).[26]

[24] For a history of Berber, see for instance Mohamed Benrabah, *Langue et pouvoir en Algérie* (Paris: Éditions Séguier, 1999), pp. 28–31.
[25] Giuliva Milò, *Lecture et pratique de l'histoire dans l'oeuvre d'Assia Djebar* (Brussels: Peter Lang, 2007), p. 148.
[26] Benrabah remarks of Algerians, "l'absence de haine à l'encontre du non-musulman, de l'étranger, français notamment," *Langue et pouvoir en Algérie*, p. 23.

Yet Djebar like Woolf read *Antigone* as a play that holds colonial powers to account. Both had read some Greek and had witnessed the performance of Greek plays.[27] Barbara Goff and Michael Simpson in *Crossroads in the Black Aegean* have studied the adaptation of Sophocles' plays by African and Caribbean dramatists that makes the Aegean a "zone of cultural transmission among Africa, ancient Greece, and contemporary Europe."[28] The complex matter of cultural transmission significantly complicates the translation from either Greek or a colonial language: "The adaptations rehearse within themselves the very ambivalence that prevails between them and their context, while this context furnishes the content as an overall explanatory model. In addition to submitting to the authority of colonial culture, as they try to bring that authority and that culture into opposition, the plays internally reproduce the terms of their submission."[29] By focusing on ambivalence and submission their argument inflects the problem of iterability, which asks questions about the life of a text in new surroundings. In *L'amour, la fantasia*, for instance, Djebar's Antigone offers an "overall explanatory model" in the sense that she reenacts the problem of burying a brother who is a combatant on the wrong side. The novel explicitly denies terms of submission, when although Algerians are entombed, the Antigone figure remains alive to imagine a future and to bind the teller to her tale.

Fantasia writes a history that weaves together written French accounts of the nineteenth-century colonial conquest of Algeria, which began in 1830, with the testimony of the mothers and sisters of twentieth-century maquisards. The counterpointing of Algerian and French narratives was particularly relevant to the postwar period, during which Algerians who wished to know their history had been forced to turn to French accounts.[30] In this setting it is not surprising that the story of the French in Algeria is a tale of translation as failed communication. The French soldiers are unable to translate the Arabic speech they hear, although they have brought with them "a horde of

---

[27] In 1993 Djebar saw a performance of *Antigone* that was staged by young Maghrebians in Strasbourg (*CV*: 238). In *Vaste est la prison* the narrator mentions her study of Greek, "grâce au grec ancient maîtrisé" (*VP*: 294). Woolf's knowledge of Greek is a matter of record. She mentions seeing a production of *Medea* in Syracuse in a letter of April 14, 1927 (*L3*: 364).

[28] Barbara Goff and Michael Simpson, *Crossroads in the Black Aegean: Oedipus, Antigone, and Dramas of the African Diaspora* (Oxford: Oxford University Press, 2007), p. 8.

[29] *Ibid.*, p. 4.

[30] Omar Carlier, "Scholars and Politicians: An Examination of the Algerian View of Algerian Nationalism," *The Maghreb in Question: Essays in History & Historiography*, ed. Michel le Goll and Kenneth Perkins (Austin: University of Texas Press, 1997), 146. Clarisse Zimra points out that the novel "makes us aware of the contested construction of subject position in the shuffling and reshuffling of competing yet mutually imbricated *versions* of the past that are, also, *visions*." "Disorienting the Subject in Djebar's *L'Amour, la fantasia*," *Yale French Studies* 87 (1995), 156.

interpreters, geographers, ethnographers, linguists, botanists, diverse scholars
and professional scribblers" (*FE*: 45). Even so, the professionals fail to understand the local dialects, so that "outside of the battlefield speech is at a
standstill and a wilderness of ambiguity sets in" (*FE*: 33). ("Hors combat,
toute parole semble gelée et un désert d'ambiguïté s'installe," *F*: 52.) The
"wilderness" that signals the failure of translation to facilitate communication
between the soldiers and the native population creates the circumstance in
which the autobiographer assumes the role of historian.

Although the name of Antigone does not appear until midway through
Fantasia, already in the opening scene the narrator begins a tale of the
separation of sisters, like that between Antigone and Ismene, on the basis of
their access to and use of the dominant language. The autobiographical scene
of "a little Arab girl going to school for the first time . . . hand in hand with her
father" (*FE*: 3) introduces the theme of education that distinguishes girls who
read, although in the eyes of the neighbors reading brings misfortune.[31]
Although the other schoolgirls use their education to write to men in
French, an act specifically forbidden by their fathers, the narrator attempts
something more daring. Whereas the language of the love letters is the
language of imprisonment, she writes an autobiography that connects personal aspiration with local history, "weighed down under the oppressive
burden of my heritage" (*FE*: 218). Such writing shares the characteristics of
both the love letters and the reports of the French. At times "such an itch to
put pen to paper reminds me of the letter-writing mania which afflicted the
cloistered girls of my childhood: sending those endless epistles out into the
unknown brought them a breath of fresh air and a temporary escape from
their confinement" (*FE*: 44–5). The war correspondence of the French, "the
killers," offers an analogy with love letters in that both war and love inspire a
fear that is assuaged by writing (*FE*: 57). The chapters of the novel alternate
the French letters and memoirs that celebrate military success, albeit with an
undercurrent of anxiety, with oral reports of the sufferings of the communities that were annihilated. Situated between the French language of the
official report and the expression in French of naive hope, the narrator holds
colonial strategy and practice up to judgment.

The problem of the relationship to the language of the brother is the
fertile soil in which narration becomes linked to translation. During the war

[31] A character in Woolf's short story, "A Society," makes a similar point: "'If we hadn't learnt to read,'
she said bitterly, 'we might still have been bearing children in ignorance and that I believe was the
happiest life after all . . . I've done my best . . . to prevent my little girl from learning to read, but what's
the use?'" (*CSF*: 128).

of 1956–62 with France the relationship of sister to brother was intensified by secrecy, since many women either supported the maquisards with food and clothing, or joined them as nurses and soldiers. In the presence of foreign soldiers the language of the brother/sister relationship came under scrutiny, as it does in *Antigone* and in *Three Guineas*. The word *brother* assumed several meanings, as when a French soldier questions a young woman, who replies "I've been brought up according to the Arab word! The 'Brothers' are my brothers" (*FE*: 134). In another section of the novel a sister and brother who have been separated by war meet again on a city street. He lets fall the single word from their childhood, *hannouni*, a word of endearment "peculiar to the speech of our tribe – half-way between the Berber language of the highlands and the Arabic of the nearby city," that serves to identify them to each other, and to recall their childhood in the village. The word, which means something like "tender-hearted," is untranslatable into French or English. The untranslatable word is also a reminder of the taboos that are the basis of civilization. It suggests to the sister dreams of love and her "flirtatious" manner towards the brother, and "the barrier of incest" that separates them. Goff and Simpson note that the plays of the Sophoclean trilogy "fluctuate around the very access to civilization, almost before culture, where those taboos that are the conditions and grounds of social being, against incest, patricide, and the exposure of the dead, are inaugurated and tested."[32] Unlike the signifier *brother* that became the subject of contention, the "little language of love" between brother and sister escapes challenge because it is untranslatable.

Fantasia reenacts the Antigone myth as colonial history. Not only does it focus attention on the struggle between the state and patterns of kinship as Antigone understands them, but it spells out the horrors of live burial in more overtly political terms than the language of interment in *The Years*, as though the Greek text had articulated offstage an actual moment of colonial history. In 1845 the French in an outstandingly cruel maneuver herded the fifteen hundred members of the Ouled Riah tribe and their cattle into caves, and then built fires at the entrances, so that in a few hours all were asphyxiated. Nor does the matter end there, for Djebar's narrative is marked by the language of entombment. Matriarchs who are silenced and sequestered are said to endure "a living death" (*FE*: 181). The narrator writes of the colonized people's French as "this language [that] was formerly used to entomb my people . . . By laying myself bare in this language I start a fire which may consume me. For attempting an autobiography in the former

---

[32] Goff and Simpson, *Crossroads in the Black Aegean*, p. 19.

enemy's language" (*FE*: 215). ("Cette langue était autrefois sarcophagi des miens ... Me mettre à nu dans cette langue me fait entretenir un danger permanent de déflagration. De l'exercice de l'autobiographie dans la langue de l'adversaire d'hier," *F*: 300.) *Cave* also infiltrates the vocabulary, in an ominous sense. The poet's word for the cave, *antre*, suggests retreat into an obscure and unknown locus. Djebar puns on her position between – *entre*, French, Arabic and Berber, as "'antre', un antre – en anglais *a cave* – c'est-à-dire un ventre noir, une cave obscure" (*CV*: 33).[33]

A section entitled "Voice" invokes Antigone in the character of Cherifa, a sister who joins her two brothers in the maquis. When her younger brother is killed while trying to escape a French raid, Cherifa waits in a tree until the next day, and returns to his body. She tries to move it to a stream so that she can wash the corpse: "I wanted to wash him, at least to moisten his face. I took water in the palms of my hands; I started to sprinkle it over him, as one does for one's ablutions, without realizing that I was crying, sobbing all the time" (*FE*: 121). ("Je voulais le laver, lui mouiller au moins le visage. J'ai pris de l'eau dans mes paumes: j'ai commencé à l'en asperger, comme pour des ablutions, sans me rendre compte qu'en même temps je pleurais, je sanglotais," *F*: 173–4.) In the following section the narrator writes of Cherifa as a thirteen-year-old girl, "a new Antigone, mourning for the adolescent lying on the grass, stroking the half-naked corpse with henna-stained hands" (*FE*: 122). ("nouvelle Antigone pour l'adolescent étendu sur l'herbe, elle palpe, de ses doigts rougis au henné, le cadavre à demi dénudé," *F*: 175.) As in Sophocles' play her mourning cry "takes wing," like the cry of a bird. It is the cry of the mother who bore him, the cry of his sisters, the voices of the old women who are the traditional mourners. Twenty years later, when the narrator meets Cherifa, ailing and housebound, her voice recreates "the fear, the defiance, the intoxication in that forgotten place" (*FE*: 143). Although Cherifa's oral account, delivered from a sequestered place, like a voice from the tomb, serves to authenticate the narrative, at the same time its translation separates her from the narrator: "Strange little sister, whom henceforth I leave veiled or whose story I now transcribe in a foreign tongue" (*FE*: 141). The feminine subject that is released by a cry of mourning is inevitably compromised by translation into the language of the occupier: "I have captured your voice; disguised it with my French without clothing it" (*FE*: 142). ("Petite soeur étrange qu'en langue étrangère j'inscris désormais, ou que je voile ... Ta voix s'est prise au piège; mon parler français la déguise sans l'habiller," *F*: 201–2.)

---

[33] In *Between the Acts* Isa mutters to herself a line that suggests female entombment: "To what dark antre of the unvisited earth, or wind-brushed forest, shall we go now?," p. 51.

For a long time the literature of the Maghreb has been characterized by a discourse of liberation that was identified with the nation. Djebar has been praised for a courageous exploration that goes beyond questions of national identity to an understanding of the complex rapport among societies, cultures, and peoples.[34] She has rejected the alternatives of prophecy or report: "I do not claim to be either a fortune-teller or a scribe. On the territory of dispossession, I would that I could sing" (*FE*: 142) ("Je ne m'avance ni en diseuse, ni en scripteuse. Sur l'aire de la dépossession, je voudrais pouvoir chanter," *F*: 202.) That is, removed from the discourse of identity her Antigone stands for a lyricism that offers potentiality, what she *would*. Whereas the bird whose cry is heard when Antigone scatters dust on her brother's corpse marks the boundary between metamorphosis that might save her as it did Philomela, and metaphor that has no such power, in *Fantasia* the narrator actively seeks that territory and its risks, on the margin between languages and between prose and song. Yet a position so constructed comes at the cost of the relationship to her sisters. The conclusion is stark: "Torch-words which light up my women-companions, my accomplices; these words divide me from them once and for all" (*FE*: 142). ("Mots torches qui éclairent mes compagnes, mes complices; d'elles, définitivement, ils me séparent," *F*: 203.) Education in French and English, which makes translation the instrument of colonial history, has clearly reshaped the myth. Yet Antigone's attempt to revise the dominant language and its literary forms begins, as in the play, with the relationship of a girl to her brothers and sister, outside the gates of the city.

In responding to Cherifa the narrator questions literary terminology and reimagines her role. Cherifa herself, though a "conteuse," does not "raconte" (*F*: 201). Hers is a "récit," imbued with "nostalgie" (*F*: 202). That is, she does not merely describe the events of her life but creates a narrative of imagination. The narrator who would capture the voice of Cherifa advances "naked – since I have shed memories of childhood – I think of myself as bearing offerings, hands outstretched to whom? – to the Lords of yesterday's war, or to the young girls who lay in hiding and who now inhabit the silence that succeeds the battles . . . And I offer what?" (*FE*: 142).[35] ("Corps nu – puisque je me dépouille des souvenirs d'enfance –, je me veux porteuse d'offrandes, mains tendues vers qui, vers les Seigneurs de la guerre d'hier, ou vers les fillettes rôdeuses qui habitant le silence succédant

---

[34] Hafid Gafaïti, "Assia Djebar, l'écriture et la mort," *Assia Djebar*, ed. Najib Redouane and Yvette Benayoun-Szmidt (Paris: Harmattan, 2008), 227–38.
[35] Translation mine.

aux batailles ... Et j'offre quoi," *F*: 202.) This is the dilemma of the writer who translates an oral narrative: to do so disorients both her sense of the addressee and of literary forms, while focusing attention on the unavoidable complicity of the writing hand. The hand is the instrument of the sexualized body: "When the hand writes, slow positioning of the arm, carefully bending forward or leaning to one side, crouching, swaying to and fro, as in an act of love" (*FE*: 180). ("Quand le main écrit, lente posture du bras, précautionneuse pliure du flanc en avant ou sur le côté, le corps accroupi se balance comme dans un acte d'amour," *F*: 255.) In this new situation the feminine subject, assuming a position that is not supine, seems to court her jeopardy, while evolving towards an as yet to be identified reader.

In Djebar's telling the play becomes a tale of hands – Antigone's hands and the narrator's. As in Loraux's reading of hands in *Antigone*, what is at issue in the sentry's linking her to the deed of burying her brother is the authority of representation. The closing passage of *Fantasia* identifies Fromentin as "the painter who has accompanied me throughout my wanderings like a second father figure. Eugène Fromentin offers me an unexpected hand – the hand of an unknown woman he was never able to draw" (*FE*: 226). In 1853 as Fromentin was leaving an oasis where six months earlier a massacre had occurred, he picked up the severed hand of a woman: "I seize on this living hand, hand of mutilation and of memory, and I attempt to bring it the *qalam* [the Arabic word for *pen*]" (*FE*: 226). ("Plus tard, je me saisis de cette main vivante, main de la mutilation et du souvenir et je tente de lui faire porter le 'qalam,'" *F*: 313.) The narrator tentatively offers the pen to the hand that has been marked by a history of mutilation and murder.

Vaste est la prison opens and closes with the Woolfian image of the driven hand: "while my hand races and the father's language (the language now, moreover, transformed into a father tongue) slowly but surely undoes the wrapping cloths from a dead love ... while my hand races on" (*VPE*: 11–12). ("alors que ma main court, que la langue du père (langue d'ailleurs muée en langue paternelle) dénoue peu à peu, sûrement, les langes de l'amour mort ... alors que ma main court," *VP*: 11.) The novel ends with a repeated reminder of the urgent voices of the dead: "As my hand races across pads of paper, my voice is patiently wrested from me, or rather, and this is something I do not really understand, the sound of my heart is stripped from my body. The dead return to us; what do they desire in this sudden desert?" (*VPE*: 346). ("au fur et à mesure que ma main court sur les tablettes, la voix patiemment m'est arraché, ou plutôt, et je le comprends à peine, on m'écharne du son de mon coeur! Les morts nous reviennent et ils désirent quoi, dans ce soudain desert?," *VP*: 335.) The image of the racing hand transforms the autobiographical aspect of the narrative into a tale of the female writer's becoming a subject. In *Ces voix* Djebar wrote that she was besieged by the voices of her fictional characters, the sound of whose harsh breathing haunts her (*CV*: 29). The voices that only she can hear, far from being a symptom of mental disorder, are the voices that empower the subject to emerge. Mireille Calle-Gruber reads the image of the racing hand as a gesture of giving birth. It severs the connection with the matrilineal line in order to couple the language of the father as oppressor and at the same time as the giver of the gift of writing that becomes the language of emancipation.[36]

Reading Woolf's well-known description of completing *The Waves* in the context of the opening and closing passages of *Vaste est la prison* suggests the potential energy and unsettling aftermath of the *abusive* translation. On February 7, 1931 she wrote in her diary: "Here in the five minutes that remain, I must record, heaven be praised, the end of The Waves. I wrote the words O Death fifteen minutes ago, having reeled across the last ten pages with some moments of such intensity & intoxication that I seemed only to stumble after my own voice, or almost, after some sort of speaker (as when I was mad). I was almost afraid, remembering the voices that used to fly ahead" (*D4*: 10). Whereas in *Antigone* the difficulty of attributing the deed to her hand may be the sign of the gods, Daniel Ferrer approaches the matter from psychoanalysis, when he characterizes Woolf's lines as "opening on to the place from which the text as a whole is uttered . . . the place from which language draws back in the very acts of its enunciation."[37] Translation illuminates the occasion for such withdrawal. As a visual simile the image may be read in the historical context of the nineteenth-century hysteric responding to hypnotic suggestion. Djebar's image of herself as a child holding her father's hand as he leads her to the French school is a differently historicized image of writing in the brother's language. But in her novel the experience of the narrator's no less fraught passage into "the father's language" in Maghrebian culture does not carry the stigma of incapacitating disease.

Gayatri Spivak might interpret these passages as an instance of value formation in postcolonial writing: "You take positions in terms not of the discovery of historical or philosophical grounds, but in terms of

---

[36] Mireille Calle-Gruber, "Résistances de l'écriture ou l'ombilic de l'oeuvre à propos de *Vaste est la prison* d'Assia Djebar," *Postcolonialisme & autobiographie*, ed. Alfred Hornung and Ernstpeter Ruhe (Amsterdam and Atlanta: Rodopi, 1998), 139–40.

[37] Daniel Ferrer, *Virginia Woolf and the Madness of Language*, trans. Geoffrey Bennington and Rachel Bowlby (London and New York: Routledge, 1990), pp. 95–6.

reversing, displacing, and seizing the apparatus of value-coding."[38] The hand codes the value of the relationship between the body and the mind, and between the dead and the living. Woolf recognized that moments when the body is in control provided an opportunity to "seize the apparatus of value-coding," when she wrote in "On Being Ill" that "the poverty of the language" means that in order to write of illness and the body we require "a new language ... more primitive, more sensual, more obscene" (*E5*: 196). Yet in nearly all of the more than one thousand appearances of *hand* in her novels it is used to hold objects, grasp another hand, beat time, wave, etc. It emerges from the water in a brief passage in *To the Lighthouse*, and in *The Voyage Out* and *Orlando* the hand grasps a pen. Laura Marcus focuses on the insistence of Leonard and Virginia that, as the Hogarth Press expanded, "we shall continue to print the smaller editions with our own hands," a position that illuminates "the new relationship between the hand and the machine in the context of 'writing' in modernity."[39]

"The Evening Party" (*c.* 1918) weaves together the theme of the predicament of the writer in colonial society with an image of the hand, in the context of abusive writing. Against the planetary imagery of sky and ocean a group of readers and writers who are "unsubstantial figures" rehearse two models of writing. One is focused on the figure of an elderly professor who is an expert on Shelley's commas; the other model is built on "some imperceptible shock" experienced in childhood that encounters "a vast renunciation" when "some one talks of negroes" or a rubber plantation (*CSF*: 92–3). In a colonial society the writer who is forced to compromise between academic correctness and an inner vision of childhood faces a dilemma whose image is the hand that has "never for a second since I was born ceased to tell me of hot and cold, damp or dryness, I'm amazed that I should use this wonderful composition of flesh and nerve to write the abuse of life. Yet that's what we do. Come to think of it, literature is the record of our discontent" (*CSF*: 93).[40] *Abuse* in the English sense prompts the narrator's reticence when faced with the task of challenging a colonial society in which writing is premised upon "something visible to each of

---

[38] Gayatri Spivak, "Poststructuralism, Marginality, Post-Coloniality and Value," *Literary Theory Today*, ed. Peter Collier and Helga Geyer-Ryan (Ithaca, N.Y.: Cornell University Press, 1990), 226–8.

[39] Laura Marcus, "Virginia Woolf as Publisher and Editor: The Hogarth Press," *The Edinburgh Companion to Virginia Woolf and the Arts*, ed. Maggie Humm (Edinburgh: Edinbugh University Press, 2010), 263–74.

[40] Woolf wrote in her Greek diary of 1906 that "it is amusing to be able to abuse entirely." See chapter two, p. 28.

them" (*CSF*: 93).[41] Yet the writing hand that is notably absent from the image of the Woolf who "stumbles after" the language of the brother frames Djebar's narrative of the emergence of the woman writer from the colonial subject. Translation redefines the sense of what constitutes abuse, as Djebar transforms the personal suffering in the English text into an image of the subject who creates her historical circumstance.

If interpellation, in Althusser's sense of the term, is the subject's enactment into history, then we may read the scene in which the female writer's hand responds as the first step in which the subject is hailed in the dominant language. But whereas Woolf in the diary entry images herself as a woman whose voice in solitude is ventriloquized, Djebar assumes the perspective of the historian, and places her scene in the context of colonial education. In an image that she repeats throughout her work, the daughter who at first is led by the father's unusual gift of education seizes for her own uses the language that he teaches. The title of her book of essays, *Ces voix qui m'assiègent*, explains her inhibitions about writing autobiography in the context of the colonial culture of the Maghreb, which forbids the use of the first person, so that the mother's receiving a postcard addressed to her by her husband is considered a challenge to social mores. In both writers' work the process by which the subject acquires her language is the work of a lifetime, and the image of empowerment as a kind of seizure by or of the dominant language is its poetic.

Djebar prefaced Part One of *Vaste est la prison*, entitled "La Sieste," with the final line of Woolf's "A Haunted House": "Oh, is this *your* buried treasure? The light in the heart" (*CSF*: 117), translated as: "Est-ce donc cela votre trésor caché? Cette clarté au coeur." The citation, one among a half-dozen that Djebar chose from various writers, represents hegemony by an image of haunting that is a signature of the work of both. Woolf wrote "A Haunted House" in 1918–19, towards the end of World War I. In the midst of the influenza epidemic that she compared to "the black death," "buried treasure" suggests the thousands of war-related casualties (*D1*: 209). The story was published in time of war, in the posthumous *A Haunted House and Other Short Stories* (1944), and reappeared in Djebar's novel during a period of violence in Algerian history.

The story concerns the mode of presence of the phantom that in Derrida's phrase "inhabits without residing."[42] A couple lying in bed hear

---

[41] Among Woolf's references to the weariness of her hand as she wrote *Roger Fry*, see *D5*: 191, 217, 240.
[42] Jacques Derrida, *Specters of Marx: The State of the Debt, the Work of Mourning, and the New International*, trans. Peggy Kamuf (New York and London: Routledge, 1994), p. 18.

but do not reply to their spectral selves, as though, Woolf wrote of Walter Scott, they were "ghosts living within ourselves" (*E*2: 218–19).[43] Nena Skrbic observes that "the story is haunted by its open-ended and multiple signage, in which the sense of the unseen is coincident with the play of narrative."[44] The signage of the unseen is suggested by the shutting and opening of a door heard "gently knocking like the pulse of a heart" (*CSF*: 117). The narrative is structured by doubling: "My hands were empty," and the house is "all empty." The pair "Whatever hour you woke" and "it wasn't you that woke us" unsettles the reference of "you," and the possibility of dialogue. "Buried treasure" is repeatedly attributed, but is without a referent until the final line brings closure to the story and to the sign at the moment of awakening. Throughout the story the known is paired with the unknown, the actual with the virtual. The phantoms and the sleepers, divided by death ("death was between us"), inhabit the adjoining worlds of the visible and the invisible that become accessible to each other during sleep. The ghosts, who address only each other, are overheard, and become visible as shadows and reflections in the window pane. This sense of adjoining worlds upsets the conventions of representation, and suggests the need for a new way of reading. In fact the narrative "one," and later the "I" who has access to both worlds, is a reader holding a pencil.[45]

"A Haunted House" gives the coordinates of a ghostly past, a somnolent present, and a future figured as awakening. It captures the moment when, in Ranjana Khanna's study of colonial melancholy: "the phantom of the secret manifests itself in language as symptom when the secret is in danger of being revealed."[46] What is unsayable in colonialism manifests itself as "a spectral remainder of the inassimilable colonial structure of the nation state," with the result that melancholy is not an illness but a critical term for the analysis of colonialism. "A Haunted House" is Woolf's critique of colonial ideology as a secret, the "it" for which the ghosts are searching upstairs, in the garden, and in the drawing room, a search that ends when "it" is named by the

---

[43] After the death of Julian Bell, Woolf wrote of him as a ghost walking beside her, and hearing his voice from the grave (*D*5: 107, 110, 164).

[44] Nena Skrbic, *Wild Outbursts of Freedom: Reading Virginia Woolf's Short Fiction* (Westport, Conn.: Praeger, 2004), p. 137.

[45] Although I prefer to reserve *translation* to refer to the relationship between two texts, Freud used it and *transformation* to refer to the work of the narrator who deals with "the preconscious remains of the day" by "translating it into action." Sigmund Freud, *The Interpretation of Dreams*, trans. Joyce Crick (Oxford: Oxford University Press, 1999), chapter seven, "The Psychology of the Dream-Processes," especially pp. 334, 346–8, 365, and 375.

[46] Ranjana Khanna, *Dark Continents: Psychoanalysis and Colonialism* (Durham, N.C.: Duke University Press, 2003), p. 25.

sleeper who wakes and cries: "Oh, is this *your* buried treasure? The light in the heart." The secret is encoded in the history of exploration and domestic confinement as romanticized gender roles. The "ghostly couple" moves from house to garden during light and darkness, summer and winter, while the narrator leaves her book to search the house: "What did I want to find?" The search widens to image exploration on a global scale: "He left it, left her, went North, went East, saw the stars turned in the Southern sky" (*CSF*: 116). The passage prefigures the image in *To the Lighthouse* of Mr. Ramsay's fantasies of imperial exploration, and "those fumbling airs that breathe and bend over the bed" in "Time Passes" (*TL*: 191). In the story the secret manifests itself as a marginal disturbance below the threshold of recognition, "like the pulse of a heart," or the opening and shutting of doors.

In "La Sieste" the narrator awakens from a restorative sleep that has banished an unhappy love like a bad dream, so that she is "arisen as if from a long illness." The effort to understand is superseded: "I make an effort to try to understand, then very gradually, uneasily, I sense finally with certainty, something both new and vulnerable, a beginning of something, I don't know what, something strange . . . I am carrying some change inside me, and it floods through me" (*VPE*: 21). ("Je fais effort pour comprendre peu à peu, malaisément, puis avec certitude, que quelque chose de neuf et de vulnérable à la fois, un commencement de je ne sais quoi d'étrange . . . Je porte en moi un changement et j'en sais inondée," *VP*: 20.) The novel opens with a scene of the subject at the moment when she emerges, as in *Fantasia*, undefended and anticipatory. The narrative of *Vaste est la prison* envisions what follows in a colonized society when the narrator becomes a subject as the result of an awakening in which the body is for the moment ascendant. "Clarté au coeur" shifts the emphasis of "light in the heart," to suggest that Woolf's mysterious story has prompted a historical study of female subjectivity.

One of the most elusive aspects of translation concerns the ethical question that is posed when the narrator undertakes to translate the private rituals of mourning into a dominant language. What are the costs of translating sounds of grief into the language of the state and the courts that the other mourners do not command? Whereas Djebar poses such translation as a special problem of Maghrebian culture, in some of Woolf's work it appears that the translator faces a similar alienation from the accepted uses of language. In *Vaste est la prison* an ethical problem arises when during the ritual of mourning the narrator separates herself from the group of mourners in order to translate the voice of the other. Since Djebar's narrator figures herself among the female mourners, she hesitates to translate a Berber women's ritual into the French language. In Woolf's short story "Sympathy," narrative is created when the narrator moves from a fantasy of mourning distinguished by ingestion and aggression to representing her loss, a process of recognizing the dead that constitutes the authority of the feminine subject within the constraints of print culture. In the work of both narrative fiction becomes the place to explore the ethical dimension of translation.

Although Woolf's knowledge of the language of psychoanalysis is not well documented, "Sympathy" seems to me to engage the idea of *introjection*, a term that was central to debates in the early days of the British psychoanalytic movement, and especially in the work of Melanie Klein and her associates. The term had been introduced by Sándor Ferenczi in 1909, in an essay which was translated as "Introjection and Transference," chapter two of *Sex in Psychoanalysis* (1916). He associated the term with *transference*, as the analysand's "extension of his circle of interest, i.e. introjection," in order to suppress certain unconscious associations.[47] Whereas the healthy person is aware of this activity, the neurotic manifests introjection when he transfers his feelings onto the analyst. Ferenczi developed a theory of "transference therapy ... [as] a natural way of healing ... I deny, however, that transference is harmful, and surmise rather that ... the ancient belief, which strikes its roots deep in the mind of the people, will be confirmed, that diseases are to be cured by 'sympathy.'"[48] The key terms, repeated throughout the essay, are *introjection* and *sympathy*.[49]

Nicolas Abraham and Maria Torok between 1959 and 1975 evolved new meanings of "introjection." They drew on Freud's essay "Mourning and Melancholia" (1917) and on Ferenczi's article, "On the Definition of Introjection" (1912), to analyze *incorporation* and *introjection* as two forms of mourning. After suffering a loss "incorporation" makes it tempting to substitute fantasy for the work of psychic reorganization. "If accepted and worked through, the loss would require major readjustment. But the fantasy of incorporation merely simulates profound psychic transformation through magic; it does so by implementing literally something that has only figurative meaning. So in order not to have to 'swallow' a loss, we fantasize swallowing that which has been lost, as if it were some kind of thing."[50] Such losses "stand like tombs in the life of the ego."[51]

[47] Sándor Ferenczi, *Sex in Psychoanalysis*, trans. Ernest Jones (New York: Basic Books, 1916), p. 50.
[48] *Ibid.*, p. 57.   [49] "Sympathy" is also a key word in Woolf's "On Being Ill" (1926).
[50] Nicolas Abraham and Maria Torok, *The Shell and the Kernel: Renewals of Psychoanalysis*, vol. 1, trans. Nicholas T. Rand (Chicago: University of Chicago Press, 1994), p. 126.
[51] *Ibid.*, p. 114.

Incorporation may be figured as the mouth empty of food or words: "Learning to fill the emptiness of the mouth with words is the initial model for introjection."[52] Whereas incorporation involves the fantasy that the object has been taken into the body, introjection, a more elusive term, refers to an ongoing process in which loss stimulates language and in particular the capacity for metaphor. Incorporation works like magic, but introjection requires the slow and painful process of using language to assimilate loss and to reorganize the psyche. Given the difficulty of introjection, the temptation to regress to incorporation remains a nostalgic possibility. We can see this regression "when words fail to fill the subject's void and hence an imaginary thing is inserted into the mouth in their place."[53] In the work of Woolf and Djebar the narrator moves tentatively from an understanding of incorporation to writing narrative as introjection, and in so doing translation into the dominant language becomes a problem of writing the untranslatable.

Derrida writes of incorporation and introjection, that "Everything is played out on the borderline which divides and opposes the two terms."[54] Work on the borderline is an ongoing process: "Mourning *must* be impossible. Successful mourning is failed mourning. In successful mourning I incorporate the one who has died, I assimilate him to myself, I reconcile myself with death, and consequently I deny death and the alterity of the dead other and of death as other ... Where the introjection of mourning succeeds, mourning annuls the other."[55] Yet the two states of mourning impinge on each other. In incorporation the process of keeping the dead alive within the mourner in effect shifts the emphasis from mourning to the construction of the self as a kind of jailer, who preserves not the dead other "but a certain topography it keeps safe, intact, untouched by the very relationship with the other to which, paradoxically enough, introjection is more open." Yet such is the temptation merely to "mime introjection," that the features of incorporation may reappear whenever the laborious processes of introjection falter.[56] In arguing for introjection as a process that if one is to honor the dead must be incomplete and ongoing, Derrida makes room for the emergence of the subject that signifies its presence by resistance to successful mourning. He insists on the ongoing nature of mourning as "the inevitability of the work of mourning – which is not one work among others

[52] *Ibid.*, p. 128. [53] *Ibid.*, pp. 128–9.
[54] Jacques Derrida, "Fors," trans. Barbara Johnson, *Georgia Review* 31 (1977), 70.
[55] Jacques Derrida and Elizabeth Roudinesco, *For What Tomorrow: A Dialogue*, trans. Jeff Fort (Stanford: Stanford University Press, 2004), pp. 159–60.
[56] *Ibid.*

but the overdetermining mark of all work."[57] In Djebar and Woolf the subject manifests much more than an accommodation of psychoanalytic studies of mourning to literary purposes; rather because of the special role of women as mourners it witnesses the reinstatement of feminine heritage within the domain of history: "We think the dead are absent but, transformed into witnesses, they want to write through us" (*VPE*: 357). ("Les morts qu'on croit absents se muent en témoins qui, à travers nous, désirent écrire," *VP*: 346.) In Derrida's phrase the translator protects "the language that does not present itself." That the mourning subject exists in order to resist closure and so to sustain mourning is perhaps its most important ethical claim.

"Sympathy" (*c.* 1919) seems custom-made to show how narrative is derived from the move from an imagined incorporation to introjection, while suggesting that closure is imposed by print culture. Whereas Djebar presents the problem of translating a female ritual of mourning in Berber culture, Woolf's story shows how death opens the rift between the language of grief and the dominant language that stresses inheritance. The divided subject emerges on the borderline between incorporation and introjection. The narrator, reading in the newspaper of the death of a young friend, Humphry Hammond, imagines the circumstances of his death, and the subsequent ceremonial visits and meals to be shared with his widow Celia. In the manuscript Woolf bracketed this strange image of the narrator's undefended hand: "The pity which bids me tender my hand to her to bite becomes, or will become, an impulse of compassion which in its generosity appears to her contemptuous" (*CSF*: 103). The breakdown in communication is figured when the writer puts her hand in jeopardy, "outstretched" as in Djebar's image of the poet who would sing. The image of ingestion comes up again a few sentences further on, when the narrator imagines that Celia "sucks" at a flower and discovers a nest of bird's eggs. Yet incorporation, however violent, has the advantage of encrypting the ghost: the narrator regards Celia with "envy," because "the emptiness has for her its ghost" (*CSF*: 102).

The transition away from incorporation begins, in Abraham and Torok's words, when "the wants of the original oral vacancy are remedied by being turned into verbal relationships with the speaking community at large . . . This is how the literal ingestion of foods becomes introjection when viewed figuratively."[58] So in "Sympathy" the narrator, newspaper in hand, images

[57] *Ibid.*   [58] Abraham and Torok, *The Shell and the Kernel*, p. 128.

death as an eclipse, revealing that without "impediment . . . my friends pass dark across the horizon," as they take their leave and gaily troop to the water's edge to set sail. These visual images inspired by mourning enable the narrator to hypothesize the ghost as a figure who beckons from the border: "The simple young man whom I hardly knew had, then concealed in him the immense power of death. He had removed the boundaries and fused the separate entities by ceasing . . . He silently withdrew, and though his voice was nothing his silence is profound. He has laid his life down like a cloak for us to tread over. Where does he lead us? We come to the edge and look out" (*CSF*: 104). The narrator laments that she must return to the smaller world where "the horizon [is] shut in" (*CSF*: 104). Closure is achieved with the arrival of a dinner invitation that makes clear that Humphry senior has died, the younger Humphry lives, and the narrator has attributed to Celia her own incorporation of the dead, as though mourning were the occasion to imagine another as the self. In fact Celia's mourning is expressed in terms of inheritance. The death of the older Humphry, she writes, means that "we shall I suppose, move into the big house" (*CSF*: 105). The narrator constitutes her position by the ability to imagine incorporation as violent ingestion, introjection as a painterly image of the horizon, and narrative closure as a return to the print world of the newspaper and the letter.

Although Abraham and Torok do not deal with literary language, in "Sympathy" it would seem that introjection is the goal of narrative. At first death inspires images of infantile biting and sucking that suggest violent incorporation that is the prelude to the image of a widened horizon like that seen during an eclipse, a momentary enlargement of the visible world that leaves the narrator poorer afterwards, as though a window had opened and then closed. It is the moment when the subject seizes an image of the visible, as in the party scene in *Mrs. Dalloway*, when the window opens a visual perspective beyond the language of social communication. The ghost is also the occasion of the doubling of names, Humphry son and father, that suggests parallel worlds, and of a narrator who creates Celia's world, in a language that Celia herself does not command. Is Woolf saying that although fiction resembles mourning as the privileged site of the fruitful interaction between incorporation and the attempt at introjection, the language of print culture imposes arbitrary closure on a process better left unfinished?

Several studies of Woolf associate her treatment of mourning with a modernist aesthetic that rejects Victorian rituals. John Mepham writes that "writing about the dead demanded a literary form that is in some ways more like song than story, in which image and rhythm supplant plot and commentary as the basic architectonic devices."[59] Susan Bennett Smith demonstrates Woolf's resistance to Victorian conventions and the way in which a work of art is an alternative that "allows grief to be worked through."[60] Tammy Clewell addresses "the ethics of anticonsolatory mourning" in Woolf.[61] Christine Froula situates Woolf's mourning in the context of English elegy, and the historical analysis of the aftermath of war: "As powerless as the eloquence of Keynes and Freud to forestall another civil war, Woolf's elegiac art battles alongside them on the side of Love for a future that history had not yet, in 1925, foreclosed."[62] Mark Spilka writes, in *Virginia Woolf's Quarrel with Grieving*, that although her fiction contains only two deathbed scenes, she maintained a "characteristic difficulty with grieving." Herbert Duckworth, Julia Stephen's first husband, was "the ghostly robber . . . the sorrow waiting behind her into which she privately dipped, as Virginia would later dip, for her lost dead." In fact Woolf took all the "ghosts" of Julia, Stella, Thoby, and Leslie with her into her fiction. "Her struggle to put these spirits to rest is one of the more heroic annals of modern fiction."[63] Save for Mepham's these studies all assume a self fully present to itself that necessarily excludes the subject that is manifested by the division that occurs during mourning.

In a study of "Time Passes" that has far-reaching consequences for all of Woolf's work David Sherman writes of the subject that is divided in mourning as anticipating concepts that appear in ethics and philosophy. In "Time Passes" and other works we hear "the voice of a subject that is other than and outside itself; in this difference from itself, it is able to approach the difference of others without subsuming them as the same."[64] Sherman's discussion of the self that emerges during moments of "narrative insomnia" links "A Haunted House" to the scenes from Djebar's work that I have been discussing. This subject that "enters the text to lament the fatal constrictions of identity" is the Antigone of Djebar and Woolf, whose

---

[59] John Mepham, "Mourning and Modernism," *Virginia Woolf: New Critical Essays*, ed. Patricia Clements and Isobel Grundy (London: Vision Press, and Totowa, N.J.: Barnes & Noble, 1983), 143.

[60] Susan Bennett Smith, "Reinventing Grief Work: Virginia Woolf's Feminist Representations of Mourning in *Mrs. Dalloway* and *To the Lighthouse*," *Twentieth Century Literature* 41 (1995), 323.

[61] Tammy Clewell, "Consolations Refused: Virginia Woolf, the Great War, and Modernist Mourning," *Modern Fiction Studies* 50 (2004), 208.

[62] Christine Froula, "*Mrs. Dalloway*'s Postwar Elegy: Women, War, and the Art of Mourning," *Modernism/Modernity* 9 (2002), 157.

[63] Mark Spilka, *Virginia Woolf's Quarrel with Grieving* (Lincoln: University of Nebraska Press, 1980), pp. 36 and 46.

[64] David Sherman, "A Plot Unraveling into Ethics: Woolf, Levinas, and 'Time Passes,'" *Woolf Studies Annual* 13 (2007), 166.

"authority is derived not from omniscience, but from its mastery of frag-mentariness, contingency and irony."[65] I would add that the subject Sherman analyzes is a postwar phenomenon, and that its ability "to look at interiority from its beyond" is the aspect of Woolf's work that invites translation into other languages and cultures.

At the heart of *Vaste est la prison* is a chapter on the narrator's mother, whose incorporation of her dead son is linked to Berber as a dead language, in contrast to the narrator's attempts at introjection. Two deaths are represented, that of a daughter and a son, in terms of their impact on the language of mourning. The female mourners hear a Berber lament that they cannot translate, while the narrator shows that the process from incorpor-ation to introjection depends precisely on translation. As in the story of the Tower of Babel, the scene of translation is linked to questions of genealogy and fecundity. The narrator is the daughter of Bahia: "I, Isma, the narrator, the descendant through the youngest daughter" (*VPE*: 234). The chapter is one of seven that tell of "the arable woman," a term that Djebar drew from an agricultural economy to figure the potential fecundity of the female subject.

During an outbreak of typhoid fever, Bahia, the narrator's mother, as a six-year-old child watches beside the body of her eldest sister, who has died. During the vigil over the corpse, two women recite verse. A woman from the capital who speaks a learned language ("une langue savante," *VP*: 236) recites in French "O my other self, my shadow, my one so like me, / You are gone, you have deserted me, left me arable, / Your pain, a plowshare, turned me over and seeded me with tears." A second woman tears her face. Shaken by a spasm, she improvises in Berber, a language that the others do not understand: "*Meqqwer lhebs iy inyan / Ans'ara el ferreg felli*" (*VPE*: 236). Another sister, speaking to "those of you who do not understand the language of our ancestors," translates the words into French: "So vast the prison crushing me / Release, where will you come from?" (*VPE*: 243). ("Vaste est la prison qui m'écrase / D'où me viendras-tu, déliverance?" *VP*: 237.) The child Bahia, as she repeats to herself the words of the lament in Arabic or in Berber, becomes mute. On the first anniversary of the death, when she is taken to visit a sorceress who is skilled in freeing a person who has been kidnapped by a beloved who is now among the dead, her speech is suddenly restored, as if by magic. When as a young woman, Bahia gives birth to an infant who dies at six months, she refuses to visit his grave. It is, writes the narrator, because the two bereavements together had the effect of

[65] *Ibid.*

burying the language, "as if the language vanished into thin air" (*VPE*: 251). "And the dead child remained entombed in her memory forever" (*VPE*: 251). ("Et l'enfant mort est resté toujours, en sa mémoire-tombe, l'enfant endormi," *VP*: 246.)

The association of Berber with death and lamentation seems to have removed it from the world, as in fact the death of an older generation can turn an oral language into a ghost.[66] Yet lines from the Berber song entitle the novel. Mireille Calle-Gruber argues that the narrative of the deaths in the life of Bahia creates consequences that are analogical rather than logical; the phenomenon becomes an emblem, the anecdote a symptom.[67] Bahia is always at the point of losing language or losing the other.[68] The story of the maternal language is paradigmatic in the sense that in the life story of the mother we find the place where language is lost, and reborn as lyric, song, trance, cry, and silence.[69] The sense of sororal grieving becomes a form of knowledge, of knowing that it is necessary to grieve: "Bref, écrire comme on porte le deuil."[70] Calle-Gruber has identified the task that the subject faces, that is to make signs of sounds, in order to create from historically disparate experiences a narrative that reflects the history of the Berber language in another register.

The narrator of *Mrs. Dalloway* interprets the song of the old woman at the tube station that focuses the novel around the loss of others and the loss of language as a problem of translation. The passage poses the question, how to protect a language that over time has become untranslatable in the sense of becoming foreign to itself. At the moment when Peter Walsh realizes the hopelessness of his love for Clarissa, which he generalizes as the female failure to understand passion, he is interrupted, and his feelings restated in another register, by the sound of a beggar woman singing of lost love. The song

issued ... from a tall quivering shape, like a funnel, like a rusty pump, like a wind-beaten tree for ever barren of leaves, which lets the wind run up and down its branches singing

> *ee um fah um so*
> *foo swee too eem oo.*
>
> (*MD*: 80–1)

---

[66] Djebar describes her writing as "ce travail d'exhumation ... ramener toujours ce qui est enterré" (*CV*: 48).

[67] Mireille Calle-Gruber, *Assia Djebar ou la résistance de l'écriture: regards d'un écrivain d'Algérie* (Paris: Maisonneuve et Larose, 2001), p. 87.

[68] *Ibid.*, p. 86.   [69] *Ibid.*, p. 88.   [70] *Ibid.*, p. 95.

J. Hillis Miller, who interprets Woolf's novel as "a resurrection of ghosts from the past," reads the song as a paraphrase of Richard Strauss' "Allerseelen," on the basis that lines from the English translation are silently quoted in the novel. The title of the song commemorates the occasion of a collective resurrection of the spirits that links Peter Walsh and the other guests at Clarissa's party.[71] The ancient song of love is untranslatable, or as the narrator puts it, sung "with an absence of all human meaning." The voice echoes "the age of tusk and mammoth," that sings of a future "earth, now become a mere cinder of ice" (*MD*: 81). Not only does the song allude to a time commensurate with the life cycle of the planet and its species, but it dissolves the nature/culture distinction as well: the voice "of no age or sex," whose song is "the voice of an ancient spring ... fertilizing" (*MD*: 80–1). It is followed by the narrator's disquisition on love "which has lasted a million years," which rather than translate responds to loss in another register, from the perspective of the last day of the universe.

What is the emotional force of the sounds that Djebar calls "a deep song strangled in the throat," whether "*ee um fah*" or "*Meqqwer lhebs*," which focuses not only a particular scene but the poetics of mourning and the role of the untranslatable in the entire novel? What are the peculiar powers of sounds that disavow any claim to agency or representation? Do Woolf and Djebar impose a new test on the iterability that in Derrida's terms is the condition of historicity?[72] The songs are untranslatable in the sense that they open a perspective on history that is older than text or alphabet. They envision iterability as a movement from the ancient Berber tongue or from the time of mammoth and mastodon to the present. From a point in a future that Woolf measured in astronomical time they open a window on a past unrepresented by records, whose power and value lie precisely in being untranslatable.

When the dead reappear in Woolf's novels they are often a reminder that mourning is a kind of blind spot in national history. In *Mrs. Dalloway* Clarissa Dalloway and Peter Walsh are each haunted by "spectral presences" (*MD*: 56). Unlike Septimus Smith's dead comrade Evans, these specters from the unconscious realm lack an identity, yet they have the power to motivate Clarissa's hatred of Miss Kilman, and Peter's dream of irremediable loss. A sentence that appears only in "Mrs. Dalloway on

---

[71] J. Hillis Miller, *Fiction and Representation: Seven English Novels* (Cambridge, Mass.: Harvard University Press, 1982), pp. 189–91.

[72] Jacques Derrida, "'This Strange Institution Called Literature': An Interview with Jacques Derrida," *Acts of Literature*, ed. Derek Attridge (New York and London: Routledge, 1992), 64.

Bond Street" suggests what is at stake. As Clarissa looks at the books in the shop window, she recalls the line from *Cymbeline*: "Fear no more the heat o' the sun ... And now can never mourn, can never mourn, she repeated ... for it ran in her head; the test of great poetry; the moderns had never written anything one wanted to read about death, she thought" (*CSF*: 149). It is as though Clarissa seeks in literature the means to introjection, in order to represent the loss she suffers. The specters serve as a reminder of the political consequences when introjection fails, so that hatred and loss become entombed as the residue of war. In this respect Woolf may be closer to Djebar than to English modernists, in her emphasis on the consequences for the feminine subject when mourning has been prevented.

In *To the Lighthouse* the contrast between Cam and Lily plays out the significance of introjection in the lives of two women. The ghosts in the last section figure the comparison between Cam's passage to womanhood and Lily Briscoe's painting. Cam, trapped in a small boat with her father and brother, longs for a freedom that she images as an island peopled by "ghosts" that are "free to come and go." To associate the ghost with freedom is the mark of Lily's initial misapprehension of Mrs. Ramsay as "ghost, air, nothingness, a thing you could play with easily and safely at any time of day or night, [until] ... she put her hand out and wrung the heart thus" (*TL*: 170). When Lily cries out the name of her friend, at first silently, but then aloud, does her cry summon the ghost who appears, albeit as "some trick of the painter's eye"? (*TL*: 172). As in "Sympathy" narrative involves a movement from what Lily considers "these emotions of the body" towards a painterly image, Mrs. Ramsay wearing a "wreath of white flowers." And, curiously, when Lily thinks of Mr. Carmichael, who has the capacity to hear her unspoken thoughts, she imagines a pool and an image of the literally disembodied hand: "something would emerge. A hand would be shoved up" but it is a hand that does not yet hold the brush or pen (*TL*: 170). In comparison to Cam, whose suffering remains mute, Lily moves towards assimilating her loss of Mrs. Ramsay. When she is able, after encountering her friend as a ghost, to create "a sense of someone there," she becomes the subject who has "had her vision," distinguished from the painter by her capacity as a mourner whose work is necessarily unfinished (*TL*: 198).

Whereas all the figures in *The Waves* recall Percival in moral terms, as "the body of the complete human being whom we have failed to be, but at the same time, cannot forget," Bernard's characterization is figured on the borderline that divides and opposes incorporation and introjection (*W*: 185).

In Derrida's phrase he carries "the dead other in me."[73] In the holograph draft Woolf wrote of "the spectral landscape wh. becomes visible in the last chapter" (*Hol W*: 758). There Bernard says simply, "I carry a dead body about the world with me" (*Hol W*: 719). The published version reveals a Bernard whose creative agency is linked to his negotiations with the spectral. In the well-known scene in which he sees himself as "a man without a self," he experiences the loss of his multiple selves: "No more to hear echoes, no more to see phantoms, to conjure up no opposition, but to walk always unshadowed, making no impress upon the dead earth" (*W*: 191–2). He is "thin as a ghost," as though his social identity offered him protection from the spectral (*W*: 192). Those ghosts that haunt Bernard are "shadows of people one might have been; unborn selves"; their absence leaves him impoverished (*W*: 194). Percival has become a phantom in the sense that although constantly present he eludes representation: "What is startling, what is unexpected, what we cannot account for, what turns symmetry to nonsense – that comes suddenly to my mind, thinking of him. The little apparatus of observation is unhinged" (*W*: 162). Bernard's continuing sense of personal and narrative incompleteness situates his narrative on the border between incorporation of the dead body and the labor of introjection. His position is figured at the end of the novel by the solitary meal he consumes – "We have been taking into our mouths the bodies of dead birds" – and the train journey home, a kind of closure that he is reluctant to undertake (*W*: 196). Yet far from extending his hand as an invitation, he sees it in language like that in "The Evening Party": "I could worship my hand even, with its fan of bones laced by blue mysterious veins and its astonishing look of aptness, suppleness and ability to curl softly or suddenly crush – its infinite sensibility" (*W*: 194). Rather than being the hand of the subject that grasps the pen or gestures towards the other, it is an executive hand that commands his adoration.

In order to mourn the deaths of her friends among western and Algerian writers Djebar welcomed the ghost as a necessary element of her subjectivity. She spoke on the violence of 1993 in Algeria in an address to the Strasbourg Parliament of Writers, convened in order to protest the violence in Sarajevo and Eastern Europe as well as in Algeria. It was the first time, writes Clarisse Zimra, that Djebar "has come publicly in voice as well as in print, to an openly political position regarding current events in her

---

[73] Jacques Derrida, "The Deaths of Roland Barthes," *Philosophy and Non-Philosophy since Merleau-Ponty*, trans. Pascale-Anne Brault and Michael Naas, ed. Hugh J. Silverman (London: Routledge, 1988), p. 267.

country ... She indicts the official governmental policy ... But she also indicts a whole generation of writers and thinkers, herself among them, who have not spoken soon enough and loudly enough."[74] As Mildred Mortimer reminds us, Djebar "comes to autobiography fully aware that subjectivity in life and fiction are transgressions in Algerian culture ... Islamic culture is bound to the *non-dire*, or unspoken, in other words, to silence; it prohibits personal disclosure."[75] At this charged moment of history Djebar spoke of her personal sense of haunting: "For I am haunted, personally – in the calm before the storm – by the long and abiding state of morbidity in which Algerian culture has lingered.[76] Although some of the specters in her fiction are her maternal forebears, like the paternal grandmother mourned by the narrator of *Vaste est la prison*, more often Djebar's ghosts are those of the war dead. In the printed version of *Le blanc de l'Algérie* (1995) Djebar mourns the death of friends who haunt her as though they had not been buried. She turns to a European model of subjectivity, in this passage on Dante, who writes of "the absent dear to us": "I ask nothing: only that they continue to haunt us, that they live within us. But in which language?"[77] To ask "nothing" says that the subject makes no appeal, and does not attempt to open a dialogue, but rather suspends speech and the self, so as to be in a position actively to receive, all the more necessary when as we see in the last sentence translation is both central and problematic.

The Woolf whose work was attractive to Djebar can be glimpsed in some recent attempts to study her attitudes towards race and class from a perspective that moves beyond the concepts of personal and national identity. Mark Hussey counters the frequent attacks on Woolf and Bloomsbury on the grounds of patriotism and class by arguing that "her narratives set individual consciousness in tension with [the] mass mind" that represents the values of Thatcher's Britain.[78] Woolf typically marked her text as spoken by a subject, from a specified standpoint, for instance "the educated man's daughter" in *Three Guineas*.[79] Patricia McManus broadens

---

[74] Clarisse Zimra, "Assia Djebar: The White of Algeria: Introduction," trans. Andrew Benson, *Yale French Studies* 87 (1995), 138–41.

[75] Mildred Mortimer, "Assia Djebar's *Algerian Quartet*: A Study in Fragmented Autobiography," *Research in African Literatures* 28 (1997), 103.

[76] Zimra, "Assia Djebar: The White of Algeria," 142.

[77] Assia Djebar, *Algerian White*, trans. David Kelley and Marjolijn de Jager (New York and London: Seven Stories Press, 2000), p. 52.

[78] Mark Hussey, "Mrs. Thatcher and Mrs. Woolf," *Modern Fiction Studies* 50–1 (2004), 10.

[79] *Ibid.*, p. 21. See also Urmila Seshagiri, who argues that Lily Briscoe's "Chinese eyes" associate Woolf's art with non-western traditions, in "Orienting Virginia Woolf: Race, Aesthetics, and Politics in *To the Lighthouse*," *Modern Fiction Studies* 50 (2004), 58–84.

the conception of the public sphere in which as an intellectual Woolf positioned herself by studying "not Woolf's understanding of her historical moment but the conditions which enabled, which provided terms of, that understanding ... and the sense of that position's historical vulnerability."[80] Woolf's engagement with translation as a means to subvert the dominant discourse created the conditions in which Djebar, who records her agonizing decision to represent her mother tongue and its culture in the language of the colonial occupier, found Woolf's position habitable.

Reading *Antigone* in wartime conditions suggests why a key text of colonial education dramatized the struggle to create a language that could challenge the limitations of kinship and nation. It suggests that war offers women the opportunity to envision and to represent their subjectivity. It involves the interaction of inter-intralingual translation that is the chief feature of twentieth-century *Antigone*'s heroism in German classical studies. Yet Djebar and Woolf read her differently. Confronted with the deaths during war of her friends and her family, Djebar put more emphasis on burial, *sépulture*, as in the title *La femme sans sépulture* (2002), and in the many scenes throughout her work of grieving women. Woolf's inability to mourn ("I felt nothing") may illustrate an aspect of British culture that resulted in her emphasis on the aftereffects of war. That is, mourning in her work is experienced less directly as grief than as the search for a narrative that comes into existence as the transition from incorporation to introjection, the mourning process that in *Vaste* is enacted as a social ritual. In this circumstance narrative originates in the unmediated cry of the grieving bird/ sister that both invites and defies translation. When de Man queried Benjamin's assigning the central role to the translator rather than to the poet/reader, he seemed to assume that translation necessarily involves readers, whereas the figure of Antigone involves the larger challenge to translation of utterance in the natural world.

New translations have questioned the assumption that the Tower of Babel represents colonial discord. Paul Ricoeur reconsiders the Chouraki translation of Genesis into French (mentioned in the Introduction), and finds no violence in the action of the Lord that scattered men abroad: rather the census of tongues and nations that introduces the story suggests that there is no single standard for a good translation. Although in our culture, Ricoeur argues, certain texts are translated over and over, a perfect translation cannot be achieved, and we must settle for "an equivalence without

[80] Patricia McManus, "The 'Offensiveness' of Virginia Woolf: From a Moral to a Political Reading," *Woolf Studies Annual* 14 (2008), 96.

identity." The translation as an act of "*linguistic hospitality*" arises from the fact that the translator serves two masters, "the foreigner in his strangeness, the reader in his desire for appropriation."[81] His translator, who is "at the risk of serving and of betraying two masters," recalls Djebar's image of the poet who tenders her hand both to "les Seigneurs de la guerre d'hier" and to the young Algerian girls whom the war reduced to silence. Ricoeur's translator recalls as well the implications for translation in Woolf's assertion at the close of *Three Guineas* that "we are ourselves" the figure that "is called in German and Italian Führer or Duce; in our own language Tyrant or Dictator" (*TG*: 129). Faced with the political and ethical implications of translation, Woolf's urgent call to "find new words" established a kind of forward position that years after her death could be read as welcoming the critical transformations that are endemic to translation.

[81] Paul Ricoeur, *On Translation*, trans. Eileen Brennan, introduction by Richard Kearney (London and New York: Routledge, 2006), pp. 22–3.

Conclusion

Throughout this study I have been concerned with the effects on Woolf's writing practice of those translations from Greek, Russian, and French by means of which she created the historical moment when feminist history might challenge the assumptions of the dominant culture. Her response to translation reveals the importance of language in her methods as a historian, in a narrative that is marked by her position as an imperial subject. Woolf first studied foreign languages within the institutions of the British educational system, whose ideals are reflected in the essays of Matthew Arnold. His position is the referent of her theories of "knowing" Greek and of translation as focused largely on semantics. Her major translation essay, "On Not Knowing Greek," was written when, after completing her university courses, she undertook, with Janet Case, an education in Greek philosophy and tragedy that was the backbone of her writing career. In her early translation of the ancient Greeks she worked in the shadow of Arnold, the effects of whose ideas persisted throughout her life. Although she resisted his attempts to maintain the dominant paradigm, some of her lifelong habits suggest that she continued to work within the limits that Arnold imposed on the translator, in particular his attention to the translation of individual words. His preoccupation with semantics assumes that to establish equivalence between the vocabularies of two languages is the central task of the translator. Woolf's tendency to focus on the translation of *love* or *soul,* for instance, maintains links not only with Arnold's methods but with her own marginal retranslation of individual words in *Agamemnon* as well.

Yet a theory of translation that is now considered outmoded led Woolf into new territory, as though a single word might open onto another world. She wrote in 1938 that reading "translations of Greek verse ... is like an aeroplane propeller invisibly quick and unconscious" (*D5*: 131). The startling image suggests the immediacy of her surrender to a Greek text, as well as its centrifugal effect on her mind. For instance the continuing effect of Shelley's translation of the *Symposium*, in particular the untranslated word for *love* between men, is apparent in the many ways that she too sought to bring into the public domain a discourse in which language might name same-sex love. Translations from other languages had a similar effect. In the work of Dostoyevsky and Proust she discovered an attention to *soul* that was missing in the work of the British novelists of her generation. Her diary as well as her fiction reveals that *soul*, a key word in their fiction that was never adequately translated, kept open a window onto the unknown and untranslatable that was the lodestar of her spiritual search for what eludes representation. The extraordinary significance of key words in her novels – *light* in *Jacob's Room*, *plunge* in *Mrs. Dalloway*, or *flounder* in *To the Lighthouse* – suggests the capacity of the single word to organize narrative.

The change in Woolf's career that has been observed after *Jacob's Room* coincided with her reading of Proust, which began in 1922 and lasted most of her life. Her reading notes suggest that her theory of the relationship of language to the unconscious was derived from the C. K. Scott Moncrieff translation of *À la recherche du temps perdu*. His mistranslation of Proust's rich vocabulary of words for thought as either *conscious* or *unconscious* offered a view of the mind that unlike Freud's focuses on the power of the artist. Proust attributes it to his/her ability at the moment of awakening from sleep to inhabit both worlds. As a view of the capacity of language Proust's theory brought together several of Woolf's preoccupations, not only with the language of spirituality, but with what she called in "The Hours" manuscript "something that lies below words." His emphasis on *soul* corroborated what she had admired in the Russians, especially in Chekhov and Dostoyevsky, but expressed in a language and culture closer to her own. Proust's theory of mind/body strengthened the position from which she attacked the realism of her contemporaries, and provided a model for the awakening to gender reversal in *Orlando*.

Lawrence Venuti explores the question of translation and cultural identities in the tendency of translators to "rewrite the foreign text in domestic dialects and discourses" that are familiar to readers and publishers. "Whether the effects of a translation prove to be conservative or transgressive depends fundamentally on the discursive strategies developed by the translator, but also on various factors in their reception."[1] Woolf's translation essay, "On Not Knowing Greek," nicely balances the question of cultural identities as she considers both the discursive strategy of the translator and its reception by the reader. The essay is conservative to the extent that it shares the

[1] Lawrence Venuti, *The Scandals of Translation: Towards an Ethics of Difference* (London and New York: Routledge, 1998), p. 68.

ethnographic bias that is endemic to translation, when she writes of Penelope and Nausicaa that "they are no more self-conscious than children," or of the *Odyssey* as "instinctive story-telling" (*E4*: 50). Yet she acknowledges the "sources of misunderstanding, of distorted and romantic, of servile and snobbish passion" that condition any reading (*E4*: 49–50). The balance between "conservative" and potentially "transgressive" creates the opportunity to redefine the reader who although benefiting from the increase in literacy in Britain did not attend university. The new readers of translations, among whom she counts herself, share the strange cultural imperative to make sense of the Greeks, though "with what slight resemblance to the real meaning of Greek, who shall say?" (*E4*: 38–9). Here and elsewhere Woolf seized a moment of historical change as an opportunity when translation might reshape the cultural identity of the reader.

Translation as it is practiced in postcolonial literature challenges the monolingual reader by expanding the referential world of empire, so that "translation becomes an integral part of the reading experience."[2] After Woolf's great translation essay, key scenes in her novels shift attention to the effects of translation in colonial culture. The reluctance of Louis in *The Waves* and Edward in *The Years* to translate would narrow the reader's world to present-day England. The refusal to translate highlights as well Woolf's own position when on occasion she too silently refused. But she was more "hospitable" to the demands of new readers both British and foreign.

The lineaments of a position that she did not articulate in an essay stand out clearly in relationship to the theories of Derrida and Benjamin. Derrida's frequent emphasis on his relationship to a language not his own, and to the language of mourning, illuminates large areas of Woolf's concern and provides a vocabulary that enables us to read her work along new lines. In several interviews Derrida traced to his experience as an Algerian diasporic Jew his sense of merely inhabiting, rather than appropriating, the French language. That position established the linguistic perspective of his well-known criticism of western metaphysics. He argues that the system of signifier/signified must always be provisional, since it leaves open the possibility of a concept present for thought, but independent of language. Translation is a test case in the sense that it calls in question not only signifier/signified, but also the quest for the "transcendental signified" that is implicit in our language and culture. Derrida's redefinition of translation is part of its deconstruction: "For example, no translation would be possible without it.

---

[2] Samia Mehrez, "Translation and the Postcolonial Experience," *Rethinking Translation: Discourse, Subjectivity, Ideology*, ed. Lawrence Venuti (London and New York: Routledge, 1992), 122.

In effect, the theme of a transcendental signified took shape within the horizon of an absolutely pure, transparent, and unequivocal translatability. In the limits to which it is possible, or at least *appears* possible, translation practices the difference between signified and signifier. But if this difference is never pure, no more so is translation, and for the notion of translation we would have to substitute a notion of *transformation*: a regulated transformation of one language by another, of one text by another."[3] The process of "transformation" by means of translation is Woolf's vision of a language suitable for women's writing.

A comparison of their positions also identifies what is attributable to Woolf alone. The significant starting point for my argument is Derrida's "iterability," or the capacity of a text to signify in the absence of both sender and receiver: "There is no history without iterability, and this iterability is also what lets the traces continue to function in the absence of the general context or some elements of the context."[4] In Woolf's work the translation is the primary instance of the iterable text, both in the sense that it has been removed from its original cultural setting, and more importantly in the sense that its appearance in another language reveals the traces of a history of repressed struggle. In other words the iterable text, for instance Shelley's translation of the *Symposium*, reveals the history of the reception of certain words in English.

Derrida suggests that a national language affirms its identity in relation to translation: "The identity of a language can only affirm itself as identity to itself by opening itself to the hospitality of a difference from itself or of a difference with itself."[5] In the final chapter of *The Years* translation structures the limits of hospitality within the Pargiter family as it finds itself unable to cross boundaries between the class lines of an imperial culture. Translation as an act of hospitality appears as well in Djebar's discussion of French as the language of the other: "the heredity of blood transmuted into a welcoming language" as "the true welcome" is the aim rather than the outcome of the family party in *The Years*. Although reading *Antigone* in a family setting seems to promise a fruitful exchange between generations, and between London and the empire, that path is blocked by Edward's refusal to translate, and by the alienation of the Pargiters' native language so that an act of intralingual translation becomes necessary as well. The iterable

---

[3] Derrida, *Positions*, p. 20.
[4] Jacques Derrida, "'This Strange Institution Called Literature': An Interview with Jacques Derrida," *Acts of Literature*, ed. Derek Attridge (New York and London: Routledge, 1992), 64.
[5] Derrida, *Aporias*, p. 10.

text is the line in which Antigone declares to Creon, "'Tis not my nature to join in hating but in loving." The theme of *love* and *hate* elsewhere in the chapter suggests that the line, perhaps because never translated, moulds the behavior of characters who are struggling to express their desire for "a different life." North perceives that Peggy's wounding words represent "her feeling, not her words; he felt her feeling now; it was not about him; it was about other people; about another world, a new world" (*Y*: 369–70). As in Woolf's earlier novels, a search for the language of feeling prompts the reader to seek a new world. But if these two members of the family cannot handle the import of Antigone's line, none is equal to the song of the two lower-class children near the end of the chapter. The *harsh* and *hideous* sound of the children's singing alienates their language. "Etho passo tanno hai" is not presented as an ancient song of love, as are the nonsense syllables in *Mrs. Dalloway*. Rather the alphabet not used to think or write is greeted with hostility. The syllables are alien utterance, as though without intra-lingual translation talk across the lines of class were impossible. Refusing both inter- and intralingual translation the Pargiter family remains barri-caded, statuesque figures standing in the window. The strained atmosphere of the party suggests that the lack of hospitality is the sign of its historical moment, when the borders of family and empire that were intended to protect in fact confine.

Benjamin's injunction to the translator, to "expand and deepen his lan-guage by means of the foreign language," was in the broadest sense Woolf's goal as well.[6] But the messianic goal of translation as leading to "a realm of reconciliation and fulfillment," where language becomes adequate to divine revelation, is not matched by Woolf's emphasis on the temporal contingency of the sign. As a result she moves in a direction directly opposite to Benjamin's "no poem is intended for the reader," and his dismissal of any translation that is "meant for readers who do not understand the original." In his argument the translation that "undertakes to serve the reader" is by definition a bad translation, suitable only for communicating information.[7] Woolf, equally mistrustful of restricting language to communication, devel-oped a more flexible theory. Perhaps because the translator habitually finds himself both striving for accuracy and aware of the tastes of the reader, throughout her work she occupied a double position. She was both the reader who read Greek and the reader who did not, a position facilitated at a time when in England learning Greek was the mark of gender difference.

---

[6] Benjamin, *Selected Writings*, vol. 1, p. 262. [7] *Ibid.*, p. 253.

These significant differences may be focused on their distinction between the translatable and the untranslatable text. In Benjamin's essay translatability is "an essential quality of certain works," part of the "afterlife" of a work "in the age of its fame."[8] Woolf's sense of history forbade an emphasis on "essential quality." Although in Benjamin's essay only a translation is untranslatable, some of the most interesting moments in Woolf's work occur when the untranslatable word, for same-sex love for instance, requires intralingual translation as well, and in so doing draws attention to a still unresolved historical struggle. In *Orlando* for example, as the reader of a translation of Proust she worked along Benjamin's lines, "to liberate the language imprisoned in a work in his re-creation of that work," but "liberation" for her as for Proust referred to the legal and cultural restraints on the language of naming. Although Woolf lived in the worlds of both Benjamin and Derrida, she preserved a sense that language is imprinted less by any sacred text than by the struggles of local history.

The iterable text that crosses boundaries in a colonial culture calls in question the relationship between languages. The play that causes such trouble at the Pargiters' party is the subject in Djebar's and Woolf's work of an "abusive" translation that sends the reader back to reconsider the more problematic scenes of *Antigone*. The cry of mourning tests the translator's ability to maintain both the domestic and foreign aspects of the play. The cry of the kitchen maid in *Three Guineas* and the scene of mourning women in *Vaste est la prison* focus on the act of translation that divides the narrator from her sisters. It marks the difficult moment when Antigone as female mourner defends the space between the cry of grief and the dominant language. It is that "something that lies below words" that is suggested in "The Hours" manuscript, in which the untranslatable word draws attention to the contingency of the sign and the possibility of the transformation of language.

In "A Haunted House" the sleepers hear the voices of the dead couple whose house they inhabit, and their awakening is marked by a cry that the narrator translates, "Is this *your* buried treasure?" When Djebar translated the last lines of "A Haunted House" as the prelude to the first section of *Vaste est la prison*, she chose one of the short stories in which Woolf experimented with the difficulties of narration in a colonial society. Yet Djebar's translation of the final line, "the light in the heart," as "Cette clarté au coeur" marks a significant difference between their understanding of translation. In Djebar's novel *clarté* is a quality of recognition that the

---

[8] *Ibid.*, pp. 254–5.

narrator locates in her body as she awakens from a healing sleep: "Je porte en moi un changement et j'en suis inondée" (*VP*: 20). ("I am carrying some change inside me, and it floods through me," *VPE*: 21.) Woolf's "light in the heart" suggests the possibility of a spiritual awakening yet to be realized. Djebar's *clarté*, associated here with physical change, suggests the light of reason, lucidity, and precision, qualities that are associated as well with her French education. In Djebar's novel the ghost that troubles sleep and motivates awakening introduces a narrative about the film maker's reentry into her native culture in the role of translator.

Djebar's invitation to the ghost of Dante, to continue to haunt, and her query – in what language? – points to the condition of postcolonial writing where translation keeps alive and available the several languages that are necessary to write the history of a diaspora. As the citizen of a colonial power Woolf wrote in *A Room of One's Own* of herself and other daughters as colonized subjects who might free themselves from patriarchy by learning foreign languages. Although Woolf's understanding of the potential for the "abuse" of language suggests a real constraint, she too was a translator who welcomed ghosts. The subject who advances with outstretched hand figures their vulnerability, a figure and a position that long after Woolf's death Djebar might inhabit as her own.

Bibliography of works cited

Abel, Elizabeth. *Virginia Woolf and the Fictions of Psychoanalysis*. Chicago: University of Chicago Press, 1989.

Abraham, Nicolas and Torok, Maria. *The Shell and the Kernel: Renewals of Psychoanalysis*. Trans. Nicholas T. Rand. Vol. i. Chicago: University of Chicago Press, 1994.

Alexiou, Margaret. *The Ritual Lament in Greek Tradition*. Cambridge: Cambridge University Press, 1974.

Althusser, Louis. "Ideology and Ideological State Apparatuses." *Lenin and Philosophy and Other Essays*. Trans. Ben Brewster. New York: Monthly Review Press, 1971. 127–86.

Arnold, Matthew. *Complete Prose Works of Matthew Arnold*. Ed. R. H. Super. ii vols. Ann Arbor: University of Michigan Press, 1960–77.
  Essays in Criticism: Second Series. London: Macmillan, 1888.

Asad, Talal. "The Concept of Cultural Translation in British Social Anthropology." *Writing Culture: The Poetics and Politics of Ethnography*. Ed. James Clifford and George E. Marcus. Berkeley: University of California Press, 1991. 141–64.

Auerbach, Eric. *Mimesis: The Representation of Reality in Western Literature*. Trans. Willard Trask. Garden City, N.Y.: Doubleday & Company, 1957.

Avery, Todd and Brantlinger, Patrick. "Reading and Modernism: 'Mind Hungers' Common and Uncommon." *A Concise Companion to Modernism*. Ed. David Bradshaw. Oxford: Blackwell, 2003. 243–61.

Bakhtin, M. M. *The Dialogic Imagination: Four Essays by M. M. Bakhtin*. Trans. Caryl Emerson and Michael Holquist. Ed. Michael Holquist. Austin: University of Texas Press, 1981.
  "Response to a Question from the *Novy Mir* Editorial Staff." *Speech Genres and Other Later Essays*. Trans. Vern W. McGee. Ed. Caryl Emerson and Michael Holquist. Austin: University of Texas Press, 1986. 1–9.

Barber, Stephen M. "States of Emergency, States of Freedom: Woolf, History, and the Novel." *Novel: A Forum on Fiction* 42 (2009), 196–205.

Bassnett, Susan and Lefevere, André, eds. *Constructing Cultures: Essays on Literary Translation*. Clevedon, Somerset and Philadelphia, Pa.: Multilingual Matters, 1998.

Beard, Mary. "The Invention (and Re-Invention) of 'Group D': An Archeology of the Classical Tripos, 1879–1984." *Classics in 19th and 20th Century Cambridge.* Cambridge: Cambridge Philological Society, 1999. 95–134.

The Invention of Jane Harrison. Cambridge, Mass.: Harvard University Press, 2000.

Beer, Gillian. "Hume, Stephen, and Elegy in *To the Lighthouse.*" *Essays in Criticism* 34 (1984), 33–55.

Virginia Woolf: The Common Ground. Ann Arbor: University of Michigan Press, 1996.

"'Wireless': Popular Physics, Radio and Modernism." *Cultural Babbage: Technology, Time and Invention.* Ed. Francis Spufford and Jenny Uglow. London and Boston, Mass.: Faber and Faber, 1996. 149–66.

Belknap, Robert. "Novelist Technique." *The Cambridge Companion to the Classic Russian Novel.* Ed. Malcolm V. Jones and Robin Feuer Miller. Cambridge: Cambridge University Press, 1998. 233–50.

Bell, Clive. *Old Friends: Personal Recollections.* London: Chatto & Windus, 1956.

Proust. New York: Harcourt, Brace & Company, 1929.

Benardete, Seth. *Sacred Transgressions: A Reading of Sophocles' "Antigone".* South Bend, Ind.: St. Augustine's Press, 1999.

Benjamin, Walter. *Selected Writings.* Vol. 1: *1913–1926.* Ed. Marcus Bullock and Michael W. Jennings. Cambridge, Mass.: Belknap Press of Harvard University Press, 1996.

Benrabah, Mohamed. *Langue et pouvoir en Algérie.* Paris: Éditions Séguir, 1999.

Berman, Antoine. *L'âge de la traduction: "La tâche du traducteur" de Walter Benjamin: un commentaire.* Paris: Presses Universitaires de Vincennes, 2008.

Bourdieu, Pierre. "The Production and Reproduction of Legitimate Language." *Language and Symbolic Power.* Trans. Gino Raymond and Matthew Adamson. Ed. John B. Thompson. Cambridge, Mass.: Harvard University Press, 1991. 43–65.

Bowie, Malcolm. *Freud, Proust and Lacan: Theory as Fiction.* Cambridge: Cambridge University Press, 1987.

Breay, Claire. "Women and the Classical Tripos 1869–1914." *Classics in 19th and 20th Century Cambridge.* Cambridge: Cambridge Philological Society, 1999. 49–70.

Briggs, Julia. *Reading Virginia Woolf.* Edinburgh: Edinburgh University Press, 2006.

Butler, Judith. *Antigone's Claim.* New York: Columbia University Press, 2000.

"Imitation and Gender Insubordination." *Inside/Out: Lesbian Theories, Gay Theories.* Ed. Diana Fuss. New York and London: Routledge, 1991. 13–31.

The Psychic Life of Power. Stanford: Stanford University Press, 1997.

Calle-Gruber, Mireille. *Assia Djebar ou la résistance de l'écriture: regards d'un écrivain d'Algérie.* Paris: Maisonneuve et Larose, 2001.

"Résistances de l'écriture ou l'ombilic de l'oeuvre à propos de *Vaste est la prison* d'Assia Djebar." *Postcolonialisme & autobiographie.* Ed. Alfred Hornung and Ernstpeter Ruhe. Amsterdam and Atlanta, Ga.: Rodopi, 1998.

Caravelli, A. "The Bitter Wounding: The Lament as Social Protest in Rural Greece." *Gender and Power in Rural Greece.* Ed. J. Dubisch. Princeton: Princeton University Press, 1986. 169–94.

Carlier, Omar. "Scholars and Politicians: An Examination of the Algerian View of Algerian Nationalism." *The Maghreb in Question: Essays in History & Historiography.* Ed. Michel le Goll and Kenneth Perkins. Austin: University of Texas Press, 1997.

Casanova, Pascale. *The World Republic of Letters.* Trans. M. B. DeBevoise. Cambridge, Mass.: Harvard University Press, 2004.

Caughie, Pamela. *Virginia Woolf & Postmodernism: Literature in Quest & Question of Itself.* Urbana: University of Illinois Press, 1991.

   "Virginia Woolf's Double Discourse." *Discontented Discourses: Feminism/Textual Intervention/Psychoanalysis.* Ed. Marleen S. Barr and Richard Feldstein. Urbana: University of Illinois Press, 1989. 41–53.

Caws, Mary Ann. *Surprised in Translation.* Chicago: University of Chicago Press, 2006.

   Women and Bloomsbury: Virginia, Vanessa and Carrington. New York and London: Routledge, 1990.

Caws, Mary Ann and Luckhurst, Nicola, eds. *The Reception of Virginia Woolf in Europe.* London: Continuum, 2002.

Caws, Mary Ann and Wright, Sarah Bird. *Bloomsbury and France: Art and Friends.* Oxford and New York: Oxford University Press, 2000.

Cheyfitz, Eric. *The Poetics of Imperialism: Translation and Colonization from "The Tempest" to "Tarzan."* New York and Oxford: Oxford University Press, 1991.

Clarke, Stuart. *Orlando: The Holograph Draft.* London: S. N. Clarke, 1993.

Clewell, Tammy. "Consolations Refused: Virginia Woolf, the Great War, and Modernist Mourning." *Modern Fiction Studies* 50 (2004), 197–223.

Cory, Mark E. "Soundplay: The Polyphonous Tradition of German Radio." *Wireless Imagination: Sound, Radio, and the Avant-Garde.* Ed. Douglas Kahn and Gregory Whitehead. Cambridge, Mass.: MIT Press, 1992. 331–65.

Cuddy-Keane, Melba. "Virginia Woolf and the Varieties of Historicist Experience." *Virginia Woolf and the Essay.* Ed. Beth Carole Rosenberg and Jeanne Dubino. New York: St. Martin's Press, 1997. 59–77.

   "Virginia Woolf, Sound Technologies, and the New Aurality." *Virginia Woolf in the Age of Mechanical Reproduction.* Ed. Pamela L. Caughie. New York: Garland, 2000. 69–96.

   Virginia Woolf, the Intellectual and the Public Sphere. Cambridge and New York: Cambridge University Press, 2003.

Curtiss, Mina, ed. and trans. *Letters of Marcel Proust.* New York: Helen Marx Books, 2006.

Dalgarno, Emily. *Virginia Woolf and the Visible World.* Cambridge: Cambridge University Press, 2001.

Davenport-Hines, Richard. *A Night at the Majestic: Proust and the Great Modernist Dinner Party of 1922.* London: Faber and Faber, 2006.

Davis, Lydia, trans. *Du côté de chez Swann, The Way by Swann's.* By Marcel Proust. London: Penguin, 2002.

de Gay, Jane. *Virginia Woolf's Novels and the Literary Past.* Edinburgh: Edinburgh University Press, 2006.

De Lisle, Leconte. *Sophocle: traduction nouvelle.* Paris: Alphonse Lemerre, 1877.

de Man, Paul. *The Resistance to Theory*. Minneapolis: University of Minnesota Press, 1986.

Derrida, Jacques. *Aporias*. Trans. Thomas Dutoit. Stanford: Stanford University Press, 1993.

"The Deaths of Roland Barthes." *Philosophy and Non-Philosophy since Merleau-Ponty*. Trans. Pascale-Anne Brault and Michael Naas. Ed. Hugh J. Silverman. London: Routledge, 1988.

"Deconstruction and the Other." *Debates in Continental Philosophy: Conversations with Contemporary Thinkers*. Ed. Richard Kearney. New York: Fordham University Press, 2004. 139–56.

Deconstruction and the Possibility of Justice. Ed. Drucilla Cornell, Michel Rosenfeld, and David Gray Carlson. New York and London: Routledge, 1992.

"Des Tours de Babel." *Difference in Translation*. Ed. Joseph P. Graham. Ithaca, N.Y.: Cornell University Press, 1985. 165–248.

"D'un ton apocalyptique adopté naguère en philosophie." *Les fins de l'homme: à partir du travail de Jacques Derrida*. Paris: Éditions Galilée, 1981. 445–79.

The Ear of the Other: Otobiography, Transference, Translation. Trans. Peggy Kamuf. Ed. Christie McDonald. Lincoln: University of Nebraska Press, 1985.

"Fors." Trans. Barbara Johnson. *Georgia Review* 31 (1977), 64–116.

Glas. Trans. John P. Leavey, Jr. and Richard Rand. Lincoln: University of Nebraska Press, 1986.

Limited Inc. Trans. Samuel Weber and Jeffrey Mehlman. Evanston, Ill.: Northwestern University Press, 1988.

"Living On: Border Lines." Trans. James Hulbert. *Deconstruction and Criticism*. By Harold Bloom, Paul de Man, Jacques Derrida, *et al*. New York: Seabury Press, 1979. 75–176.

Margins of Philosophy. Trans. Alan Bass. Chicago: University of Chicago Press, 1982.

Monolingualism of the Other; or, The Prosthesis of Origin. Trans. Patrick Mensah. Stanford: Stanford University Press, 1998.

Positions. Trans. Alan Bass. Chicago: University of Chicago Press, 1981.

"The *Retrait* of Metaphor." *Enclitic* 2:2 (1978), 3–32.

"Sending: On Representation," *Social Research* 49 (1982), 294–326.

Specters of Marx: The State of the Debt, the Work of Mourning, and the New International. Trans. Peggy Kamuf. New York and London: Routledge, 1994.

"'This Strange Institution Called Literature': An Interview with Jacques Derrida." *Acts of Literature*. Ed. Derek Attridge. New York and London: Routledge, 1992. 33–75.

Writing and Difference. Trans. Alan Bass. Chicago: University of Chicago Press, 1978.

Derrida, Jacques and Roudinesco, Elizabeth. *For What Tomorrow: A Dialogue*. Trans. Jeff Fort. Stanford: Stanford University Press, 2004.

DeSalvo, Louise and Leaska, Mitchell. *Letters of Vita Sackville-West to Virginia Woolf*. New York: William Morrow, 1985.

Dick, Susan. "The Restless Searcher: A Discussion of the Evolution of 'Time Passes' in *To the Lighthouse*." *English Studies in Canada* 5 (1979), 311–29.

Diment, Gayla. "Tolstoy and Bloomsbury." *Tolstoy Studies Journal* 5 1992), 39–51.

Dion, Michel. "Between the Dialectics of Time-Memory and the Dialectics of Duration-Moment: Marcel Proust and Virginia Woolf in Dialogue." *Analecta Husserliana* 86 (2007), 155–69.

Djebar, Assia. *Algerian White*. Trans. David Kelley and Marjolijn de Jager. New York and London: Seven Stories Press, 2000.

L'amour, la fantasia. Paris: Albin Michel, 1985.

Ces voix qui m'assiègent. Paris: Albin Michel, 1999.

Fantasia: An Algerian Cavalcade. Trans. Dorothy S. Blair. Portsmouth: Heinemann, 1993.

La femme sans sépulture. Paris: Albin Michel, 2002.

So Vast the Prison. Trans. Betsy Wing. New York: Seven Stories Press, 1999.

Vaste est la prison. Paris: Albin Michel, 1995.

"Writing in the Language of the Other." *Lives in Translation: Bilingual Writers on Identity and Creativity*. Ed. Isabelle de Courtivron. Basingstoke and New York: Palgrave Macmillan, 2003. 19–27.

Donadey, Anne. "The Multilingual Strategies of Postcolonial Literature: Assia Djebar's Algerian Palimpsest." *World Literature Today* 74 (2000), 27–36.

Doyle, Laura. "Introduction: What's Between Us." *Modern Fiction Studies* 50 (2004), 1–7.

Dubino, Jeanne. "A Dialogue with Imperialist Discourse." *Virginia Woolf: Emerging Perspectives: Selected Papers from the Third Annual Conference on Virginia Woolf*. Ed. Mark Hussey and Vara Neverow. New York: Pace University Press, 1994. 38–43

duBois, Page. "Antigone and the Feminist Critic." *Genre* 19 (1986), 370–83.

Dünkelsbühler, Ulrike. *Reframing the Frame of Reason: Trans-lation In and Beyond Kant and Derrida*. Trans. Max Statkiewicz. Amherst, N.Y.: Humanity Books, 2002.

Eide, Marion. "'The Stigma of Nation': Feminist Just War, Privilege, and Responsibility." *Hypatia: A Journal of Feminist Philosophy* 23 (2008), 48–60.

Eikhenbaum, Boris. *Tolstoy in the Sixties*. Trans. Duffield White. Ann Arbor, Mich.: Ardis, 1982.

Ellenberger, Henri F. *The Discovery of the Unconscious: The History and Evolution of Dynamic Psychiatry*. New York: Basic Books, 1970.

Ergal, Yves-Michel. *"Sodome et Gomorrhe": L'écriture de l'innommable*. Paris: Éditions du Temps, 2000.

Ferenczi, Sándor. *Sex in Psychoanalysis*. Trans. Ernest Jones. New York: Basic Books, 1916.

Fernald, Anne. *Virginia Woolf: Feminism and the Reader*. New York: Palgrave Macmillan, 2006.

Ferrer, Daniel. *Virginia Woolf and the Madness of Language*. Trans. Geoffrey Bennington and Rachel Bowlby. London and New York: Routledge, 1990.

Feuer, Kathryn B. *Tolstoy and the Genesis of War and Peace.* Ed. Robin Feuer Miller and Donna Tussing Orwin. Ithaca, N.Y.: Cornell University Press, 1996.

Finch, Alison. "Love, Sexuality and Friendship." *The Cambridge Companion to Proust.* Ed. Richard Bales. Cambridge: Cambridge University Press, 2001. 168–82.

Flint, Kate. "Reading Uncommonly: Virginia Woolf and the Practice of Reading." *YES* 26 (1996), 187–98.

Fodor, Alexander. "Ambiguities in Tolstoy's Views on Patriotism." *Lev Tolstoy and the Concept of Brotherhood.* Ed. Andrew Donskov and John Woodsworth. New York: Legas, 1996. 181–93.

Tolstoy and the Russians: Reflections on a Relationship. Ann Arbor, Mich.: Ardis, 1984.

Foley, Helen P. "The Politics of Tragic Lamentation." *Tragedy, Comedy and the Polis: Papers from the Greek Drama Conference, Nottingham, 18–20 July 1990.* Ed. Alan H. Sommerstein, Stephen Halliwell, Jeffrey Henderson, and Bernhard Zimmerman. Bari: Levante Editori, 1990. 101–43.

Forster, E. M. *Maurice.* New York: Norton, 1971.

Fowler, Rowena. "'On Not Knowing Greek': The Classics and the Woman of Letters." *Classical Journal* 78 (1982–3), 340–6.

"Virginia Woolf: Lexicographer." *English Language Notes* 39 (2002), 54–70.

France, Peter. "Literatures of Medieval and Modern Europe: French." *The Oxford History of Literary Translation in English.* Vol. IV: *1790–1900.* Ed. Peter France and Kenneth Haynes. Oxford: Oxford University Press, 2006. 230–45.

France, Peter and Haynes, Kenneth, eds. *The Oxford History of Literary Translation in English.* Vol. IV: *1790–1900.* Oxford: Oxford University Press, 2006.

Freud, Sigmund. *The Interpretation of Dreams.* Trans. Joyce Crick. Oxford: Oxford University Press, 1999.

Standard Edition of the Complete Psychological Works of Sigmund Freud. Trans. James Strachey in collaboration with Anna Freud. London: Hogarth Press, 1953 (vol. V), 1957 (vol. XIV), 1961 (vol. XIX).

Friedman, Susan. "Virginia Woolf's Pedagogical Scenes of Reading: *The Voyage Out, The Common Reader,* and Her 'Common Readers.'" *Modern Fiction Studies* 38 (1992), 101–23.

Froula, Christine. "*Mrs. Dalloway*'s Postwar Elegy: Women, War, and the Art of Mourning." *Modernism/Modernity* 9 (2002), 125–63.

Virginia Woolf and the Bloomsbury Avant-Garde: War/Civilization/Modernity. New York: Columbia University Press, 2005.

Gafaïti, Hafid. "Assia Djebar, l'écriture et la mort." *Assia Djebar.* Ed. Najib Redouane and Yvette Benayoun-Szmidt. Paris: Harmattan, 2008. 227–38.

Garnett, Constance, trans. *The Idiot.* By Fyodor Dostoyevsky. London: Heinemann, 1913, reprint 1969.

War and Peace. By Leo Tolstoy. London: Heinemann, 1900, reprint 1994.

Gasché, Rodolphe. "Saturnine Vision and the Question of Difference: Reflections on Walter Benjamin's Theory of Language." *Studies in Twentieth Century Literature* 11 (1986), 69–90.

Gättens, Marie-Luise. *Women Writers and Fascism: Reconstructing History.* Gainesville: University of Florida Press, 1995.

Gay, Peter. *Freud: A Life for our Time. New York and London:* W. W. Norton, 1988.

Gellner, Ernest. *Nations and Nationalism.* Ithaca, N.Y.: Cornell University Press, 1983.

Ginzburg, Lydia. *On Psychological Prose.* Trans. Judson Rosengrant. Princeton: Princeton University Press, 1991.

Goff, Barbara and Simpson, Michael. *Crossroads in the Black Aegean: Oedipus, Antigone, and Dramas of the African Diaspora.* Oxford: Oxford University Press, 2007.

Goldhill, Simon. *Who Needs Greek? Contests in the Cultural History of Hellenism.* Cambridge: Cambridge University Press, 2002.

Gottlieb, Laura Moss. *"The Years*: A Feminist Novel." *Virginia Woolf Centennial Essays.* Ed. Elaine K. Ginsberg and Laura Moss Gottlieb. Troy: Whitsun Publishing Conpany, 1983.

Guiguet, Jean. *Virginia Woolf et son oeuvre: l'art et la quête du réel.* Paris: Didier, 1962.

Guyomard, Patrick. "Sur l'éclat d'Antigone." *Lacan avec les philosophes.* Paris: Albin Michel, 1991. 61–6.

Hale, Terry. "Readers and Publishers of Translations in Britain." *The Oxford History of Literary Translation in English.* Vol. IV: *1790–1900.* Ed. Peter France and Kenneth Haynes. Oxford: Oxford University Press, 2006. 34–47.

Hall, Stuart. "The Local and the Global: Globalization and Ethnicity." *Dangerous Liaisons: Gender, Nation, and Postcolonial Perspectives.* Ed. Anne McClintock, Aamir Mufti, and Ella Shohat. Minneapolis: University of Minnesota Press, 1997. 173–87.

Hankins, Leslie Kathleen, "*Orlando*: 'A Precipice Marked V': Between 'A Miracle of Discretion' and 'Lovemaking Unbelievable: Indiscretions Incredible.'" *Virginia Woolf: Lesbian Readings.* Ed. Eileen Barrett and Patricia Cramer. New York and London: New York University Press, 1997. 180–202.

Harrison, Jane. *Prolegomena to the Study of Greek Religion.* Cambridge: Cambridge University Press, 1903. Reprinted New York: Meridian Books, 1957.
Reminiscences of a Student's Life. London: Hogarth Press, 1925.

Haynes, Kenneth. "Greek and Latin Literature: Introduction." *The Oxford History of Literary Translation in English,* Vol. IV: *1790–1900.* Ed. Peter France and Kenneth Haynes. Oxford: Oxford University Press, 2006.
"Translation and British Literary Culture." *The Oxford History of Literary Translation in English.* Vol. IV: *1790–1900.* Ed. Peter France and Kenneth Haynes. Oxford: Oxford University Press, 2006. 1–20.

Hermans, Theo. "Paradoxes and Aporias in Translation and Translation Studies." *Translation Studies: Perspectives on an Emerging Discipline.* Ed. Alessandra Riccardi. Cambridge: Cambridge University Press, 2002. 10–23.

Herzfeld, Michael. "The Unspeakable in Pursuit of the Ineffable." *Translating Cultures: Perspectives on Translation and Anthropology.* Ed. Paula G. Rubel and Abraham Rosman. Oxford and New York: Berg, 2003. 109–34.

Hobsbawm, Eric. *Nations and Nationalism since 1780*. Cambridge: Cambridge University Press, 1990.

Holoka, James P. Review: "Flashar, Hellmut. *Altertumswissenschaft in den 20er Jahren: Neue Fragen und Impulse*. Stuttgart: Franz Steiner Verlag, 1995." *Bryn Mawr Classical Review* 96 (1996), 504–11.

Hughes, Edward J. *Marcel Proust: A Study in the Quality of Awareness*. Cambridge: Cambridge University Press, 1983.

Humm, Maggie, ed. *The Edinburgh Companion to Virginia Woolf and the Arts*. Edinburgh: Edinburgh University Press, 2010.

Hussey, Mark. "Mrs. Thatcher and Mrs. Woolf." *Modern Fiction Studies* 50–1 (2004), 8–30.

"To the Lighthouse and Physics: The Cosmology of David Bohm and Virginia Woolf." *New Essays on Virginia Woolf*. Ed. H. Wussow. Dallas, Tex.: Contemporary Research Press, 1995. 79–97.

Virginia Woolf A–Z. Oxford: Oxford University Press, 1995.

Jacobs, Carol. *In the Language of Walter Benjamin*. Baltimore, Md.: Johns Hopkins University Press, 1999.

Jacobus, Mary. "The Difference of View." *Women Writing and Writing About Women*. Ed. Mary Jacobus. London: Croom Helm in association with Oxford University Women's Studies Committee, 1979. 10–21.

Jakobson, Roman. "On Linguistic Aspects of Translation." *On Translation*. Ed. Reuben Brower. Cambridge, Mass.: Harvard University Press, 1959. 232–9.

Jameson, Fredric. *Nationalism, Colonialism and Literature: Modernism and Imperialism*. Derry: Field Day Theatre Company, 1988.

Jebb, R. C. *Sophocles: The Plays and Fragments, Part III, The Antigone*. Cambridge: Cambridge University Press, 1891.

Johnson, Patricia J. "Woman's Third Face: A Psycho/Social Reconsideration of Sophocles' Antigone." *Arethusa* 30 (1997), 369–98.

Jones, Christine Kenyon and Snaith, Anna. "'Tilting at Universities': Woolf at King's College London." *Woolf Studies Annual* 16 (2010), 1–44.

Jones, Frederick L., ed. *The Letters of Mary W. Shelley*. Vol. II. Norman: University of Oklahoma Press, 1944.

Josipovici, Gabriel. "Fail Again. Fail Better." *Times Literary Supplement* 5461 (November 30, 2007), 14–16.

Kaplan, Alice Yaeger. *Reproductions of Banality: Fascism, Literature, and French Intellectual Life*. Minneapolis: University of Minnesota Press, 1986.

Keynes, John Maynard. *Two Memoirs: Dr. Melchior: A Defeated Enemy and My Early Beliefs*. London: Rupert Hart-Davis, 1949.

Khanna, Ranjana. *Dark Continents: Psychoanalysis and Colonialism*. Durham, N.C.: Duke University Press, 2003.

Klemperer, Victor. *The Language of the Third Reich: LTI – Lingua Tertii Imperii: A Philologist's Notebook*. London and New Brunswick, N.J.: The Athlone Press, 2000.

Kolocotroni, Vassiliki. "Greek Lessons in Early Virginia Woolf." *Modern Language Review* 100 (2005), 313–22.

Koselleck, Reinhart. *Futures Past: On the Semantics of Historical Time.* Trans. Keith Tribe. Cambridge, Mass.: MIT Press, 1985, reprint New York: Columbia University Press, 2004.

Koster, Cees. "The Translator In Between Texts: On the Textual Presence of the Translator as an Issue in the Methodology of Comparative Translation Description." *Translation Studies: Perspectives on an Emerging Discipline.* Ed. Alessandra Riccardi. Cambridge: Cambridge University Press, 2002. 24–37.

Koteliansky, S. S. and Woolf, Virginia. *Talks with Tolstoi.* Trans. A. B. Goldenveiser. London: Hogarth Press, 1923.

Kuper, Adam. *The Invention of Primitive Society: Transformations of an Illusion.* London and New York: Routledge, 1988.

Lacan, Jacques. *The Seminar of Jacques Lacan; Book VII: The Ethics of Psychoanalysis 1959–1960.* Trans. Dennis Porter. Ed. Jacques-Alain Miller. New York and London: W. W. Norton, 1992.

Ladenson, Elisabeth. *Proust's Lesbianism.* Ithaca, N.Y.: Cornell University Press, 1999.

Leaska, Mitchell A., ed. *The Pargiters: The Novel-Essay Portion of "The Years."* New York: Harcourt Brace Jovanovich, 1977.

Lecercle, Jean-Jacques. *The Violence of Language.* London and New York: Routledge, 1990.

Lee, Hermione. *Virginia Woolf.* London: Chatto & Windus, 1996.

Lefevere, André. "Translation Practice(s) and the Circulation of Cultural Capital: Some Aeneids in English." *Constructing Cultures: Essays on Literary Translation.* Ed. Susan Bassnett and André Lefevere. Clevedon, Somerset and Philadelphia, Pa.: Multilingual Matters, 1998. 41–56.

"Why Waste our Time on Rewrites?: The Trouble with Interpretation and the Role of Rewriting in an Alternative Paradigm." *The Manipulation of Literature: Studies in Literary Translation.* Ed. Theo Hermans. London and Sydney: Croom Helm, 1985. 215–43.

Leonard, Miriam. *Athens in Paris: Ancient Greece and the Political in Post-War French Thought.* Oxford: Oxford University Press, 2005.

Leontis, Artemis. *Topographies of Hellenism: Mapping the Homeland.* Ithaca, N.Y.: Cornell University Press, 1995.

Levenback, Karen. *Virginia Woolf and the Great War.* Syracuse: Syracuse University Press, 1999.

Lewis, Andrea. "The Visual Politics of Empire and Gender in Virginia Woolf's *The Voyage Out.*" *Woolf Studies Annual* 1 (1995), 106–19.

Lewis, Philip E. "The Measure of Translation Effects." *Difference in Translation.* Ed. Joseph E. Graham. Ithaca, N.Y.: Cornell University Press, 1985. 31–62.

Lienhardt, Godfrey. *"Modes of Thought." The Institutions of Primitive Society: A Series of Broadcast Talks.* Oxford: Basil Blackwell, 1967. 95–107.

Lloyd-Jones, Hugh. "Introduction to the English Edition." *Sophocles.* Trans. Hazel Harvey and David Harvey. Oxford: Basil Blackwell, 1979.

Loraux, Nicole. "La main d'Antigone." *Metis* 1 (1986), 165–96.

The Mourning Voice: An Essay on Greek Tragedy. Trans. Elizabeth Trapnell Rawlings. Ithaca, N.Y.: Cornell University Press, 2002.

Lubbock, Percy. *The Craft of Fiction.* New York: Charles Scribner's Sons, 1921.

MacIntyre, Alasdair. *The Unconscious: A Conceptual Analysis.* Revised edition. New York and London: Routledge, 2004.

Mackenzie, Robin. "Proust's 'Livre intérieur.'" *Modernism and the European Unconscious.* Ed. Peter Collier and Judy Davies. New York: St. Martin's Press, 1990. 149–64.

Maine, Henry Sumner. *Ancient Law: Its Connection with the Early History of Society and its Relation to Modern Ideas.* New York: Holt, 1861; reprint edition Tucson: University of Arizona Press, 1986.

Malley, Henry. "A Rediscovered Eulogy: Virginia Woolf's 'Miss Jane Case: Classical Scholar and Teacher.'" *Twentieth Century Literature* 28 (1982), 290–301.

Marchand, Suzanne L. *Down from Olympus: Archeology and Philhellenism in Germany 1750–1970.* Princeton: Princeton University Press, 1996.

Marcus, George E. "Contemporary Problems of Ethnography in the Modern World System." *Writing Culture: The Poetics and Politics of Ethnography.* Ed. James Clifford and George E. Marcus. Berkeley: University of California Press, 1991. 165–93.

Marcus, Jane. *Art and Anger: Reading Like a Woman.* Columbus: Ohio State University Press, 1988.

  "Britannia Rules *The Waves.*" *Decolonizing Tradition: New Views of Twentieth-Century "British" Literary Canons.* Ed. Karen Lawrence. Urbana: University of Illinois Press, 1992. 136–62.

  Hearts of Darkness: White Women Write Race. New Brunswick, N.J.: Rutgers University Press, 2004.

  "Thinking Back Through our Mothers." *New Feminist Essays on Virginia Woolf.* Ed. Jane Marcus. Lincoln: University of Nebraska Press, 1989. 1–30.

Marcus, Laura. "The European Dimensions of the Hogarth Press." *The Reception of Virginia Woolf in Europe.* Ed. Mary Ann Caws and Nicola Luckhurst. London: Continuum, 2002. 328–56.

  "Introduction." *Translations from the Russian by Virginia Woolf and S. S. Koteliansky.* Ed. Stuart N. Clarke. London: Virginia Woolf Society of Great Britain, 2006. vii–xxiv.

  "Virginia Woolf and the Hogarth Press." *Modernist Writers and the Marketplace.* Ed. Ian Willison, Warwick Gould, and Warren Chernaik. London: Macmillan, 1996. 124–50.

  "Virginia Woolf as Publisher and Editor: The Hogarth Press." *The Edinburgh Companion to Virginia Woolf and the Arts.* Ed. Maggie Humm. Edinburgh: Edinburgh University Press, 2010. 263–79.

Mares, Cheryl. "Woolf's Reading of Proust." Reprinted in *Reading Proust.* Ed. Mary Ann Caws and Eugène Nicole. New York and Paris: Peter Lang, 1990. 185–93.

Marshik, Celia. *British Modernism and Censorship.* Cambridge: Cambridge University Press, 2006.

McCall, Marsh. "Divine and Human Action in Sophocles: The Two Burials of the *Antigone.*" *Yale Classical Studies* 22 (1972), 103–17.

McDonald, Christie. *The Proustian Fabric: Associations of Memory.* Lincoln: University of Nebraska Press, 1991.

McIntire, Gabrielle. "Heteroglossia, Monologism, and Fascism: Bernard reads *The Waves*." *Narrative* 13 (2005), 29–45.

McManus, Patricia. "The 'Offensiveness' of Virginia Woolf: From a Moral to a Political Reading." *Woolf Studies Annual* 14 (2008), 91–138.

McNeillie, Andrew, ed. *Virginia Woolf: The Common Reader: First Series.* New York: Harcourt Brace Jovanovich, 1984.

McQuade, Molly. "Life Sentences." *Woolf Studies Annual* 14 (2008), 53–67.

McVicker, Jeanette. "Woolf in the Context of Fascism: Ideology, Hegemony and the Public Sphere." *Virginia Woolf: Texts and Contexts: Selected Papers from the Fifth Annual Conference on Virginia Woolf.* Ed. Beth Rigel Daugherty and Eileen Barrett. New York: Pace University Press, 1996. 30–4.

Mehlman, Jeffrey. *Revolution and Repetition: Marx/Hugo/Balzac.* Berkeley: University of California Press, 1977.

Mehrez, Samia. "Translation and the Postcolonial Experience." *Rethinking Translation: Discourse, Subjectivity, Ideology.* Ed. Lawrence Venuti. London and New York: Routledge, 1992. 120–38.

Mepham, John. "Mourning and Modernism." *Virginia Woolf: New Critical Essays.* Ed. Patricia Clements and Isobel Grundy. London: Vision Press, and Totowa, N.J.: Barnes & Noble, 1983.

Meylaerts, Reine. "Heterolingualism in/and Translation: How Legitimate Are the Other and his/her Language? An Introduction." *Target* 18 (2006), 1–15.

Mignolo, Walter. "Colonial and Postcolonial Discourse: Cultural Critique or Academic Colonialism?" *Latin American Research Review* 28 (1993), 120–34.

"Globalization, Civilization Processes, and the Relocation of Languages and Cultures." *Cultures of Globalization.* Ed. Fredric Jameson and Masao Miyoshi. Durham, N.C.: Duke University Press, 1998. 37–43.

Miller, Christopher. *Nationalists and Nomads: Essays on Francophone African Literature and Culture.* Chicago: University of Chicago Press, 1998.

Miller, J. Hillis. *Fiction and Repetition: Seven English Novels.* Cambridge, Mass.: Harvard University Press, 1982.

Milo, Giuliva. *Lecture et pratique de l'histoire dans l'oeuvre d'Assia Djebar.* Brussels: Peter Lang, 2007.

Minow-Pinkney, Makiko. "'The Meaning on the Far Side of Language': Walter Benjamin's Translation Theory and Virginia Woolf's Modernism." *Virginia Woolf Across Cultures.* Ed. Natalya Reinhold. New York: Pace University Press, 2004. 79–84.

Virginia Woolf and the Problem of the Subject. New Brunswick, N.J.: Rutgers University Press, 1987.

Moncrieff, C. K. Scott, trans. *À la recherche du temps perdu.* By Marcel Proust. New York: Random House, 1932–4. Reprint edition 1951–7.

Moncrieff, C. K. Scott, ed. *Marcel Proust: An English Tribute.* London: Chatto & Windus, 1923.

Morson, Gary. *Hidden in Plain View: Narrative and Creative Potential in "War and Peace."* Stanford: Stanford University Press, 1987.

Mortimer, Mildred. "Assia Djebar's *Algerian Quartet*: A Study in Fragmented Autobiography." *Research in African Literatures* 28(2) (1997), 102–17.

Neverow, Vara S. "Freudian Seduction and the Fallacies of Dictatorship." *Virginia Woolf and Fascism: Resisting the Dictators' Seduction.* Ed. Merry M. Pawlowski. Basingstoke and New York: Palgrave Macmillan, 2001. 56–72.

Neverow, Vara S. and Pawlowski, Merry. "A Preliminary Bibliographic Guide to the Footnotes of *Three Guineas*." *Woolf Studies Annual* 3 (1977), 170–210.

Niranjana, Tejaswini. *Siting Translation: History, Post-Structuralism, and the Colonial Context.* Berkeley: University of California Press, 1992.

Notopoulos, James A. *The Platonism of Shelley: A Study of Platonism and the Poetic Mind.* Durham, N.C.: Duke University Press, 1949.

Oldfield, Sybil. "Virginia Woolf and Antigone – Thinking Against the Current," *South Carolina Review* 29 (1996), 45–57.

Orwin, Donna. "Tolstoy and Patriotism." *Lev Tolstoy and the Concept of Brotherhood.* Ed. Andrew Donskov and John Woodsworth. New York: Legas, 1996. 51–70.

Parker, Robert. "Through a Glass Darkly: Sophocles and the Divine." *Sophocles Revisited: Essays Presented to Sir Hugh Lloyd-Jones.* Ed. Jasper Griffin. Oxford: Oxford University Press, 1999. 11–30.

Phillips, Kathy J. *Virginia Woolf Against Empire.* Knoxville: University of Tennessee Press, 1994.

Prins, Yopie. "OTOTOTOI: Virginia Woolf and 'The Naked Cry' of Cassandra." *"Agamemnon" in Performance 458 BC to AD 2004.* Ed. Fiona Macintosh, Pantelis Michelakis, Edith Hall, and Oliver Taplin. Oxford: Oxford University Press, 2005. 163–85.

Proust, Marcel. *À la Recherche du temps perdu.* Vols. I–III. Trans. C. K. Scott Moncrieff and Terence Kilmartin. New York: Random House, reprint 1981.

Putzel, Steven. "Virginia Woolf and British 'Orientalism.'" *Virginia Woolf Out of Bounds: Selected Papers from the Tenth Annual Conference on Virginia Woolf.* Ed. Jessica Berman and Jane Goldman. New York: Pace University Press, 2001. 105–13.

Radin, Grace. *Virginia Woolf's "The Years": The Evolution of a Novel.* Knoxville: Kentucky University Press, 1981.

Reinhardt, Karl. *Sophocles.* Trans. Hazel Harvey and David Harvey. Oxford: Basil Blackwell, 1933, reprinted 1941, 1947.

Reinhold, Natalya. "Virginia Woolf's Russian Voyage Out." *Woolf Studies Annual* 9 (2003), 1–27.

Renan, Ernest. "What is a Nation"? Trans. Martin Thom. *Nation and Narration.* Ed. Homi Bhabha. London: Routledge, 1990. 8–22.

Riccardi, Alessandra, ed. *Translation Studies: Perspectives on an Emerging Discipline.* Cambridge: Cambridge University Press, 2002.

Rich, Susanna. "*De Undarum Natura*: Lucretius and Woolf in *The Waves*." *Journal of Modern Literature* 23 (1999–2000), 249–57.

Richter, Harvena. *Virginia Woolf: The Inward Voyage*. Princeton: Princeton University Press, 1970.

Ricoeur, Paul. "The Metaphorical Process as Cognition, Imagination, and Feeling." *On Metaphor*. Ed. Sheldon Sacks. Chicago: University of Chicago Press, 1979. 141–57.

   On Translation. Trans. Eileen Brennan. Intro. Richard Kearney. London and New York: Routledge, 2006.

   Time and Narrative. Vol. ii. Trans. Kathleen McLaughlin and David Pellauer. Chicago: University of Chicago Press, 1985.

Robinson, Douglas, ed. *Western Translation Theory from Herodotus to Nietzsche*. Manchester and Northampton, Mass.: St. Jerome Publishing, 1997. Second edition 2002.

Rosenbaum, S. P., ed. *Women & Fiction: The Manuscript Versions of "A Room of One's Own."* By Virginia Woolf. Oxford: Blackwell, 1992.

Rosenfeld, Natania. "Monstrous Conjugations: Images of Dictatorship in the Anti-Fascist Writings of Virginia and Leonard Woolf." *Virginia Woolf and Fascism: Resisting the Dictator's Seduction*. Ed. Merry M. Pawlowski. Basingstoke and New York: Palgrave Macmillan, 2001. 122–36.

Rubenstein, Roberta. *Virginia Woolf and the Russian Point of View*. New York: Palgrave Macmillan, 2009.

Sackville-West, Vita. "A Week in France with Virginia Woolf." *Virginia Woolf: Interviews and Recollections*. Ed. J. H. Stape. London: Macmillan, 1995. 34–6.

Schehr, Lawrence. *The Shock of Men: Homosexual Hermeneutics in French Writing*. Stanford, Calif.: Stanford University Press, 1995.

Scott, Bonnie Kime, ed. *Gender in Modernism: New Geographies, Complex Intersections*. Urbana: University of Illinois Press, 2007.

   The Gender of Modernism: A Critical Anthology. Bloomington: Indiana University Press, 1990.

Sedgwick, Eve. *Epistemology of the Closet*. Berkeley: University of California Press, 1990.

Segal, Charles. "The Female Voice and its Contradictions: From Homer to Tragedy." *Religio Graeco-Romana: Festschrift für Walter Pötscher*. Ed. Joachim Dalfen, Gerhard Petersmann, and Franz Ferdinand Schwarz. Horn/Graz: Berger, 1993. 57–75.

   "The Gorgon and the Nightingale: The Voice of Female Lament and Pindar's Twelfth Pythian Ode." *Embodied Voices: Representing Female Vocality in Western Culture*. Ed. Leslie C. Dunn and Nancy A. Jones. Cambridge: Cambridge University Press, 1994. 17–34.

Seshagiri, Urmila. "Orienting Virginia Woolf: Race, Aesthetics, and Politics in *To the Lighthouse*." *Modern Fiction Studies* 50 (2004), 58–84.

Shattuck, Roger. *Marcel Proust*. New York: Viking Press. 1974.

Shelley, Mary W. *Letters*. Ed. Frederick L. Jones. Vol ii. Norman: University of Oklahoma Press, 1944.

Sherman, David. "A Plot Unraveling into Ethics: Woolf, Levinas, and 'Time Passes.'" *Woolf Studies Annual* 13 (2007), 159–80.

Silver, Brenda. "Textual Criticism as Feminist Practice: Or, Who's Afraid of Virginia Woolf Part II." *Representing Modernist Texts: Editing as Interpretation.* Ed. George Bornstein. Ann Arbor: University of Michigan Press, 1991. 193–222.

Virginia Woolf's Reading Notebooks. Princeton: Princeton University Press, 1983.

Skrbic, Nena. *Wild Outbursts of Freedom: Reading Virginia Woolf's Short Fiction.* Westport, Conn. and London: Praeger, 2004.

Smith, Susan Bennett. "Reinventing Grief Work: Virginia Woolf's Feminist Representations of Mourning in *Mrs. Dalloway* and *To the Lighthouse.*" *Twentieth Century Literature* 41 (1995), 310–27.

Snaith, Anna. "Conversations in Bloomsbury: Colonial Writers and the Hogarth Press." *Virginia Woolf's Bloomsbury.* Vol. II: *International Influence and Politics.* Ed. Lisa Shahriari, and Gina Potts. London: Palgrave Macmillan, 2010. 138–57.

Spilka, Mark. *Virginia Woolf's Quarrel with Grieving.* Lincoln: University of Nebraska Press, 1980.

Spiropoulou, Angeliki. *Virginia Woolf, Modernity and History: Constellations with Walter Benjamin.* London: Palgrave Macmillan, 2010.

Spivak, Gayatri. "Poststructuralism, Marginality, Post-Coloniality and Value." *Literary Theory Today.* Ed. Peter Collier and Helga Geyer-Ryan. Ithaca, N.Y.: Cornell University Press, 1990. 219–44.

Sproles, Karyn Z. *Desiring Women: The Partnership of Virginia Woolf and Vita Sackville-West.* Toronto: University of Toronto Press, 2006.

Stalla, Heidi. "William Bankes: Echoes of Egypt in Virginia Woolf's *To the Lighthouse.*" *Woolf Studies Annual* 14 (2008), 21–34.

Stape, J. H., ed. "A Week in France with Virginia Woolf." *Virginia Woolf: Interviews and Recollections.* London: Macmillan, 1995. 34–6.

Steiner, George. *Antigones.* Oxford: Oxford University Press, 1984.

Stewart, Garrett. *Reading Voices: Literature and the Phonotext.* Berkeley: University of California Press, 1990.

Stray, Christopher. *Classics Transformed: Schools, Universities, and Society in England, 1830–1960.* Oxford: Clarendon Press, 1998.

Stubbs, Jeremy. "Between Medicine and Hermeticism: 'The Unconscious' in *Fin-de-siècle* France." *Symbolism, Decadence and the Fin-de-siècle: French and European Perspectives.* Ed. Patrick McGuinness. Exeter: University of Exeter Press, 2000. 144–72.

Swanson, Diana. "An Antigone Complex? The Political Psychology of *The Years* and *Three Guineas.*" *Woolf Studies Annual* 3 (1997), 28–45.

Tate, Trudi. "*Mrs. Dalloway* and the Armenian Question." *Textual Practice* 8 (1994), 467–86.

Taxidou, Olga. *Tragedy, Modernity and Mourning.* Edinburgh: Edinburgh University Press, 2004.

Thompson, Hilary. "Time and its Countermeasures: Modern Messianisms in Woolf, Benjamin, and Agamben." *Modernism and Theory: A Critical Debate.* Ed. Stephen Ross. London and New York: Routledge, 2009. 86–98.

Tolstoy, Leo. *War and Peace.* Trans. Constance Garnett. New York: Modern Library, 1994.

Venuti, Lawrence. *Rethinking Translation: Discourse, Subjectivity, Ideology.* London and New York: Routledge, 1992.

The Scandals of Translation: Towards an Ethics of Difference. London and New York: Routledge, 1998.

The Translator's Invisibility: A History of Translation. London and New York: Routledge, 1995.

Venuti, Lawrence, ed. *Translation Studies Reader.* New York and London: Routledge, 2000.

Vernant, J. P., and Vidal-Naquet, P. *Myth and Tragedy in Ancient Greece.* Trans. Janet Lloyd. New York: Zone Books, 1988.

Villeneuve, Pierre-Eric. "Communities of Desire: Woolf, Proust, and the Reading Process." *Virginia Woolf & Communities: Selected Papers from the Eighth Annual Conference on Virginia Woolf.* New York: Pace University Press, 1999. 22–8.

Wachtel, Andrew. *An Obsession with History: Russian Writers Confront the Past.* Stanford: Stanford University Press, 1994.

Wallace, Jennifer. *Shelley and Greece: Rethinking Romantic Hellenism.* London: Macmillan, 1997.

Webb, Timothy. *The Violet in the Crucible: Shelley and Translation.* Oxford: Clarendon Press, 1976.

Weir, Justin. "Anna Incommunicada: Language and Consciousness in *Anna Karenina*." *Tolstoy Studies Journal* 8 (1995–6), 99–111.

Whitworth, Michael. "Physics: 'A Strange Footprint.'" *A Concise Companion to Modernism.* Ed. David Bradshaw. Oxford: Blackwell, 2003. 200–20.

Whyte, Lancelot Law. *The Unconscious Before Freud.* New York: Basic Books, 1960.

Wilson, Emma. *Sexuality and the Reading Encounter: Identity and Desire in Proust, Duras, Tournier, and Cixous.* Oxford: Clarendon Press, 1996.

Winterer, Caroline. *The Culture of Classicism: Ancient Greece and Rome in American Intellectual Life, 1780–1910.* Baltimore, Md.: Johns Hopkins University Press, 2002.

Wolin, Richard. *Walter Benjamin: An Aesthetic of Redemption.* Berkeley: University of California Press, 1994.

Wollager, Mark. "Woolf, Postcards, and the Elision of Race: Colonizing Women in *The Voyage Out*." *Modernism/Modernity* 8 (2001), 43–75.

Woolf, Leonard. *Downhill All the Way: An Autobiography of the Years 1919–39.* London: Hogarth Press, and New York: Harcourt Brace Jovanovich, 1967.

Wussow, Helen M., ed. *Virginia Woolf "The Hours": The British Museum Manuscript of "Mrs. Dalloway."* New York: Pace University Press, 1996.

Young, John Wesley. *Orwell's Newspeak and Totalitarian Language: Its Nazi and Communist Antecedents.* Charlottesville: University of Virginia Press, 1991.

Zimra, Clarisse. "Assia Djebar: *The White of Algeria*: Introduction." Trans. Andrew Benson. *Yale French Studies* 87 (1995), 138–41.

"Disorienting the Subject in Djebar's *L'Amour, la fantasia.*" *Yale French Studies* 87 (1995), 149–70.

"'When the Past Answers our Present': Assia Djebar Talks About *Loin de Médine.*" *Callaloo* 16 (1993), 116–31.

Zwerdling, Alex. *Virginia Woolf and the Real World.* Berkeley: University of California Press, 1986.

Index

Abel, Elizabeth 41, 109
Abraham, Nicolas and Torok, Maria 176–7
  incorporation/introjection 176–7, 178–9
Agamemnon 3, 65
Alexiou, Margaret 61, 62
Althusser, Louis 53
Antigone 5–6, 16, 38–68, 88, 151, 165, 166,
  167, 169, 187
Arnheim, Rudolf 63
Arnold, Matthew 4, 21–2, 74
Asad, Talal 27–9
Auerbach, Eric 98
Avery, Todd and Brantlinger, Patrick 27 n 29

Bakhtin, M. M. 89
Beard, Mary 44
beauty 123–5
Beer, Gillian 33, 42 n 18, 64 n 98, 147 n 42
Belknap, Robert 76
Bell, Clive 120
Benardete, Seth 58
Benjamin, Walter
  "The Medium through Which Works
    of Art Continue to Influence Later Ages"
    149 n 48
  "On Language as Such and on the Language of
    Man" 139
  "The Task of the Translator" 8–10, 137–9
Benrabah, Mohamed 164 n 26
Berber 160–1, 162–4, 182
Berman, Antoine 9
Blanchot, Maurice 18
Bourdieu, Pierre 160
Bowie, Malcolm 113, 114 n 40
Breay, Claire 44 n 27
Briggs, Julia 67 n 108
Butler, Judith 53, 56, 125–6

Calle–Gruber, Mireille 171, 182
Caravelli, A. 61
Carlier, Omar 165 n 30

Casanova, Pascale 161 n 16
Case, Janet 2
Caughie, Pamela 32, 66, 86 n 62, 127 n 76
Caws, Mary Ann 98, 99–100
Cheyfitz, Eric 10 n 22
Chouraqui, André 11
Clewell, Tammy 180
conscious/unconscious 108, 109–11, 112–14, 113 n
  37, 115, 118
cry 17, 57, 60, 61–5
Cuddy-Keane, Melba 25–6, 49 n 50, 109,
  114 n 41

Davis, Lydia 108 n 26
De Lisle, Leconte 40
de Man, Paul 145, 146
Derrida, Jacques 10–11, 34, 66–7
  Aporias 5, 51
  "Deconstruction and the Other" 67 n 106
  Deconstruction and the Possibility of Justice
    67 n 109
  "Des Tours de Babel" 142–4
  "Force of Law: The 'Mystical Foundation of
    Authority'" 67–8
  "Fors" 177 n 54
  Glas 66, 67 n 106
  Limited Inc 149 n 49
  "Living On: Border Lines" 133, 152
  Monolingualism of the Other 143 n 25
  Positions 10
  "Sending: On Representation" 34 n 54
  "Signature Event Context" 149
  Specters of Marx 156
  Writing and Difference 36 n 62
Derrida, Jacques and Elizabeth Roudinesco, *For
  What Tomorrow: A Dialogue* 144
Dick, Susan 96
Diment, Gayla 71 n 7
Dion, Michel 110 n 31
Djebar, Assia 15–16, 157–8
  L'amour, la fantasia 159, 165–70

Le blanc de l'Algérie 186
Ces voix qui m'assiègent 160, 171
Loin de Médine 161
Vaste est la prison 162–3, 164, 170, 181–2
Donadey, Anne 161
Dostoyevsky 92–3
  The Idiot 93
dreams 93–4
Dubino, Jeanne 148 n 44
duBois, Page 39 n 3
Dünkelsbühler, Ulrike 59

Eide, Marion 89 n 67
Eikhenbaum, Boris 77–80
Ergal, Yves-Michel 121

feeling 101–3, 119
Ferenczi, Sándor 176
Fernald, Anne 157 n 4
Ferrer, Daniel 171
Feuer, Kathryn B. 79
Finch, Alison 120
Flint, Kate 148 n 45
Fodor, Alexander 72 n 9
Foley, Helen P. 62
Fowler, Rowena 24 n 16, 51 n 58
Freud, Sigmund 112–13, 174 n 45
Fromentin, Eugène 170
Froula, Christine 42 n 18, 180

Gafaïti, Hafid 169 n 34
Garnett, Constance 69
Gasché, Rodolphe 159
Gellner, Ernest 90
gender 126–8, 175
Goff, Barbara and Simpson,
  Michael 165, 167
Goldhill, Simon 42
Guiguet, Jean 98

Hale, Terry 99 n 11
Hall, Stuart 161
hand 58–9, 170–3
Hankins, Leslie 119 n 53
Harrison, Jane 43–5
Haynes, Kenneth 24 n. 20
Headlam, Walter 42
Hermans, Theo 31
Herzfeld, Michael 28
Hitler 62
Hobsbawm, Eric 86
Hogarth Press 6, 69–70
Holoka, James P. 46 n 36
Hughes, Edward J. 126
Hussey, Mark 33, 186

Jacobs, Carol 138
Jaeger, Werner 46
Jakobson, Roman 3
Jameson, Fredric 90
Jebb, R. C. 42, 48
Jones, Christine Kenyon and Snaith, Anna 2 n 2
Josopovici, Gabriel 133 n 1
Julian the Apostate 141

Keynes, John Maynard 120 n 56
Khanna, Ranjana 174
kinship 145–6
Klemperer, Victor 51
Kolocotroni, Vassiliki 65 n 101
Koselleck, Reinhart 50
Koster, Cees 32

Lacan, Jacques 60
Lecercle, Jean-Jacques 124
Lee, Hermione 2, 88, 98
Lefevere, André 4, 27
Leonard, Miriam 38
Leontis, Artemis 29 n. 35
Levenback, Karen 76, 82
Lewis, Andrea 30 n. 39
Lewis, Philip E. 10–12, 115
Loraux, Nicole 57–8, 61
Lubbock, Percy 72–3, 110

MacIntyre, Alasdair 112–13
Maine, Sumner 29
Marchand, Suzanne L. 18–19
Marcus, Jane 66, 135, 154 n 61
Marcus, Laura 70, 172
Mares, Cheryl 99 n 8
Marshik, Celia 119 n 53
McCall, Marsh 59
McDaniel, James 128
McDonald, Christie 117
McIntire, Gabrielle 135
McManus, Patricia 186
McNeillie, Andrew 36 n 61
McQuade, Molly 1 n 1
McVicker, Jeanette 51 n. 58
Mehlman, Jeffrey 129 n 80
Mepham, John 179
Mignolo, Walter 163 n 23
Miller, Christopher L. 161
Miller, J. Hillis 99, 116 n 48, 183
Milò, Giuliva 164
Mirrlees, Hope 67
Moncrieff, C. K. 13, 107–9
Morson, Gary 74–5, 80, 84
Mortimer, Mildred 186
mourning 42, 54–5, 177–82, 183–6

nation 7, 86–7, 89–91
Newman, Francis 22–3
Niranjana, Tejaswini 160

Oldfield, Sybil 39
Orwin, Donna 84

Phillips, Kathy 158
Plato
    Symposium 24, 25
primitive 29–30
Prins, Yopie 20 n 5, 65
Proust, Marcel 12–13, 99, 104, 120–1
    Du coté de chez Swann
        ("hours" scene) 103–5
    Guermantes 118–19
    Sodome et Gomorrhe 121–2,
        123, 126–7

Radin, Grace 82, 83
Reinhardt, Karl 46–8
Reinhold, Natalya 70
Renan, Ernest 89
representation 32–7, 56–7, 160
Rich, Susanna 154 n 60
Richter, Harvena 98
Ricoeur, Paul 107, 187–8
Rosenbaum, S. P. 44
Rosenfeld, Natania 41
Rubenstein, Roberta 91, 92 n 71, 95

Sackville-West, Vita 1, 100 n 14, 121
Schehr, Lawrence 123
Scully, Stephen 52 n 59
Sedgwick, Eve Kosofsky 122
Segal, Charles 60
Seshagiri, Urmila 186 n 79
Shattuck, Roger 108 n 25
Shelley, Mary 24
Shelley, Percy 24
Sherman, David 180–1
Silver, Brenda 45, 72
Skrbic, Nena 174
Smith, Susan Bennett 180
Snaith, Anna 159
soul 7, 36, 91–2, 94–6
Spilka, Mark 180
Spiropoulou, Angeliki 138 n 12
Spivak, Gayatri 171
Steiner, George 38
Stewart, Garrett 147
Strachey, Lytton 1
Stray, Christopher 19
Stubbs, Jeremy 115 n 44
Swanson, Diana 41

Tate, Trudi 158 n 8
Taxidou, Olga 39, 45
Thompson, Hillary 9 n 19
Tolstoy, Leo 6–7, 71 n 8, 71–2
    Anna Karenina 73–4
    War and Peace 83–4, 86
Tower of Babel 8, 14, 138, 147–8
translation 1, 89, 109
    "abusive" 131–2, 156–7
    and ethics 175, 178
    and ethnography 27–8, 160

University of London 2

ventriloquism 63
Venuti, Lawrence 94, 109, 125
Vernant, Jean-Pierre 49 n 48, 58 n 73
Vernant, Jean-Pierre and Vidal-Naquet,
        P. 49 n 48
Verrall, A. W. 3, 42–3
Villeneuve, Pierre-Eric 7 n 11, 98

Wachtel, Andrew 77
Warr, George 2
Webb, Timothy 25 n 21
Weir, Justin 75
Whitworth, Michael 33
Whyte, Lancelot Law 112 n 33
Wilson, Emma 130
Winterer, Caroline 39 n 3
Wollager, Mark 30
Woolf, Leonard 70
Woolf, Virginia
    essays
        The Common Reader 20, 38
        "How It Strikes a Contemporary" 38
        "How Should One Read a Book?" 33
        "The Leaning Tower" 158
        "Letter to a Young Poet" 124
        "On Being Ill" 100–1, 147–8
        "On Not Knowing French" 110
        "On Not Knowing Greek" 18, 20–1
        "Phases of Fiction" 111–12
        "Reading at Random" 145 n 35
        "A Sketch of the Past" 55
        "Speech of January 21, 1931" 114, 148
        Three Guineas 40, 47, 49–50, 52–3, 56–7,
            65–7
        "Women and Fiction" 52
    novels
        Between the Acts 141–2,
            168 n 33
        "The Hours" manuscript 106–7
        Jacob's Room 140–1
        "Melymbrosia" 102

Mrs. Dalloway 75–6, 93–4, 101, 116–17,
    182–4
Night and Day 92
Orlando 13, 119, 123–4, 127–31, 132
To the Lighthouse 34–5, 119, 184
The Voyage Out 29–30, 149–50
The Waves 13, 134–7, 152–5, 184–5
The Years 14–15, 56, 80–3, 84–6, 87–8, 151–2
short stories
    "The Evening Party" 172

"A Haunted House" 16–17, 173–5
"Mrs. Dalloway on Bond
    Street" 183
"A Society" 166 n 31
"Solid Objects" 35–6
"Street Haunting" 159 n 10
"Sympathy" 176, 178–9

Zimra, Clarisse 165 n 30, 185
Zwerdling, Alex 66